COLD WAR THEATRE

Cold War Theatre provides an account of the theatrical history of the post forty years within the context of East/West politics. Its geographical span ranges from beyond the Urals to the Pacific Coast of the US, and asks whether the Cold War confrontation was not in part due to the cultural climate of Europe.

Taking the McCarthy era as its starting point, this readable history considers the impact of the Cold War upon the major dramatic movements of our time, East and West. The author poses the question as to whether European habits of mind, fostered by their cultures, may not have contributed to the political stalemates of the Cold War. 'In time', he suggests, the Cold War may come to be seen as 'a schism in the Enlightenment, as remote as the religious feuds which darkened the Middle Ages.'

A wide range of actors from both the theatrical and political stages are discussed, and their contributions to the theatre of the Cold War examined in a hugely enjoyable and enlightening narrative. John Elsom has been an active observer to the events he describes, having been a writer and critic for thirty years and the Chair of the Liberal Party Arts and Broadcasting Panel for ten years. As the President of the International Association of Theatre Critics, a UNESCO organisation, since 1985, he has witnessed at first hand the changes brought about by *glasnost* and *perestroika*. He is a lecturer in the Department of Arts Policy and Management at the City University, London. His previous books include *Post-War British Theatre* and *Is Shakespeare Our Contemporary?*, both published by Routledge.

COLD WAR
THEATRE

John Elsom

London and New York

First published 1992
by Routledge
11 New Fetter Lane, London EC4P 4EE

Simultaneously published in the USA and Canada
by Routledge
a division of Routledge, Chapman and Hall, Inc.
29 West 35th Street, New York, NY 10001

Typeset in Palatino by
Falcon Typographic Art Ltd, Fife, Scotland
Printed and bound in Great Britain by
Clays Ltd, St Ives plc

British Library Cataloguing in Publication Data
Elsom, John.
Cold war theatre.
I. Title
792.09

Library of Congress Cataloging in Publication Data
Elsom, John
Cold War theatre/John Elsom.
p. cm.
Includes bibliographical references and index.
1. Theater – History – 20th century. 2. Theater – Political aspects.
I. Title.
PN2189.E45   1992
792'.09'045 – dc20   91–47104

ISBN 0–415–00167–6
0–415–08108–4 (pbk)

To Sarah and Thomas

CONTENTS

Acknowledgements   ix

1 THE CONSCIENCE OF A DIPLOMAT:
  AN INTRODUCTION   1

2 THE TRIAL OF ARTHUR MILLER   13

3 BINKIE BEAUMONT'S WEST END   25

4 THE HEAT IN BRECHT'S COOLNESS   37

5 AT THE BACK OF THE MIND   49

6 OLIVIER PASSES THE BATON   61

7 THE VELVET PRISON   73

8 THE SECULAR BAPTIST   85

9 THE AGE OF AQUARIUS   97

10 THE FLOATING ISLAND   109

11 TOWARDS MUSIC   120

12 THE NATIONAL THEATRE IS YOURS   132

13 BROADWAY BABIES   144

14 THE UNRAVELLING   156

15 THEME AND EXPOSITION   168

   Notes   180
   Index   186

ACKNOWLEDGEMENTS

This book has required help from too many people to thank them all by name. I must record my gratitude to those colleagues within the International Association of Theatre Critics who took the trouble to explain the situations in their countries to me and, in particular, to Eleanor Bromley, Ion Caramitru, Welton Jones, Carlos Tindemans, Serge Volynets and Dan Vasilieu for supplying valuable material. I must also thank my colleagues in the Department of Arts Policy and Management at City University, London, and the British Council for helping me to travel. I have been lucky enough to receive loving support from my family and friends in Britain, who have read my various drafts and tolerated my obsessions without giving too many signs of being bored by them. Those who commented in detail include Judith Elliott, Anthony Field, Ian Herbert, Tony Macadam, John Pick, Iphigenia Taxopoulou, Peter Thompson, Nick White and my editors at Routledge, Helena Reckitt and Talia Rodgers. This book would probably not have been written without the support over many years of the late Rosalind Wade, formerly the editor of *Contemporary Review*, but it is dedicated to my grandchildren, Sarah and Thomas, who are members of the first post Cold War generation.

1

THE CONSCIENCE OF A DIPLOMAT
An Introduction

'I can do anything better than you'
(From *Annie Get Your Gun*, 1946)

In September 1950, one architect of the Cold War, George Kennan, asked for an indefinite leave of absence without pay from his post within the US State Department, where he was an adviser on foreign affairs to the Truman administration. He was 46, too young to retire, too old to back down when he thought he was right, and a 'small, inward voice' was telling him, 'You have despaired of yourself. Now despair of your country!'[1]

The Cold War was with us for so long, and penetrated so many aspects of our lives, that it is tempting to believe that it was an inevitable response to events outside our control, at least in the West, and that if Kennan had not existed, somebody would have had to invent him. In fact, his views were not thought to be self-evident when he first put them forward and they were developed along lines which he neither liked nor anticipated.

Kennan was a career diplomat who returned home from Moscow in 1946, appalled by the chaos in Europe and the strident anti-Americanism of Soviet foreign policy under Stalin. In the United States, he found the public in a state of post-war euphoria, for whom Uncle Joe was almost a national hero. He thus wrote an article for *Foreign Affairs* (July 1947) under his cipher 'X', in which he described the threat of Soviet expansion and how it could be contained and this essay, 'The source of Soviet conduct', became the first public blueprint for the Cold War.

Kennan was a strategist on a grand, almost eighteenth-century, scale, of liberal views, educated at Princeton, and blind to neither the political nor the human realities of what he was preaching. He spoke Russian, was a student of Russian history and had witnessed the purges of the 1930s and the misery caused by the collectivisation of the land. He was thus under no illusions about Stalin. He also knew that the Soviet distrust of the West had deep roots, dating back at least to 1919

1

when fourteen foreign armies fought on Russian soil to overthrow the Bolshevik revolution.[2] Marxist-Leninism endorsed this fear, and made it intellectually respectable, elevating it as part of the struggle between the forces of capitalism and communism, in which the proletariat would eventually triumph. Kennan did not believe that the Soviet Union, exhausted by war already, would want to invade Western Europe unless it was tempted or provoked into doing so, two possibilities which he was determined to prevent.

He was more alarmed by the thought that the Western Allies might simply give way to Soviet demands from disunity or peace-seeking generosity. Examples of such political weakness were fresh in his mind – from Munich before the war and Yalta six years later where President Roosevelt had allowed Stalin to annex most of Eastern Europe, from the Baltic to the Balkans. Of course, Roosevelt, who was by then a dying man, had merely agreed that countries like Poland, Czechoslovakia and Hungary should stay within the Soviet zone of influence until the time when, with the war and its aftermath cleared away, they could be returned to their independent governments. Kennan did not believe that Stalin would slacken his grip on the land left in his keeping and he did not want to see the mistakes of Yalta repeated, in Austria, Finland or who knew where.

How should the Soviet threat be met? By military alliances or by diplomatic pressure? By trying to de-stabilise the Soviet Union or by assassinating Stalin? In time, all these alternatives were contemplated, but Kennan thought that containment should be achieved through economic means rather than military ones, with the armed forces standing by for emergencies. He was thus a supporter of General George Marshall who in the midsummer weeks of 1946 was explaining to Harvard students how to regenerate Europe with the help of US dollars. Marshall did not rule out the possibility of giving assistance to the Soviet Union as well, and the countries under its spell in Eastern Europe, whereas Kennan believed that the provision of aid should be tied to political conditions, such as free elections in the countries which received it. By such tactics the Cold War should be conducted.

That was Kennan's theory, but he did not know how it would be received in the White House. Harry Truman had the reputation of being a political barnstormer with little interest in foreign affairs. The subtleties of Kennan's approach might be expected to elude him, but this was not so. 'Containment' became the new diplomatic watchword and in 1947, Kennan was elevated to the post of Director, Policy Planning Unit, in the State Department, a key adviser to the Secretary of State himself, Dean Acheson.

These were heady times. Kennan had the rare political chance to bring into being his own policies. He could help to implement the Marshall

Plan for Europe and comment influentially on other containment strategies, such as the establishment in 1949 of the North Atlantic Treaty Organisation (NATO). He also had the grim satisfaction of watching his prophecies come true. The communist *coups d'états* in Eastern Europe, accompanied by a barrage of propaganda and acts of harassment, demonstrated that Stalin would never grant his buffer states any real independence.

Even while he was being proved right, Kennan sensed that things were not going according to plan. Having alerted public opinion to the Soviet threat, he was alarmed by the fear of the Red Menace which had spread throughout the United States. A scare seemed to have been started for political reasons, just before the 1948 presidential election, by Truman's Republican opponents. Senator Joe McCarthy accused the Democrats of letting Soviet spies into their administration. A Senate Committee was established to investigate Un-American Activities, which claimed the right even to censor schoolbooks.

At first, Truman was able to brush the charges aside as a red herring, and won the election, but McCarthy was a persistent man, who thought that he had the Democrats on the run. He made speeches on radio and television, waving a sheaf of papers, claiming that they proved the existence of some 'two hundred card-carrying Communists' within the State Department itself. Kennan's immediate response was one of 'head-shaking wonder', but he thought grimly, 'Now he will have to prove it! Then we will have an end to the matter!'[3]

But Kennan was wrong. There was a conspiracy and there were spies near the centre of government. Alger Hiss, at Roosevelt's side in Yalta, was acquitted of spying, but given a jail sentence for perjury. The Rosenburgs were sent to the electric chair. Some of Kennan's friends were held under suspicion, including Robert Oppenheimer, the physicist who had designed the first atomic bomb and was now trying to live with the consequences.

Kennan discovered that the trouble with democracies was that subtle ideas could become simple-minded, and then mad, in a direct ratio to their vote-winning potential. To sell the idea of containment to the American people, it had been necessary to turn it into something like a Holy War. There was no alternative. It would otherwise have been dismissed as an expensive folly. But can you ever fight a Holy War without sliding into a similar bigotry from which you are so anxious to protect mankind?

In 1948, the Central Intelligence Agency (CIA) was established, with Kennan's approval, to investigate what the Soviet fifth column was doing in the United States and to set up a counter-spy system. The CIA was then asked to undertake black propaganda for the military. Its role had therefore changed, from gathering intelligence in a peaceful way to

3

spreading false rumours. It might even be said that the CIA was trying to de-stabilise governments with whom the United States was not officially at war. It was a reckless step in the wrong direction, for which Kennan blamed the Pentagon. He had never been able to explain his theory of containment to the generals. 'The American military . . . abhorred the concept of limited warfare and were addicted to doing things only in the most massive, ponderous and unwieldy manner'.[4] They still talked of surrounding the Euro-Asian continent with military bases from which they could launch a pre-emptive, and nuclear, strike.

This fearful prospect confirmed the Soviet suspicions of the West. The Cold War was in danger of becoming a self-fulfilling prophecy. The Pentagon, in its efforts to contain Stalin, was producing those conditions which encouraged Stalinism to thrive. In 1949, despite US aid, General Chiang Kai-Shek's Nationalist army was driven to the offshore island of Formosa (Taiwan) by Mao Tse-Tung's People's Liberation Army. A vast new communist state was brought into being, allied to the Soviet Union. In 1950, almost as a geo-political footnote to the war in China, the Korean war began and there were other regional conflicts on the horizon.

The disintegration of the old European empires – British, French, Belgian, Dutch and Portuguese – accounted for many of them. The patterns were often very similar. A rebel force, armed with old Soviet weapons, would start a guerrilla campaign in the hills against a colonial government, which appealed to the US and its allies for support. It was often hard to tell whether this was some machiavellian plot to de-stabilise the West or if it sprang from genuine injustice, or both, or neither.

Kennan warned that if the West believed that every little local difficulty were masterminded by Moscow, the West would find itself propping up some unpleasant regimes and dragged into disastrous wars. His prophecies fell on deaf ears, which was why, having watched helplessly the early reverses of the Korean war as General MacArthur tried to take on China and failed, he declared himself redundant at the State Department and ventured into that wilderness from which only Princeton travellers readily return.

He had a family to support and no private income, but he wanted to take a long, hard look at the civilisation he was trying to save. He travelled by train across the mid-West, irritated by the canned music in his carriage, playing 'Ave Maria' and selections from 'Rose Marie'. He did not like what he saw. St Louis was 'a grim waste of criss-crossing railroads, embankments, viaducts, junk lots, storage lots, piles of refuse, and the most abject specimens of human habitation'.[5] In Pennsylvania, he was asked to run for the Senate as a Democrat, although he was not a party member. Flattered, he accepted; and his county chairman gave him

4

some advice: 'If you're a drinkin' man, keep on drinkin'. If you're chasin' women, keep on chasin' women. They're goin' to know it anyway.'[6]

Eventually, he had to withdraw his nomination, because he could not afford the costs of his campaign. 'The lesson was a severe one', he recorded.[7] The American political system was not as open and democratic as he had been led to believe. Money mattered more than morals if you were running for office. Mr Smith could rarely go to Washington, except on a coach trip, and if he were black, he might have to go on a separate bus.

All this depressed Kennan mightily, but the Institute for Advanced Study at Princeton offered him a home and an income, where he could think about world affairs and how his personal intervention in them had gone wrong. He wrote a second article for *Foreign Affairs* (April 1951) in which he tried to dispel the thought that the West could actually win the Cold War. That should not even be its aim. His hope was that in time 'gradual, peaceful change' would come over the Soviet Union itself, if it could be helped by a positive example from the West.[8]

> If only the necessary alternatives could be kept before the Russian people in the form of an existence elsewhere on this planet of a civilization which is decent, hopeful and purposeful, the day must come – soon or late, and whether by gradual process or otherwise – when that terrible system of power which has set a great people's progress back for decades and has lain like a shadow over the aspirations of all civilization will be distinguishable no longer as a living reality, but only as something surviving partly in recorded history and partly in that sediment of constructive organic change which every human upheaval, however unhappy in its other manifestations, manages to deposit on the shelf of time.[9]

He must have hoped that the elevated tone of this article, with its long sentences and rolling, parenthetical phrases, would strike a chord in the hearts of his fellow-citizens. But, sadly, they were more likely to be glued to their television screens by the proceedings of the House Un-American Activities (HUAC), which had turned its attention to Hollywood. There was a parade of supposed 'fellow-travellers' who had innocently signed petitions in the 1930s and who, eager to ingratiate themselves, laid charges against others. Some protested, some stayed silent, but the purge continued and McCarthy's power increased, until by 1954, he was prepared to take on the Pentagon itself. After harassing a Brigadier-General, he enraged President Eisenhower, was condemned by Congress and then declined into insignificance.

Joe McCarthy died in 1957, but McCarthyism went on, leaving, according to Kennan, a 'lasting mark on American political life'.[10] In 1954, President Eisenhower outlawed the Communist Party of the

United States, although by that time it was scarcely necessary. Unless somebody had been caught with a membership card, or forced by fair means or foul to confess, it was hard to tell whether he or she was a communist. Civil rights workers, uncooperative trade unionists and troublemakers in general were tarred with the same brush. They were suspected of being communists or fellow-travellers unless they could prove otherwise, and was this how a free society should behave?

Kennan's sharpest attack on McCarthyism was delivered in 1953 in a speech made at the opening of a centre for the fine arts at the University of Notre Dame, Indiana. In it, he complained about the narrow chauvinism of the American right, which 'looked with suspicion both on the sources of intellectual and artistic activity [in the United States] and upon impulses of this nature coming to us from abroad'.[11] Strong cultures, he argued, depend upon the free exchange of ideas and upon the relationship between past and present values that the arts embody. If anything could keep communism at bay, and fascism too, and other violent swings to the left or right, it was the presence of sturdy, critical instincts, fostered by the humanistic traditions of Western art.

This is where this book really begins.

My aim is to consider the impact of the Cold War upon the cultures of various countries, taking the theatre as my point of departure, and to speculate about whether the Cold War itself may not have been affected by the cultural climates in which it was being conducted. Some readers may instantly suspect that I am giving show-business a status that it does not deserve. The theatre is a game, nothing more, and what most people want when they go to a show is a good night out.

But why, if this is so, should Joe McCarthy and his allies have wasted time in persecuting actors? The answer could be that by doing so HUAC gained useful publicity for its cause. How many Americans would recognise their local Congressman in the street, or fail to recognise Ethel Merman? The theatre may not deliver profound messages for mankind, it may not alter the direction of political events (except rarely), but it could command a deal of public attention and influence the mood within which politicans had to operate. The impresarios of Broadway had close links with Hollywood and television, and promoted stars whose faces were known wherever there were screens to display them.

Stars are seen in roles, and roles help to develop plots, and audiences all over the world seem to want the good guys to win and the bad ones to lose, although it may not be so easy to decide which is which. In the B-feature Westerns in which Ronald Reagan used to appear, the hero was the white man with short hair who had a long-standing relationship with his horse, but elsewhere the moral framework might be more complicated. The expectation that right will win in the end has always been a powerful and somewhat mysterious theatrical force.

Audiences may like to feel re-assured that they live in a just world under a benevolent God or perhaps this may simply be the way in which we have come to write plays. The aim of Greek tragedy, on whose principles much Western drama has been modelled, was to encourage virtue and to discourage vice. If justice is expected to triumph, audiences look for clues in the plot as to what constitutes 'goodness'. These may not be moral in a Christian sense. They could be fashionable, patriotic or racial, but if the public fails to be convinced, its reaction may be one of unease, even outrage, although it is more likely to avoid the show.

In the Broadway musicals of the early 1950s, the innocent girl usually married the hero, while the flighty one got stuck with the no-good gambler. By such means, audiences could be persuaded that these were the norms of behaviour, whether they tallied with real life or not. It could be described as a kind of moral massage and in those days, the best masseur on Broadway was the director, George Abbott, who has since become a super-veteran who turned 100 in 1987.

Abbott was born in 1887 and first acted on Broadway in 1913. He started to direct in the 1920s, mainly tough-guy melodramas and comedies. He became a producer, a play-doctor and dramatist, a director of musicals, the supreme professional who became *guru* to the young Harold Prince. He had a dry wit, an imposing presence and was more of a technician than a theorist. He liked to make each scene tick like clockwork and scorned the inward, symbolic stuff which he left to amateurs and eggheads.

One of his favourite words during rehearsals was 'phony', which he applied to anything which rang false to his scheme of values. This might mean something as slight as a Ronald Colman moustache or something as fundamental as a motive which seemed to him somewhat un-American by being not red-blooded enough, or buoyant enough, or not emotionally clear-cut. The baseball musical, *Damn Yankees* (1955), is a good example of an Abbott show. This was the heyday of the musical, when Rodgers and Hammerstein, Frank Loesser, Irving Berlin, Cole Porter and Leonard Bernstein all provided smash-hits. If the transformation of the musical during the 1950s can be illustrated by the contrast between *Call Me Madam* (1950), which Abbott directed, and *West Side Story* (1958), which he did not, it is worth remembering that the *West Side Story* team consisted largely of Abbott protégés, Prince, Bernstein and the choreographer, Jerome Robbins.

Abbott was instinctively patriotic, but not crassly so, and suspicious of most politicians, but left-wingers in particular. His style, as well as his shows, provided ideal material for a Hollywood purged by Joe McCarthy. McCarthy's attempts to control the myth-making process were simple-minded in comparison with those of a professional like Abbott. McCarthy wanted to ensure that God was always perceived to be on the side of America. He was supported by the leagues of patriotism and decency which brought additional pressure on the Hollywood studios, who knew anyway that virtue, if properly handled, was good box-office. For ten years, Hollywood was whisker-clean of any trace of communist corruption. Its films were awe-inspiring in their optimism. Clean-living folk (James Stewart, Doris Day) triumphed over disasters caused by foreigners, suspect politicians and even God, who might want to give their faith a good testing.

Whatever else may be said against McCarthyism, it did not prevent US show-business from providing the dominant popular culture of the 1950s. Its films were in most Western cinemas, its songs blared out from every radio, its stars were pinned up on walls around the world. Pirated reels of Errol Flynn and Johnny Weissmuller movies were popular with the students at the Stromynka hostel where Mikhail Gorbachev lived while studying for his law degree at the Moscow State University.[12] Decades later, the tattered icons of a buoyant America – Crosby, Grable, Presley and Monroe – could be found in Mexican slums and Siberian cottages. This was salesmanship of a high order, promoting not just a product but a way of life, the American Dream. It was a vision not of a classless society but of one where an ordinary guy could win through and marry the girl of his imagination, and made more irresistible by the dances, the music, the wit and irreverence, the talents drilled into a team by such directors as Abbott.

What damaged its effectiveness as propaganda was the impact of the HUAC show trials. These were shown around the world, with relish in communist countries, for they demonstrated that the Free World was not free at all and that the Hollywood visions of a proletarian paradise were almost as false as the Soviet films of rosy-cheeked girl tractor drivers. They went some way towards providing a defence for the Soviet McCarthyism, Zhdanovshchina.

Unlike the United States, the Soviet Union had an official cultural policy, Socialist Realism, whose instigator, Andrey Zhdanov, became Stalin's right-hand man after the war, until he died from poisoning in 1948. Zhdanov outlined the principles of Socialist Realism at the First All-Union Congress of Soviet Writers in 1934. Its aim was to affirm the mission of the Soviet workers to lead the world towards the triumph of revolutionary communism. It was messaianic and nationalistic; and its tunnel vision excluded anything deemed superfluous or subversive. This meant not just Abstract art or Expressionism, but private love and domestic affection, whatever distracted the worker from his central task. Socialist Realism was very puritanical.

Students were taught how to apply its principles to films and the theatre. Plays had to be realistic, which meant that they imitated the surfaces of life. They featured 'positive' heroes who came from the working classes and who knew in any situation what needed to be done. 'Conflict' was to be avoided, that is, internal doubts and hesitations, although the class struggle was all-important. A distinction was made between the internal message of the play, which had to follow standard Marxist-Leninist lines, and its external trappings, which were expected to promote a region. Socialist Realism combined local prides with an international destiny. 'Under Stalinism,' wrote the Hungarian dissident, Miklosz Haraszti, 'artists are soldiers to be drafted into battle to consolidate socialism'.[13]

Zhdanov was responsible for the purges of intellectuals in the late 1930s in which the director, V.E. Meyerhold, and the dramatist, Mikhail Bulgakov, died; and after the war, he tried to root out all traces of Western influence or 'cosmopolitanism' from Soviet culture. On this ground, he condemned the dissonant music of Prokofiev and Shostakovitch and the 'decadence' of Anna Akhmatova's love poetry. He ordered the history books to be re-written to make them sound more encouraging and supported the agronomist Trofim Lysenko in his efforts to make agriculture respond to the principles of Marxist-Leninism.

Arthur Miller's play *The Crucible* (1953), about the seventeenth-century witch hunts in Salem, can be better applied to Zhdanovshchina than McCarthyism. Those who fell foul of HUAC risked losing their jobs rather than lives and their families were not likely to be slaughtered, as Meyerhold's wife was hacked to pieces in her flat. The HUAC trials were televised and held in some check by a relatively free press and the prospect of elections. There was another curb on US propaganda, the box-office. Audiences may be gullible, but they are not composed entirely of idiots. When the American Dream became too radiant, producers noticed a falling-off in their receipts. They added a touch of realism, teenage rebellion, corruption in high places. In the Soviet Union, the film and theatre industries were funded by the state. Producers did not have to woo their public from other amusements. Workers were bussed to the theatre. What mattered was the approval of the Ministry of Culture.

There were, however, telling likenesses between McCarthyism and Zhdanovshchina. As Zhdanov provided ideological guidelines to the Soviet secret police (the KGB), so McCarthy's men instructed the Federal Bureau of Investigation (FBI) how to recognise communists and where they might be found. Arthur Miller has described how at his old campus, the University of Michigan at Ann Arbor, students and teachers were asked to inform on each other.[14] It was as if the United States like the Soviet Union was sliding towards that nightmarish future prophesied by George Orwell in his novel, *1984* (1949), where the eyes of Big Brother watched you from every street corner and thought was controlled through the manipulation of language.

'Was there something in the modern air,' mused Kennan, 'which meant that once you had cut loose from the traditional liberal principle of post-Jacksonian democracy you could find no stopping place until you had accepted the whole forbidding baggage of Soviet outlook and practice.'[15] He answered 'No' to his rhetorical question, but the signs were not encouraging. Even liberal governments, wedded in theory to the open market and free speech, were not above manipulating the arts in practice.

The wave-like assaults upon the arts which have characterised the twentieth century – the burning of the books in Nazi Germany, Zhdanovshchina in the Soviet Union and the Cultural Revolution in Mao's China – were extreme examples of a prevailing mood in which the arts were not to be respected in their own right but as a means to an end, social engineering. In such company, McCarthyism was a minor offender. In the 1950s, forward-looking universities were starting to include the arts within their Departments of the Behavioral Sciences. A new cultural theory, Structuralism, gripped the imagination of intellectuals. It stemmed from the work of a Swiss linguistics professor, Ferdinand de Saussure, who died in 1913, although his influential book, *A Course in General Linguistics*, was not published in the United States until that same year.

Saussure pointed out that all languages were arbitrary in two senses, because there was no link between a human experience and the word or signifier chosen to represent it, and because the signifier splits up our perception of the world in arbitrary ways. We know what a word means because it is distinguished from other words in a structure of signs called language. Saussure offered an analogy with a chess set. The material from which the pieces are made does not matter, only their relative positions on the board. 'In language', he said, 'there are only differences.'

In one respect, however, a language is not arbitrary. It is held in place by common usage. All sign systems are products of the societies from which they stem and transmit the injustices of which they are part. Since it is hard for us to think at all without having a sign system to help, and we would be unable to communicate our perceptions even if we could, we are inevitably the victims of language in whatever society we may find ourselves, as well as its beneficiaries. Societies practise thought-control, simply by being societies. Saussure called for a science of signs, which he called semiotics, to study the relationship between language and society; and his arguments could be applied to all the art forms, including the theatre. Those who took up his challenge, however, were primarily Marxists who wanted to describe how languages had evolved in terms of the class struggle. From their stance, Zhdanov's re-writing of history could be seen as the correction of an injustice.

History had previously been written by the ruling classes. It was time for a proletarian version.

Kennan was horrified by the idea that the massacre of the kulaks, for example, could be relegated to a positive sounding footnote in a Soviet textbook. He was a Presbyterian who believed that there was such a thing as Truth, however dimly it might be perceived. Individuals could make moral and aesthetic choices. While the defects of language might limit their perceptions, they had a duty to speak that language truthfully. At the University of Notre Dame, Kennan spoke as if unaware of the battlefields across which he was straying, between Classicism and Modernism, absolute and relative values, determinism and free will. What appalled him most of all was what was happening to the United States. It was in danger of becoming a mirror image of its enemy.

Kennan never doubted the decision to stand firm against communism, but he feared how it was being done. Of President Eisenhower, the 'Nation's Number One Boy Scout', he scathingly observed that he had a reputation of never reading anything he could possibly avoid reading. Of Eisenhower's Secretary of State, he noted that John Foster Dulles had the reputation of being a pious man, although he had never seen any signs of it in the conduct of his office.[16] It was as if US foreign policy was being modelled on Hollywood Westerns. It assumed that what was right for America was right for the rest of the world and that safety came at the point of a ballistic missile, if it was pointing in the right direction, in short: the frontier mentality.

In 1954, Dulles warned Moscow of 'massive retaliation' if the Viet Minh gained the upper hand in French Indo-China (Vietnam), seeming to sanction the use of nuclear weapons. By 1957, such threats had lost their awesome credibility. They had not stopped the war in Vietnam nor the Soviet invasion of Hungary. Dr Henry Kissinger of Harvard University offered an alternative. In *Nuclear Arms and Foreign Policy* (1957), he proposed a series of graded military responses, moving from conventional warfare to tactical nuclear weapons to all-out nuclear war. Kennan could not understand how the proposition could be taken seriously. Didn't anyone realise that there could be no victory, moral or otherwise, in a nuclear war?

Kennan rejoined the US foreign service briefly on two further occasions, as the US Ambassador to the Soviet Union in 1952–3 on the eve of Stalin's death and as the Ambassador to Yugoslavia from 1961–3, a President Kennedy appointment. He was dismayed by the low level of public debate and looked across the Atlantic to Britain to set a better example. He visited Oxford University in 1956 and gave the Reith Lectures for the BBC, in which he caused a controversy by proposing a de-militarised zone in central Europe. Why, he wondered, did Britain, home of so many liberal values, look so shabby and sorry for itself?

His life was mostly spent at Princeton, where he struggled to 'de-mythologise' US foreign policy, to get rid of its crusading zeal and its dependence on nuclear weapons. But he quickly discovered that it is not so easy to get rid of myths once they have been brought into existence. He must have felt like the sorcerer's apprentice, vainly trying to chop up the magic broom which he had summoned to life, and finding out to his horror that the fragments refused to lie down and die, but became miniature brooms instead, determined to clean up the world completely or reduce it to a single pile of dust.

2

THE TRIAL OF ARTHUR MILLER

'Mister, you can be a hero'
(From *Damn Yankees*, 1955)

In May 1956, Arthur Miller received a HUAC subpoena in Reno, Nevada, outside the offices of a divorce lawyer, Mr Hills, who was smoothing the transition between his first wife and his second, Marilyn Monroe. He did not try to evade the summons: on the contrary. Hills, a pillar of the establishment judging by the citations on his walls, warned him that it was coming and showed him an escape by the back door, while a fellow client, Carl Royce, a rich cowboy who reminded Miller of John Wayne, offered him a haven on his ranch and a private plane to get there.

Miller described these gestures of support as 'a thoroughly American anarchism' for which he had 'developed a lot of respect as our last stand against fascist decorum.'[1] But he chose to leave by the front door and when he met the HUAC investigator by the lift, he enquired, 'Are you looking for me?' In such ways did Miller acknowledge the state's right to call its citizens to account, while reserving his right as a citizen to say 'No'.

He appeared before HUAC a year later and steadfastly refused to name names. He even went on the attack. He produced an expert witness to assert that his plays were not communist and that he himself was not under communist discipline. This was unprecedented. In previous cases, expert witnesses had only appeared for the prosecution. Eventually, the Committee fined him $500 for contempt of Congress and sentenced him to a month in jail, suspended; and in 1958, the Supreme Court reversed this decision. 'Historically,' Miller wrote, 'we were in the narrow trough between the grandiose anti-Communist crusade and the next ennobling cause, the war in Vietnam . . .'[2]

Miller was indignant that he had been convicted at all, but his light sentence almost amounted to an apology. His dignified manner at his

13

hearing may have helped. It drew the press to his side. *The New Republic*, which described him as 'the passionately self-exploring, artist-genius type', praised him for staying 'cool and unemotional' under fire. He was 'impressive'.[3] His stance evoked Hollywood memories from the old days where a young Henry Fonda battled for plain folk against corruption.

Miller had prepared his mind to cope with his ordeal and this was not surprising, for the plays on which his reputation was already securely based, and the genre to which they belong, were much concerned with how an individual stood up against malign social pressures, or failed to do so. He adapted Ibsen's *An Enemy of the People* (1950) for Broadway; and it could be argued that McCarthyism was like the poison in the system against which Dr Stockmann ardently campaigned. A closer parallel, however, was with *The Crucible*; and in *Timebends*, Miller compared his expert witness, Harry Cain, with the Reverend Hale, who tried to undo the damage caused by his previous false witness.

The likeness which struck almost everyone else was between Miller himself and John Proctor, the play's hero, because he refused to bear witness against others and in his manner of doing so, his moral stand. Technically, the character of Proctor was developed along the lines recommended for tragic heroes in A.C. Bradley's *Shakespearian Tragedy* (1904), one reason why *The Crucible* was considered to be more of a tragedy than Miller's other plays which also ended in calamity: *All My Sons* (1947), *Death of a Salesman* (1949) and *A View from the Bridge* (1956). Bradley's book was a standard text in English-speaking universities and influenced many dramatists of the period, including T.S. Eliot and Eugene O'Neill. Bradley's theories were based upon Aristotle's *The Poetics* (c. 335 BC), the point of departure for most Western literary criticism, which he simplified and brought up to date to fit not only Shakespeare but other demands of the modern world.

Bradley followed Aristotle by asserting that the tragic hero should be a man (or woman) 'above average', but with a character flaw which circumstances exploit, thus bringing about his/her downfall. At the crisis, when the information about the main story has been gathered in and the outcome is in sight, a new enlightenment dawns – that, beyond the suffering, higher justice prevails. Tragic heroes rarely went quietly. Either from what they say about themselves or from what others say about them, their fates are turned into parables for mankind, a task which, according many critics, was better tackled in verse than prose.

The flaw in Proctor's character was that he had lusted after the servant-girl, Abigail, whose jealousy brought to the surface the madness in Salem. The crisis came when Proctor chose to face death rather than lend support to the witch-hunters:

> *Hale*: Man, you will hang! You cannot!
> *Proctor* (his eyes full of tears): I can. And there's your first marvel, that I can. You have made your magic now, for now I see some shred of goodness in John Proctor. Not enough to weave a banner with, but white enough to keep it from such dogs.

This may not count as poetry, but within Miller's dour restraint elsewhere in the play, it ranked as heightened prose; and the moral point was succinctly made. By standing firm, Proctor lost his life, but regained the self-respect that his affair with Abigail had nearly cost him. The crucible burnt but purified.

Something similar (without the hanging) may have happened to Miller at the HUAC hearing. As *Timebends* reveals, he was feeling guilty about his divorce. His marriage to Monroe had turned him from being a retiring writer into the kind of star (tarnished by scandal) which HUAC in its dying days needed to persecute. He could have escaped, but he did not want to subject Monroe to unwelcome publicity. He thus shouldered his burden like a man and turned defeat into a moral victory.

Miller himself was nearly a tragic hero, as defined by Bradley, but Bradley's views on this matter were not quite the same as Aristotle's. One bone of contention lay in what was meant by 'above average'. Aristotle expected that the hero should come from a noble family, a guardian of the *polis* or city state; but even for an Edwardian critic like Bradley, this sounded snobbish. Bradley extended the definition to those who were above average in ability, education and moral insight. That was one reason why Joe Keller in *All My Sons* and Willy Loman in *Death of a Salesman* were not rated as tragic heroes. Of *Death of a Salesman*, Eric Bentley remarked that 'the theme arouses pity but no terror. Man is here too little and too passive to play the tragic hero'.[4] Proctor came closer to the heroic stature, as did Miller.

Bradley established a connection between the hero's flaw and his downfall, which thus became a punishment. Aristotle was less specific. The gods must have some reason to torment him, for otherwise they would be unjust; but the hero could be the victim of someone else's flaws or of a revenge cycle which stretched back for generations. He could be under instructions from rival gods. Humility might pacify the gods, as pride would antagonise them, but Aristotle left room for the idea that the fates might simply conspire against the hero, without assistance on his part.

Bradley pointed out, however, that at some level, all of Shakespeare's heroes had caused their fates. If Lear had been less arrogant, Hamlet less indecisive, Macbeth less credulous and Othello less prone to jealousy, their downfalls could have been avoided. They had nobody to blame but themselves, however harsh this judgement may seem. The disaster was not their fault, but they had contributed to it. Bradley nudged tragic theory towards the notion that individuals were morally responsible for their lives, which, as Kennan might have pointed out, was the underlying assumption of all liberal democacies. Without it, the institutions of the Free World would collapse, trial by jury, the free press and elections. It was a principle which the West had to accept if its system of government was to survive at all.

In the 1950s, however, science and communism had in their different ways laid the burden on liberals to prove to what extent individuals could be considered to be 'free', bearing in mind that their lives were conditioned by so many factors outside their control, including language. If human beings were not free, they could not be held responsible, morally or otherwise. In an essay, 'On social plays', Miller argued that it was easier for a citizen in ancient Greece to believe that he was responsible for what happened in his society, because 'the *polis* were small units, apparently deriving from an earlier tribal organization, whose members probably knew one another personally. . . . The preoccupation of Greek drama with ultimate law, with the Grand Design, so to speak, was therefore an expression of a basic assumption of the people, who could not conceive, luckily, that any man could long prosper unless his *polis* prospered'.[5]

But the United States was too big for such a connection easily to be made, not only geographically but in the diversity and range of its ethnic groups. Beneath the formal shell of its eighteenth-century Constitution, what was left of America but a seething mass of sectional interests? This was why on one level, the idea of federal nationhood had to be sustained by flag-waving patriotism and the American Dream, while on another, the daunting size of the US drove its inhabitants into self-protecting tribal packs, smaller even than the Greek *polis*, the nuclear family, an enclave of Italian immigrants, a farm in the prairies, a huddle of settlers' shacks by the Rockies.

Show-business contributed to national stability by providing the United States with images of its scale and its compensating homeliness. The lone cowboy riding the range was one sign for the continental vastness, while another might be the whistle-stop odysseys of a Hollywood bio-pic. But America's most popular play was, and still is, Thornton Wilder's *Our Town* (1938). Grover's Corner, New Hampshire, became the Hollywood model for small-town life, where stars like Monroe played the girls-next-door.

Miller wanted to show the shadows behind the radiant screen, how neighbourliness concealed moral evasions and how the American dream of self-made success bore down heavily on middle-aged has-beens and never-weres, like Willy Loman. In his youth during the 1920s and 1930s, he had watched his father, a manufacturer, succumb to the Depression. He blamed the capitalist system and toyed with communism; but after the war, Stalinism so damaged his faith that he lost interest in party politics altogether. But he did not become disillusioned with the older definition of politics, that is, how the individual relates to the *polis*. That was his main concern for ten years until, after *A View from the Bridge* (1956), he seemed to suffer from a prolonged writer's block, which has been blamed upon his relationship with Monroe.

He wrote a film script for her, *The Misfits* (1960), but no new stage play until *After the Fall* (1964). This was taken to be an account of their marriage, but written in an odd style, with flashbacks and dream sequences, loosely connected by narration. It was as if Miller had lost confidence not only in politics and his marriage, but in his former way of looking at the world. The question marks which hovered over his social dramas and prevented some critics from calling them tragedies, had not faded with the years, but grown ever darker. His plays may have offered a strong retort to the optimism of George Abbott, they may have revealed the halo of darkness surrounding the American Dream, but they still lacked the inevitability of classical tragedy.

Would Loman, for example, have killed himself, if he had had a good year as a salesman and his son had made the football team? Probably not. Would Keller in *All My Sons* have been innocent, if his factory had supplied non-defective parts to warplanes which then went on to drop nuclear bombs on Japan? Possibly so, in which case the question arose as to the meaning of 'all'. Did it extend to all American servicemen, to all the Allied Forces – or to humanity at large? Keller and Loman did not have to contend with unseen forces or irreconcilable dilemmas, only with a society which placed a high premium on material success.

The humanisation of tragedy after Bradley led on to the idea that if societies behaved sensibly, all would be well. Soviet critics had already pronounced tragedy dead. In a modern world, controlled by scientific communism, it had no place. This seemed to be reassuring. Modern man did not need to fear the wrath of the gods. But it increased the scale of human responsibility immeasurably, beyond that of the *polis* to the world itself. There was no point where personal responsibility ended and destiny began. We were all Atlases, upholding the globe.

Classical tragedy explored the frontier between faith and reason. In ancient Greek, it was characterised by the distinction between *mythos* and *logos*, both of which simply meant a 'word' or a 'sign', but in different senses. *Logos* was used for a sign whose validity could be established by personal experience or reason; whereas *mythos* meant a sign whose validity rested upon divine revelation or unprovable assumptions. All languages were held to contain provable and unprovable elements, which made it easier to describe where reason had to give way to faith.

By the 1950s, that distinction had been long lost. Social drama assumed that there must always be a rational explanation somewhere, which was why *The Crucible* failed to generate the same degree of pity and terror as, for example, *Hamlet* or *The Bacchae* of Euripides. Miller and his audiences assumed that the devil did not exist and that what happened in Salem must have been caused by credulity, moral weakness and sexual hysteria. If this is not assumed, Proctor's dilemma becomes more alarming, for he would have to decide whether Abigail's frenzy was solely caused by jealousy or whether diabolic forces were not also at work. If he chose wrongly, all hell would break loose. The very thought of a similar possibility terrified audiences at the first performance of Aeschylus' *The Oresteia*.

This is not a fine point of dramatic theory, but a matter of perception. If we start out with the idea that there must be a logical reason for everything that happens in life, we look for explanations where none may exist. There is a kind of credulity which favours neat theories even when they don't explain much. Miller was too much of a sceptic to be fooled by quackery but he had difficulty in coping with the guilt left by the collapse of his first marriage. He briefly turned to psycho-analysis, at a time when McCarthyism was on a particular rampage.

'I could not help suspecting,' he observed, 'that psycho-analysis was a form of alienation that was being used as a substitute not only for Marxism, but for social activism of any kind.' It was an *ersatz* religion and an alternative ethic. 'The American self, a puritanical item, needed a scheme of morals to administer, and once Marx's was declared beyond the pale, Freud's offered a similar smugness of the saved.'[6]

The Cold War also laid a burden on the consciences of those who, like Miller, chose to carry it. As Arthur Koestler pointed out, it was the first time in history when men knew how to destroy the world. It required a considerable confidence in a way of life to risk defending it with so much at stake; and it was not easy for a US citizen to find out what was happening in the USSR. The choice on offer was between trusting Eisenhower's smile or being racked with a Kennan-like uncertainty, which may have been another reason why so many Americans lay on their analysts' couches each week for 45-minute confessionals.

However little value psycho-analysis may have been to Arthur Miller, Marilyn Monroe was addicted to it. She had many analysts during their marriage, and sometimes several in the same week for added protection. Psycho-analysis was part of her professional life as well, for Monroe attended Lee Strasberg's Actors Studio in New York, where a lot of Freud went a little way.

The Actors Studio, founded in 1950, was a mecca for drama students and Hollywood stars alike; and Strasberg's Method was more than a guide to acting, rather a way of life. It was based on the teachings of the Soviet director, Konstantin Stanislavski, who founded the Moscow Art Theatre (MAT) in 1898, dedicated to high standards of ensemble acting, good citizenry and public education. He was known to drama students for his two books, *My Life in Art* (1924) and *An Actor Prepares* (1926). These were not like other acting primers, but a mixture of anecdote and thoughtful discussion. Their aim was to cultivate a naturalistic style of acting, based not only on observation of how other people behaved, but also on imaginative identification with the characters concerned, acting 'from the inside out'.

MAT toured the United States in the early 1920s with great success. New York had never seen such a company before, such dedication, such naturalism, such teamwork. Many US companies were formed in imitation, among them the Group Theater in 1931, of which Strasberg was a founder-director. After the war, with Stanislavski dead and MAT in the hands of the enemy, Strasberg claimed to have inherited his mantle, although there were other contenders for that honour, including Michael Chekhov, the nephew of Anton Chekhov, whose plays were MAT's glory.

Strasberg taught the young Marlon Brando, whose performance as Stanley Kowalski in the screen version of Tennessee Williams' *A Streetcar Named Desire* (1947) established him as a major star. From then on, many actors sought Strasberg's help, including Ann Bancroft, Paul Newman and Monroe. Brando, however, remained the best advertisement for the Method, for as Kowalski, he scarcely seemed to act. He was what he was supposed to be, a virile Polish-American, who grunted rather than talked.

Strasberg brought psycho-analytical ideas to Stanislavski's teachings. Whereas Stanislavski encouraged his actors to search their memories for clues as to how they might behave in a given situation, Strasberg asked them to look inside themselves for motivating forces which they might not actually be able to remember but which, according to Freud, must be there.

In its popular Freudian model, a human being was divided into three parts, the Super-ego, the Ego and the Id. Of these, the Super-ego was the most superficial, representing Reason and what a person aspires to be. The Id was the most fundamental, the mass of animal needs and drives, mainly sexual, which motivated all human behaviour. The Ego held the balance between the two, which was not easy, for the Id might break loose anarchically or the Super-ego might try to inhibit the Id, which was destructive as well, for the Id would seek its escape in perverted ways, among them bad acting. Strasberg blamed inhibition for the hamminess which both he and Stanislavski detested, and he encouraged the actor

19

to seek a closer contact with the Id. Strasberg was more romantic than Stanislavski. He distrusted the intellect which 'murders to dissect' and urged his actors not to think but to feel. Whereas Stanislavski asked for reason and observation as well as empathy, Strasberg concentrated on motive, the more inner the better. His Method was particularly successful in training actors for the tortured melodramas of Tennessee Williams, whose heroines were those who crumpled most sensitively under pressure.

Strasberg's achievement was to develop a tradition in which actors seemed themselves without self-consciousness. This was why he was so popular in Hollywood. A Method actor provided good material for a director to shoot. A normal actor might think too much or want to push the story along. Method actors concentrated on their motivations, which gave them a self-absorbed quality. In teaching his actors how to relax, Strasberg advised them to adopt that posture in which they could most readily go to sleep.

Marilyn Monroe was his prize pupil, one of two (with Brando) whom Strasberg picked out in 1956 from the 'hundreds of actors and actresses' with whom he had worked.[7] She first attended the Actors Studio in March 1955, when she was already a star with her own production company, but an outsider cannot easily tell what influence Strasberg had on her acting, the difference, for example, between her two performances in Billy Wilder films, *The Seven Year Itch* (pre-Strasberg) and *Some Like It Hot* (post-Strasberg). Both were marvellously funny and sexy.

For Monroe, however, Strasberg was a constant source of re-assurance. He persuaded her that she was a great actress as well as the world's most beautiful woman; and that her past was not something to be wasted but to be explored in the interests of emotional fidelity. Strasberg described their first meeting: 'I saw that what she looked like was not what she really was, and what was going on inside was not what was going on outside. . . . It was almost as if she had been waiting for a button to be pushed.'[8] Monroe confided in Strasberg those intimate details which she had difficulty in explaining to her husband, and Miller, who thought Strasberg a charlatan, was not best pleased. She was a demanding pupil and when Strasberg found himself too busy to attend to her needs, Monroe turned to his wife, Paula, as the next best thing. Laurence Olivier was among several directors irritated by her deference to this higher authority.

The Strasbergs tried to boost her self-confidence with flattery but her behaviour became insanely erratic. Frightened of rejection, she took longer each day to face the outside world, let alone the cameras. She said that as a sex symbol 'everybody is always tugging at you. They would all like sort of a chunk of you.'[9] The prospect of growing old terrified her. The press did not help. The gossip columns did not take her third marriage to Miller seriously. It looked like another Hollywood stunt, a parody of *Born Yesterday* (1949), Garson Kanin's Broadway hit about a dumb blonde who marries an oh-so-sincere Washington journalist. There was life, imitating art, all over again.

But Monroe was not dumb and her relationship with Miller developed in secrecy, away from publicity; and she sought in him the stability that her life lacked. 'When we were first married,' she told a journalist, 'he saw me as so beautiful and innocent among the Hollywood wolves that I tried to be like that. But when the monster showed, Arthur could not believe it. I disappointed him when that happened.'[10] It cannot have been easy for Monroe to be married to someone of Miller's cragged earnestness. It must have felt like camping on Mount Rushmore.

Nor can it have been easy for Miller to acknowledge that he could be of so little help in her despair. While writing *The Misfits*, Miller still thought that he could 'make something of existence.'[11] *The Misfits* started with a truck ride through Reno, 'the divorce capital of the world', and ended with a parody of the great outdoors, where an ageing cowboy ventured out on the range to round up wild mustang for catfood and to demonstrate his manhood to his girl. She was more disgusted than impressed and he let the horses go. They rode back to Reno, their love renewed.

This final moment of optimism was hard to write. Miller tried out several different endings before he could decide on the right one, but it still felt as if he was trying to keep his spirits up. He separated from Monroe in 1960 and they were divorced in 1961. *The Misfits* was his last social drama.

If the Sydney-Carton-like gesture which concludes *Incident at Vichy* (1964) is discounted, his later plays are filled with uncertainty. In *The Price* (1968), Victor's altruism in supporting his father, ruined in the Depression, is as suspect as his richer brother's apparent selfishness, but neither are blamed. *The American Clock* (1980) ticked through the events of his lifetime with an ironic disbelief. In *Two-Way Mirror* (1988), two one-act plays, he dwelt upon themes of much perplexity, how to say goodbye to a dying friend and how to cope with a paranoid girl, akin to Monroe, whose fears may be justified.

Of these, only *The Price* achieved anything like the popular success of his early plays, but the appeal of his later work lies in its refusal to pass judgments. His critical essays, published collectively in 1971, indicated an impatience with social drama and speculated about how tragedies in the classical manner could come once more to be written. In a television interview in 1990, Miller gave a quick definition of tragedy: it is what happens 'when all the birds come home to roost'.[12]

If they came to roost anywhere in Eisenhower's America, it was upon Monroe. Outwardly, she was the supreme Hollywood star, tender and flirtatious, funny and sad, the girl men dreamt of and women envied, a walking, talking doll of an American Dream. Her career, as endlessly re-told in movie magazines, was a rags-to-riches story. She was christened Norma Jean Baker, brought up by foster parents and worked in her teens in a factory, where she was spotted by an army photographer who, instructed by his commanding officer, Ronald Reagan, was looking for patriotic pictures. Her first step to stardom was as the US equivalent to a Ukrainian tractor driver. Her second marriage at the age of twenty was to a baseball star, Joe DiMaggio, her third to an all-American-Jewish egghead and, at her death, it was rumoured that she was aspiring higher, to the Kennedy clan itself. There was much discussion as to how she achieved the wiggle in her walk. Some said that her bottom swayed seductively from side to side because she always placed one foot exactly in front of the other. Others argued that she cheated by filing the sides of her high heels, so that each step was slightly off-balance.

She was described in language which veered wildly from the snide to the adulatory. Strasberg said that 'she was engulfed in a mystic-like flame, like when you see Jesus at the Last Supper and there's a halo around him. There was this great white light surrounding Marilyn.'[13] But he went on to explain to reporters how she had slept her way to stardom, using the backs of cars when there were no casting couches available.

There was another side to Eisenhower's America which she epitomised, its rootlessness. While Miller clung on to family duties which might have been better discarded, she discarded where she might have clung on. Her change of name from Baker to Monroe represented a complete change of life, and there were other transformations ahead – from cheesecake to actress, from call-girl to hostess, from dumb blonde to political companion. She read avidly and took everything to heart, nuclear warfare, world famine, the plight of refugees.

She was never a paid-up member of the Beat Generation, but there were similarities. The artists of the Beat Generation are sometimes treated as if they all belonged to some embryonic class revolt, which under McCarthyism could never take place. In fact, they had few opinions in common, other than wanting to pursue a spontaneous life-style which meant drugs, sex and freewheeling across America. If they made a political gesture, it was that politics was of no importance. It simply interfered with living.

Almost everything, however, that the Beat writers, Charles Bukowski, Jack Kerouac or Alan Ginsberg ever did, was a protest against the happy American family, as featured by Hollywood. Kerouac's novel, *On The Road* (1957), set out the attractions, a loose-limbed honesty, while Jack Gelber's play, *The Connection* (1959) offered a darker side, rootless addicts waiting for a fix.

Monroe, however, drifted without protesting, took drugs without escaping, moved from place to place and man to man without tasting freedom; and her glittering career brought her everything but peace of mind. Doubting herself, she trusted nobody and anybody; and confirmed her insecurity by seeking out the untrustworthy at ever higher levels of authority. She lost the knack of sleeping. She spent the last months of her life under the surveillance of the Mafia, the FBI, the CIA and a private detective employed by Joe DiMaggio, while her analysts blamed her paranoia on her unhappy childhood. She died from an overdose of drugs in 1962 (accidentally perhaps, suicide?, manslaughter?, still unknown), the first casualty of Kennedy's Camelot.

European writers sometimes commented upon the 'middle-distance blindness' of US culture, which partly meant that while Americans might have a clear image of family life and a lofty vision of the Free World, there was a big grey area in between where anything could happen – gunfights, bar-room brawls, random lynchings. It was as if their notion of social responsibility gave out somewhere at the end of the street and did not begin again until some foreign field where they were defending Liberty. Miller expressed it differently: 'we want to create a new cosmos and each man in America is going to create that cosmos all by his little self and he is not going to need a society.'[14]

Eisenhower's America seemed bored by the poverty of the blacks, indifferent to slums and resentful of activists who tried to disturb their peace of mind. But 'middle-distance blindness' could also mean that there was nothing to fill the gap between the optimism of an Abbott musical and the pessimism of a Eugene O'Neill play; or that there were no stages between the rationality of an Arthur Miller and the blind faith of a Christian revivalist.

It was in that grey area that Marilyn Monroe came to dwell. Capable of devotion on one level and idealism on another, she became the victim of forces which neither she could control nor her doctors explain. She was 'above average' in an Aristotelian sense, for she was the living symbol of her society; and those who moralised about her downfall claimed that she had aspired too high, to marry the leader of the Free World (who was married already). If we want to take an example from real life, it was Marilyn Monroe, rather than Arthur Miller, who most closely conformed to the pattern of a Greek tragic hero.

Greek tragedy had one great aim, catharsis, which is better translated as 'purification' than 'purgation'. It was a way of trying to cure the latent panic within a society, when there are too many conflicting possibilities, some terrible, some tempting, but nobody knows which is which. The easy way out is to pretend that all is well, to ignore the doubts and fears, and to push them down deep into the soul. This can lead not only to private nightmares, in which the dangers seem more terrible for never having been confronted, but that sort of public optimism in which we march cheerfully towards self-inflicted disasters.

Aristotle described a form of theatre in which the competing claims of the gods could be publicly examined, but also where, through the downfall of the tragic hero, human limitations were acknowledged. But the docile acceptance of whatever the gods had in store could be another form of evasion. Brecht, on the part of forward-looking socialists, hated it and science had so increased our control over the world that it was hard in any case to tell where human limits began or ended. To accept limitations without knowing what they were was tantamount to superstition.

None the less, the prevailing belief that there was nothing on earth which could not eventually be controlled by man, that there were no forces to daunt the rational mind, made it difficult to write tragedies in the classical manner. The purpose of tragedy had been removed, the reconciliation of man to god. Nor is it entirely fanciful to suggest that the loss of a tragic vision was one reason why America rocked towards its hubris in Vietnam.

3

BINKIE BEAUMONT'S WEST END

'We Said We'd Never Look Back'
(From *Salad Days*, 1954)

In 1956, while waiting for the HUAC hearing, Arthur Miller and Marilyn Monroe flew to Britain to stay for a few weeks in Surrey, while Monroe was filming at Shepperton Studios. They were charmed by what they found – respectful reporters, disciplined actors, the choir of adult schoolboys who sang beneath their bedroom windows while they were trying to recover from the trans-Atlantic flight at Lord North's country estate near Windsor.

What Miller did not like was the 'trivial, voguish theatre' of the West End, 'slanted to please the upper middle class'.[1] His own play, *A View from the Bridge*, was starting its rehearsals at the New Watergate; and he asked its director, Peter Brook, why the actors who came to audition had such cut-glass accents. 'Doesn't a grocer's son,' he asked, 'ever want to become an actor?' Brook replied, 'These are all grocer's sons.'[2]

They had been trained to talk like that in drama school and most leading parts were written with such an accent in mind. An actor who could not get rid of a dialect was not unemployable, for there were always character parts. You could earn a living as a spiv (George Cole), a Lancashire lassie (Gracie Fields) or a Cockney char (Kathleen Harrison), but these were often cameos, and it could be a chastening experience just to walk on in Act Three for want of a vowel sound. The BBC also favoured Home Counties diction and in 1951, it officially stated that no 'dialect' voices should read the national news. Women were also excluded. 'People do not like momentous events such as war and disaster to be read by the female voice.'[3]

Thus the Aristotelian principle was observed that the public identi-fied with those who are better than average. With the right accent in Britain, you signalled to others that you came from a good family, had received a classical education, and could thus speak with authority. The best-known upper-class accents on the English stage came, however, from those who had no such social advantages. Ivor Novello was brought up in Cardiff, Noel Coward in Teddington, Edith Evans in Pimlico. To shake off a dialect might also mean that you were trying to get rid of your past to be someone who was fit to govern or at least to play the king.

In the theatre, as in daily life, the British were quick to catch the lapses that demonstrated that someone was not quite what he or she seemed and foreigners were struck by the stage subtleties of the genteel (Joyce Grenfell) or the upwardly mobile. The Polish artist, Feliks Topolski, described it as 'exotic'. Deference to the class system lay close to the grain of British theatre, in its characterisation, its dialogue and in the way in which plots were handled. This did not always mean open snobbery. The true aristocrat was modest and polite to social inferiors: he made them 'feel at ease'. Only a cad flaunted an old school tie, to which he may not have been entitled.

The theatre critic of the *New Statesman*, Stephen Potter, compiled a catalogue of British snubs and nuances. It was called *Gamesmanship*, or 'the art of winning games without actually cheating', and it became very popular as a radio series with several sequels, *One-Upmanship*, *Lifemanship* and *Supermanship*. Bertolt Brecht admired the irony of British actors, the coolness by which they could convey whole hierarchies of authority and obedience. Miller, however, found it very strange. British actors approached their roles in exactly the opposite way from Method actors, from the outside in, not the inside out. They bothered about their accents first and their motivations later.

He was amazed at the way in which the cast for *A View from the Bridge* created a wholly fictional world, quite unlike the Brooklyn waterfront where the play was set. They may have taken their accents from gangster movies, their gestures from Italian waiters and their proletarian roughness from John Steinbeck; but the result was 'internally consistent and wholly persuasive'.[4] The same might have been said of the West End which was full of people, on stage and off, pretending to be other than they were; and confusing innocent Americans like Miller by being so modest about it. It was as if the British class system intended to perpetuate itself by being disarmingly nice. Who could take offence at bumbling gentry (A.E. Matthews), chinless wonders (Ian Carmichael) and sensitive patriarchs (Eric Portman)?

But Miller saw flashes of the other side, the ruthlessness of the empire-builders. On a previous visit, he had watched the parliamentary procedure at work in the House of Commons. It was in 1950, the Labour Government was in power and Churchill sat on the opposition benches. A Communist MP, Willie Gallacher, was speaking 'with his thumbs hooked in the pockets of his unpressed trousers.' Churchill growled, 'Take your hands out of your pockets, man!' – and Gallacher instantly did so.[5] 'That was class talking and being obeyed,' observed Miller, 'and it was not something I had ever witnessed in the United States or thought possible, either the incredible command or the reaction to it.'

In the jargon of the times, Britain was a top-down society, whereas the United States was bottom-up. Apart from being a monarchy and not a republic, it was led by a comparatively small group of people with common religion, C. of E. by assumption, and a classical education. You still needed to pass an examination in Latin to enter Oxbridge. These values permeated down into society through the civil service, the law and such institutions as the BBC and West End Theatre. George Kennan admired the cohesive force of British culture which had held the society together through two world wars, post-war poverty and the startling reforms introduced by the Labour Party.

But what particularly impressed him, as a diplomat, was the way in which Britain was withdrawing from its empire without de-stabilising the West. The independence of India and Pakistan were prime examples; but so too was the way in which Britain was conducting its campaign against communist guerrillas in Malaysia, so unlike the French in Indo-China. The British had developed the knack of battling against so-called terrorists one month and negotiating with them the next. When they were losing a war, they granted independence, as if it was theirs to give, and left behind certain legacies of Empire – to India a civil service, to Ghana a parliament building – as if they expected their former colonies to support themselves in the manner to which they had become accustomed. Stephen Potter had a word for it, FO-manship, the Art of Losing Empires without being quite defeated.

When the ceremonies were over, the Queen welcomed them into the Commonwealth as if they were grown-up sons who had passed through troublesome adolescences. Kennan, who did not underestimate the problems or the blood shed on the way, attributed these skills to culture. The British may be old-fashioned and snobbish, but they were not vulgar. They did not waste their lives in pursuit of the fast buck. They had a wider vision.

Miller, however, distrusted British double-standards, and he had an example close to hand. The British prided themselves on having nothing quite so barbaric as the McCarthyite show trials, but these were not necessary. Every new script had to be vetted by the Lord Chamberlain's Examiner of Plays, every film by the British Board of Film Censors. The BBC observed a similar code; and programme-makers were kept under control by a government-appointed Board of Governors who were accountable, through the Postmaster-General, to Parliament. It was a secretive process. While the British censors might tolerate a more open political debate than Joe McCarthy, they were repressive on matters of religion, sex, bad language and disrespect for the monarchy.

The British might not have a wider vision than the Americans, but they did have a strong middle-distance vision. On intimate matters, such as sexual relationships, they could be tongue-tied; and resisted psycho-analytical probings. They were too pragmatic for the political or philosophical visions of the French or the Germans. But they had a clear image of the patterning of their society, where people came from and what they might do for a living, and this could be more subtle than the binary division of Marxism, bosses versus workers. They knew how to behave (or not) in public and upheld the family disciplines; and this too stemmed from a classical training, with its stoicism, its sense of form and its habit of leaving the emotions off-stage.

It often seemed as if Christianity and class conspired to keep the British in a state of suspended adolescence. It left a trail of innuendo across intimate revues. In the United States, free speech was thought to be an inalienable right. In Britain, it was a concession, granted by a paternal government protecting the best interests of its subjects. This left its theatre not only censored and class-bound, but formidably house-trained. The dancers in British musicals had such pretty frocks, the singers such sweet voices. What they lacked was energy. The strippers in tacky variety shows were not allowed to move. They had to pose, stock-still, in imitation of Greek statues.

A View from the Bridge contained two censorable subjects, homosexuality and incest, which was why Anthony Field at the Comedy Theatre had sent it along to the New Watergate for a club production. Private theatre clubs offered a loophole in the censorship laws, for they were treated as homes, not places of entertainment. But the cast was too large for the New Watergate's stage and Field consulted with lawyers about the practicality of turning the Comedy Theatre into a club. This was the first time that anybody had tried to do so with a West End theatre. Field enlisted the help of Hugh Beaumont of H.M. Tennent Ltd; and they devised a scheme whereby the law could be observed but broken.

Miller was impressed by the manoeuvre, but puzzled by British logic. Why, if you had applied for a membership card a day in advance, were you less likely to be corrupted? The answer was that club membership deterred the passerby; and women, servants and children could not be corrupted by accident. Other West End producers wondered whether the law would have been evaded so easily if the play had not been backed by H.M. Tennent Ltd.

Beaumont was then the most powerful man in British theatre, who could make and break reputations, and set next season's fashions. Miller liked him a lot. 'A tough negotiator, he seemed to love the theatre and good plays and knew what good acting was and loved that too.'[6] But Beaumont more than anybody else was responsible for the theatrical snobbery that Miller disliked so much. He had cultivated a certain class style, and marketed it, and sent it out on regional tours so that if people heard of a Tennent production, they knew exactly what to expect.

Beaumont was the funnel through which the class system penetrated so comprehensively into British theatrical life. He was born in Cardiff in 1908; and his childhood nickname which stuck, Binkie, was a local slang word for a black or a ragamuffin which was precisely what Beaumont, even as a child, was not. He came from a middle-class home and joined the local Playhouse Theatre as an apprentice manager at the age of 15. He could neither act, sing nor dance; but he had the flair of a natural showman. Among his duties, he had to look after the visiting stars. For Tallulah Bankhead, who could be hard to handle, he placed a few snacks in her dressing room, smoked salmon, some lobster mousse with black grapes, her favourite champagne. Miss Bankhead was so impressed by this handsome boy that she took him back to London as a small token of appreciation from Wales.

When she returned to New York, Beaumont sought employment elsewhere and was taken out to lunch by the Provincial Bookings Manager for Moss Empires, Mr H.M. Tennent. Harry Tennent groomed Beaumont. He introduced him to his Savile Row tailors and in other ways became a role model. Tennent had the social advantages that Beaumont lacked. He had received a First in Greats at Oxford. He was an all-round sportsman, a former President of OUDS, an accomplished pianist-singer, tall, handsome and unmarried. He came from a distinguished family, fallen on hard times, which was why he had entered trade.

What was such an Edwardian paragon doing in the Provincial Bookings Department of Moss Empires? Strange though it may now seem, this was an important and lucrative position. Tennent's immediate task was to develop a tatty collection of music halls into something more suitable for the jazz age. He was at the heart of the streamlining process which produced the numbers one, two and three touring circuits of the 1930s. The factor which prompted this transformation was the introduction of entertainments tax in 1917, a wartime measure which lasted until British theatre was on the point of collapse in 1958. It devastated the provincial managements which characterised Edwardian theatre. To meet the increased taxes, they spread production costs, which led to the habit of rehearsing shows in London which then toured; and thus metropolitan tastes prevailed over regional ones and cut-glass accents could be heard on the stage from Dumfries to Land's End.

Tennent, with Beaumont at his side, was so successful that in 1933 he was head-hunted by another theatrical chain, Howard and Wyndham, but instead of leaving Moss Empires, he persuaded them to join forces. Working together, the two companies owned or controlled large sections of British theatre. In 1936, Tennent set up an independent play-producing company, H.M. Tennent Ltd, to supply productions to these chains. Beaumont took over as managing director after Tennent's death in 1941. Together they had laid the foundations for a wider, if informal, merger of managements during the war, which became known as The Group.

In 1952, Equity, the British actors' union, produced a report which accused The Group of possessing a 'horizontal' monopoly over British theatre. It owned half the theatres in the West End and more than half of the three main touring circuits. More significantly, it also possessed a 'vertical' monopoly, a control over the companies supplying the theatres, such as actors' agencies, sheet music publishers and publicity agents. The Group had, according to Equity, a stranglehold over British theatre and the man whose thumbs were near the jugular was Binkie Beaumont. This was hard to prove. He rarely issued a contract. His word was his bond; but an actor who let him down seldom worked again.

Beaumont's war record, having been exempt from military service, was outstanding. In six years, he produced fifty-nine shows in the West End and sent out more than a hundred on tour. Of these, only seven lost money. Nor could anyone complain that this commercial success had been achieved by lowering standards. On the contrary, his standards were high, if you believed in those standards. The day war broke out, he revived *The Importance of Being Earnest* at the Golders Green Hippodrome, with John Gielgud as John Worthing and Edith Evans as Lady Bracknell. It has never been bettered. To greet the end of the war, he revived another Oscar Wilde play at the Haymarket, *Lady Windermere's Fan*, with sets by Cecil Beaton. It opened two days after the first atom bomb fell on Hiroshima. 'His sense of occasion', commented his biographer, Richard Huggett, 'was triumphant',[7] although it seems to have been somewhat untouched by events.

As an impresario, Beaumont excelled in assembling packages. He was particularly good at casting and his stars, whom he groomed and treated like stars, included most of the great names of the time – Novello, Coward, Margaret Rutherford, the Lunts, Alec Guinness, Rex Harrison and Richard Burton. Gielgud was a particular friend. Among his designers were Beaton, John Piper and Oliver Messel. His favoured dramatists included Frederick Lonsdale and Terence Rattigan, as well as Coward. He had good contacts across the Atlantic and the Channel, which he fostered. He produced plays by Jean Anouilh, Thornton Wilder and Tennessee Williams in London. His last great hit, although he continued to produce plays until his death in 1973, was the London version of *My Fair Lady* (1958).

Under his management, H.M. Tennent Ltd became the Fortnum & Mason's of British theatre, a supplier of quality goods to the gentry and those of a similar disposition. The Arts Council of Great Britain (ACGB), founded in 1946 to succeed the wartime Council for the Encouragement of Music and the Arts (CEMA), wanted to go into partnership with him and Beaumont had this in common with the subsidised sector. He was the first major impresario to use the Charity Act to evade entertainments tax. Under British law, charities can be tax-exempted if their purpose is to relieve and educate the poor. Some CEMA companies had claimed this concession on tours taking Shakespeare and the Greek classics to mining villages in Wales. Beaumont set up a non-profit-distributing subsidiary company, Tennent Productions Ltd, to produce new plays which he liked. He could then plough back the profits into the company or transfer the whole production to H.M. Tennent Ltd for marketing on a wider commercial scale.

This caused a brush with Parliament. In 1954, the Labour MP, Woodrow Wyatt, presented a bill to the Commons, whose aim was 'to control non-profit-distributing theatrical companies' and he provided figures which revealed that, under normal circumstances, N.C. Hunter's *A Day By The Sea*, from Tennent Productions Ltd., should have provided £500 to the Treasury from its weekly profits of £3,000. As it was, it yielded them nothing. Wyatt's target, however, was the scale of Beaumont's influence over British theatre. He had a dossier of complaints from those in the theatre who claimed that they had been 'black-listed'; and he asked whether Beaumont's near-monopolistic powers were healthy. After a lively debate, the House decided that they were.

Beaumont's status and aesthetic standards were thus endorsed by Parliament. But what kind of theatre did he offer? From where did these standards derive? Tennent may have been his mentor in the ways of London, but Beaumont's spiritual guide was surely Sir George Alexander, the actor-manager who ran the St James's Theatre from 1890 until 1917. Beaumont revived, and went on reviving, plays from Alexander's pre-ragtime band (by Wilde and A.W. Pinero in particular) and he looked for similar society comedies and dramas, with a hint of Edwardian subversion, a Wildean dandy or a Fallen Woman sympathetically portrayed.

The link between the two regimes can be illustrated by comparing Pinero's *The Second Mrs Tanqueray*, produced by Alexander in 1893, and Rattigan's *The Deep Blue Sea* (1952). Both plays concern 'fallen women', married to upright but boring husbands, who have lovers who betray them, and eventually contemplate or commit suicide. Both explore what it is like to feel in or out of society, what should be sacrificed to save a love affair and where passion conflicts with duty. Both share a tolerance which extends almost all the way round and in both, this broadmindedness is deceptive. Paula Tanqueray's suicide is presented as the best thing she could have done under the circumstances, an English *Hedda Gabler*, while Rattigan wanted to write about his own

31

doomed love affair with the actor, Kenneth Morgan, and Beaumont, who was gay as well, dissuaded him. He did not want trouble with the Lord Chamberlain.

Both were 'well-made plays', a boulevard form of classicism, popularised by the French in the early nineteenth century but adopted as a model throughout the Western world. They start out with a conflict which is resolved by a decision at the crisis. They progress 'from ignorance to knowledge', allowing the writers to use the time-honoured devices of suspense (the withholding of information) and pace (the provision of information); and they obey, not too slavishly, the Unities of Time, Place and Action.

Well-made plays provided the theatrical equivalent of what in architecture might be called Bankers' Georgian. In the 1950s, this pseudo-classical structure was under attack from Modernists of many persuasions. Miller disapproved of Abbott's addiction to the well-made play, Beckett poked fun at it, while Brecht provided an elaborate alternative, his Epic Theatre. They argued variously that the well-made play fostered a false sense of progress and crippled the imagination, but also that it propped up the class system by suggesting that life's decisions were best taken by heros and heroines in middle-class drawing rooms.

Whether this was so of *The Deep Blue Sea* is debatable, but Alexander and Beaumont certainly ran their theatres to appeal to the middle classes. Battling against the raffish reputation of Victorian show-business, Alexander transformed the St James's Theatre into a model of stylish respectability. He took Wilde's name off the playbills for *The Importance of Being Earnest* after his trial, but he didn't take off the play. Beaumont behaved similarly, hushing up scandals, maintaining propriety, savouring the moments when he could welcome a member of the Royal Family to the Haymarket. Sir Anthony Eden was a personal friend.

Unlike Alexander, who led by example, Beaumont was powerful enough to impose his standards, and there is another difference between the two regimes. The gentry who thronged to the St James's in the 1900s were at the heart of an empire. Their codes were of consequence from Delhi to Timbuktu. At one of Alexander's Society dramas, you did not ask 'Why am I watching these boring people?' These boring people ran the world. But in the 1950s, nobody knew what would happen to the Empire. It was a source of much anxiety. Could it be revived? Was it immoral in the first place? Could it be defended in a nuclear age and, if not, what would happen to relatives scattered over the world?

It was of little comfort to watch people behaving as if they ruled the world, if you knew that they did not, or rather (since nothing in those days was certain) thought that they might not. The West End was withering with an autumnal spirit. Dried leaves were falling everywhere

– on T.S. Eliot's *The Elder Statesman,* in Bagnold's *The Chalk Garden,* in Hunter's *A Day By The Sea.* 'Whom shall I condemn to death?' mused the dying Alexander the Great in Rattigan's *Adventure Story.* He is thinking about a possible heir. It was fashionable to be world-weary. Cynicism was smart.

In November 1956, Beaumont's empire suffered a particular blow. In the Middle East, Egyptian forces had seized the Suez Canal, thus cutting off Britain's main sea link to the Far East. With France and Israel as its allies, Britain invaded Egypt and regained the canal zone without difficulty. Beaumont's friend, the Prime Minister Sir Anthony Eden, went on television to plead with the people. 'All my life,' he said, 'I have been a man of peace . . .', but his Edwardian features looked pale and drawn. The United States was not supporting Britain. Dulles regarded the whole affair as an imperial escapade; and within days, the troops were withdrawn. The Cold War had imposed its logic; and a few days later, Eden resigned, sick in mind, body and spirits.

At that moment, the class system seemed on the brink of collapse and with it much that was perceived to be British about the British way of life: its pragmatism, its discipline, its paternal benevolence 'cruel to be kind'. The plays on which Beaumont had based his success seemed not just old-fashioned, but dangerously self-deluding and the next fifteen years can be characterised as a 'de-mythologising' of the class system, from top to bottom, from the guardians to the students' gigs. Latin ceased to be a requirement for entrance to Oxbridge.

Beaumont did not stop producing plays but lost his influence over British theatre. The first nights of Noel Coward's last plays, *A Suite in Three Keys* (1965), produced by Beaumont with the Master playing leading roles, must rank high among the sad occasions of British theatre. It was like attending a memorial service for those who were not quite dead.

In 1957, Eden's successor, Harold Macmillan, went around the country with morale-boosting speeches, whose appeal lay not to destiny but self-interest. 'Let us be frank,' he told a meeting of Conservative party workers in July, 'most of our people have never had it so good.' In one way, he was right. There was full employment and standards of living were rising; but this did not compensate for the loss of security and self-esteem which came not from nuclear weapons but from being part of a social order that was still thought to be intact. In 1957, two thousand people left Britain every week for the white Commonwealth.

'There aren't any good brave causes left,' mourned Jimmy Porter in John Osborne's *Look Back in Anger* (1956), a new play presented by a new theatrical management, the English Stage Company (ESC) at the Royal Court Theatre. The ESC was formed in 1955 to foster young writers, one of several off-centre attempts to change the course of British theatre.

Nobody knew where these new writers might come from or what they might write. The founder of the ESC, the playwright Ronald Duncan, thought that the future lay in verse drama, probably with a Christian theme, along lines pioneered by T.S. Eliot, Christopher Fry and Duncan himself. The artistic director, George Devine, had different ideas, as did other members of the ESC's first Board. They put an advertisement in the trade newspaper, *The Stage*, to see what might emerge.

Of the hundreds of scripts sent in, *Look Back in Anger* was the only one which they felt was worth producing; and they sidled it in mid-season because it was angry, roughly written and the hero wasn't better than average. Devine wrote: 'I knew my country and . . . that we ourselves had to become part of the establishment against which our hearts if not our faces were set.'[8]

In this, he showed more tactical sense than Joan Littlewood, who did not care which persons of influence she upset so long as she upset them. At her Theatre Workshop at Stratford-atte-Bowe, she assembled an un-Beaumont-like package to construct a left-wing and proletarian theatre, part music-hall, part forgotten classics and part Brecht. She searched for new plays, as did Peter Hall, a whizz-kid director from Cambridge who at 25 had donned Alec Clunes's mantle at the Arts Theatre Club. He looked overseas for inspiration and he found *Waiting for Godot*. There were some dozen smaller theatre clubs in London, engaged in a similar quest, and regional managements, notably at Coventry.

These turning-point years from 1955 to 1958 were, however, perceived by the Arts Council as ones of almost unstoppable decline. Beaumont had lost touch and The Group was selling off regional theatres to invest in commercial television and the record industry. Leicester lost two of its three theatres, Swindon its main touring house, and to crown the collapse, Alexander's St James's Theatre in the West End was demolished in 1958.

Arthur Miller noticed the signs of change in 1956. Somewhat reluctantly, Laurence Olivier took him along to see *Look Back in Anger* and Miller loved 'its roughness and self-indulgences, its flinging high in the air so many pomposities of Britishism, its unbridled irritation with life, and its verbal energy'.[9] It reminded him of the young Clifford Odets. They went backstage to meet Devine, a 'modest, cheerful little fanatic', who was sitting with Osborne. Olivier asked Osborne, 'Could you write something for me?' Osborne responded with *The Entertainer*, in which Olivier played a seedy comic, Archie Rice, heir to a famous music-hall name, who toured Britain in a patriotic revue where girls never moved without clothes. 'Don't clap too loud,' he warned anyone out there in the stalls, 'It's a very old building.'

34

The transformation of Olivier's image startled everyone; but Beaumont's stars were on the wane. Gielgud's career suffered, as did the reputations of Coward, Rattigan and Hunter. His young male hopefuls escaped to Hollywood or the Labour Exchange: his carefully groomed actresses thought it wiser to get married. His class style was turned into reverse. Regional accents replaced cut-glass ones, well-made plays were mussed around, old-fashioned politeness sounded camp. Kenneth Tynan led the attack, his target being Rattigan's Aunt Edna, the kind of person who went to matinées and admired the hats. Once, in his later years, Beaumont stopped a young actress entering his theatre in sandals and jeans. 'Don't you want to be beautiful and glamorous?' he protested. 'Don't you want to be admired by other women and pursued by men? Don't you want to be a success and a credit to your employer?'[10] She laughed in his face.

A certain residue of Beaumont's influence was left behind, the better side of Beaumont perhaps, his love of craftsmanship and stage discipline. Younger impresarios, such as Michael Codron, took over, who were equally good at assembling packages but more in tune with the times. In subsequent years, Britain never lacked dramatists who could write well-made plays, if they chose to do so, or skilled actors to perform what they wrote.

Olivier was one actor who survived the change with dignity; but in his autobiography, he wrote that 'I had reached a stage in my life that I was getting profoundly sick of – not just tired – sick'.[11] His marriage was in turmoil and he despaired of West End trivialities, some of which were appearing under his name. In 1956 he took Miller to see Vivien Leigh in Coward's *South Sea Bubble*, a Tennent production which he directed, and they exchanged a grim smile. As an actor, he was approaching the height of his powers. His cry of anguish as Titus Andronicus was described by Tynan as 'the noise made in its last extremity by the cornered human soul'. This 1955 Stratford production, directed and designed by Peter Brook (who also wrote the *musique concrète*), inspired the Polish critic, Jan Kott, to write *Shakespeare Our Contemporary* in the depths of Warsaw's political winter. Tynan, however, did not like Vivien Leigh's Lavinia who received the news that she was to be ravished on her husband's corpse 'with little more than the mild annoyance of one who would have preferred foam rubber'.[12] Leigh was wedded to West End glamour, Olivier was wedded to Leigh; and this was one reason why they were incompatible. During *The Entertainer*, Olivier found a more sympathetic partner, the actress, Joan Plowright.

There was another motive for his change of direction. In 1957, during a weekend party at the Oliviers' country estate, Notley Abbey, a Conservative MP, Oliver Lyttelton, took Olivier aside to enquire whether he would consider taking a lead in the campaign for a National Theatre with a view to becoming its first director. This was not as attractive an offer as it sounds. The campaign had been going on for 120 years without much result. It was a joke in the popular press. Olivier had been caught once before in its toils when, as co-director with Ralph Richardson and John Burrell of the Old Vic in the last years of the war, he thought that he was starting a National Theatre company, only to discover, after he had been slightingly sacked, that he wasn't.

Lyttelton, a persuasive as well as an influential man, a former member of Churchill's wartime cabinet, insisted that now was the time, after Suez, when national morale was at a low ebb, to bring into being a National Theatre for Britain. Olivier's patriotism triumphed over his experience. He decided that while he might not be 'the best man for the job', he was 'probably the only man',[13] which was why he spent the next sixteen years of his life trying to bring into being what Lyttelton described as 'one of the foundations of British Society'.[14]

4

THE HEAT IN BRECHT'S
COOLNESS

'Those who trade and live by war
Get what they don't bargain for.'
(From *Mother Courage*, 1941)

Late in the autumn of 1955, George Devine crossed the policed border
which separated the 'ghastly glitter' of West Berlin from the 'vast
sadness'[1] of the Eastern sector to see what he could make of Brecht's
Berliner Ensemble.

He was on a European tour with the Shakespeare Memorial Company
whose programme included his production of *King Lear*, starring John
Gielgud, one of those bright ideas which didn't quite work. It was
known as the 'Noguchi *Lear*', after the Japanese-American sculptor,
Isamu Noguchi, whose sets and costumes were its principal obstacle.
The intention was to rid the play of its 'historical and decorative
associations' and stress its 'universal and mythical quality'.[2] Noguchi
offered an abstract vision of the planet earth with egg-shaped forms
and ramps. This was what the *avant-garde* often meant in the 1950s,
something immense and not too specific. The holes in Lear's cloak grew
larger as the play went on to suggest a human dilemma more profound
than just having an inadequate laundry. Gielgud said that it was like
acting in a gruyère cheese.

It was Devine's 'last fling as a big institution classical director',
according to his biographer, Irving Wardle, and his last attempt to
mix-match a modern style with an old play, a compromise which
looked more radical than it was. For the English Stage Company, whose
first season he was planning, Devine wanted to find a theatrical form to
concentrate the mind on the turmoil of the times. 'Had we not seen six
million Jews murdered? Were we not seeing McCarthyism in the United
States, the emergence of the coloured races? Were we not experiencing a
scientific adjustment of all our values? No man or woman of feeling who
was not wearing blinkers could not but feel profoundly disturbed'.[3]

Bertolt Brecht came to a matinée of *King Lear* at the Hebbel Theatre and Devine seized the chance to ask his permission to stage the first London production of *The Good Person of Setzuan* (*Der gute Mensch von Setzuan*) at the Royal Court in 1956. Brecht responded cautiously, for he had hoped Binkie Beaumont might be interested, but invited Devine to see the Berliner Ensemble at his own Theater am Schiffbauerdamm in his own play, *The Caucasian Chalk Circle* (*Der kaukasische Kreidekreis*).

Devine arrived at the red neon sign of Brecht's theatre twenty minutes late. The curtain had been held for his arrival to ensure that he noticed one effect. Apart from the portraits of revolutionary heroes, the Theater am Schiffbauerdamm displayed the glories of a turn-of-the-century imperial theatre. Its auditorium 'positively dripped with gilt'[4] and cupids blessed the Fatherland by blowing trumpets at it.

The proscenium arch was apparently made of solid marble but, as the lights rose, that frame seemed to dissolve and Devine saw through the pillars, which were made of gauze, to the wings where the stagehands lingered by fly-ropes and the lighting bars hung down in rows. At a stroke Brecht sent out three signals – that there would be no attempt to sustain a naturalistic illusion, that bourgeois pretensions were gossamer-thin and that fantasies of empire was sustained by the working classes, who could say no.

Devine absorbed a somewhat different message. It was like 'the agreeable chaos of an artist's studio' with the artist himself turning up a picture and saying, 'This is more-or-less finished'.[5] The performance was less like a settled product than a process in which the audience itself played a part. The stage was bathed in white light to prevent trickery. The house lights in the auditorium were not switched off, but dimmed. This meant that friends exchanged glances with friends, conversing through eye-contact. Instead of being locked in the dark, staring at a spotlit hero, the public was on equal terms with the actors, not invited to 'suspend disbelief' but to ask questions. The whole experience was more egalitarian and less *voyeuristic*.

Devine's first impression was one of amateurishness, but he soon realised that the informality was part of the style. 'There is a scene in which twenty peasants are gradually convulsed with laughter. The detail of observation and execution was entirely remarkable and it must have been achieved with much care: one peasant in the front started laughing, the mirth rippled gradually then and overcame all twenty of them.'[6] A British director would simply have said to his cast, 'It starts with you and it goes right through. No, no. You weren't very good, and I didn't believe in your laughter, try it again. Good . . . we open on Monday.'[7] In Britain, the slick exterior masked 'affected, clichéd acting', but the Berliner Ensemble's casual presentation belied the care in the creation. It was the difference between a piece of cut-glass and a rough diamond. Devine marvelled at the amount of time, money and energy which had been spent on leaving *The Caucasian Chalk Circle* thus unfinished. It demonstrated among other matters the merits of the subsidised over the commercial theatre, but he did not know what compromises, if any, Brecht may have had to make to gain his position of privilege.

Devine admired Brecht, an 'intellectual peasant . . . shy and shrewd',[8] which was the impression Brecht liked to give, in his blue overalls and jacket, with his peaked cap cocked to one side, his fierce little cigars and his searching, quizzical expression. But Brecht was not a peasant nor did he come from a rural family, except distantly on his mother's side. In class terms, his background was not so different from Binkie Beamont's. He was born in 1898 and came, like Beaumont, from a provincial town, Augsburg, where his father was the managing director of a paper factory; but, as he later explained,

'. . . I left my own class and associated
With unimportant persons'.[9]

As Beaumont changed his name from the indelibly Welsh words by which he was christened, Hughes Griffiths Morgan, so Brecht dropped his weak-sounding forenames, Eugen Berthold, for the harder Bertolt, which he sometimes shortened to the rougher Bert.

The way in which Beaumont and Brecht labelled themselves reflect class choices, one up, one down, which stayed with them until the ends of their lives. They might have chosen differently if the outcome of the First World War had favoured Germany rather than Britain. However ruinous the war may have been in lives lost, it did not destroy the basis of the British class system and Beaumont's cultivated snobbery could be interpreted as an attempt to repair the damage to the hive. In Brecht's case, there was less of a hive to repair, an outward shell, which was one reason why he sought to build a different society altogether, one based on science, technology and the rights of the workers, and thus he altered his name, and thus his class loyalties.

He entered the war as a teenage patriot, believing in the Holy Imperial cause, but left it as a disillusioned anarchist. His local theatre at Augsburg rubbed salt into his wounds by offering a pallid programme of German classics by Goethe, Hebbel, Schiller and Shakespeare in the Schlegel-Tieck translations, roughly delivered, reverentially received, as if nothing had happened in the intervening years to ruffle the complacency. Brecht compared the passivity of the Augsburg audiences with the partisanship of sports crowds, preferring the latter.

There was one strand in German theatrical life to which he could respond. It had its origins in the turn-of-the-century satirical cabarets, one of whose stars was the dramatist Frank Wedekind. Brecht wrote an obituary in 1918 in which he described how, as the Marquis von Keith, Wedekind 'filled every corner with his personality. There he stood, ugly, brutal and dangerous, with close-cropped red hair, his hands in his trouser pockets, and one felt that the devil himself couldn't shift him.'[10] He imitated the way in which Wedekind sang his songs 'in a brittle voice, slightly monotonous and quite untrained',[11] which was exactly how such singers as Richard Taubert did not sing Schubert.

Wedekind's main influence upon Brecht lay in the way in which he wrote plays, both in form and content. By classical standards, Wedekind's plays were very untidy. The plots rambled. They muddled naturalism with symbolism and caricature, switched from funny moments to tragic ones, and were flagrantly over-theatrical. But he was ringmaster of his circus, cracking his whip across the backs of the bourgeoisie. He would name the unmentionable, masturbation, sodomy and the secret vices of the tax-collector, and turn upside down the Ten Commandments. The hero of Brecht's first performed play, *Baal* (1920), was like a male version of Wedekind's Lulu, a priapic force to match the earth spirit, courting and defying Death to the end.

Wedekind did not witness the collapse of the civilisation he so detested, but Brecht grew up in the ruins. Gloom was the common experience, but among the young radicals it amounted to a savage, cackling despair. In 1920, at an international Dada fair, Georg Grosz hung from the ceiling an effigy of a German soldier with a pig's head. Throughout Europe, the Dadaists delighted in disfiguring icons, but in Germany the movement was uniquely bitter. In Paris Marcel Duchamp scrawled a moustache on the Mona Lisa, in Zurich Tristan Tzara cut up a Shakespeare sonnet, but Grosz desecrated the memory of the dead.

Brecht left Augsburg for Munich, where his first plays were performed, and then, in 1924, for Berlin, where he served as a reluctant *dramaturg* for Max Reinhardt. Reinhardt was the grand showman of German theatre whose age, 57, misled his critics into thinking that he must be past his best. Brecht never made that mistake. Throughout his life, he absorbed powerful influences without being overwhelmed by them, except perhaps for Marxism. He acquired Reinhardt's instinct for scale, what was appropriate for small intimate theatres or for large public ones. From Reinhardt's rival, Leopald Jessner, he learnt the virtues of simple staging, plain platforms for clear-headed debates; while from the socialist director, Erwin Piscator, he gleaned the very reverse, mechanical marvels for Modernist sermons, where masses of men multiplied on flickering screens. His early plays abound in Grosz-like images, such as the man in *The Rise and Fall of the City of Mahagonny (Aufstieg und Fall der Stadt Mahagonny)* (1930) who eats his fortune and succumbs to inflation. Brecht snatched up ideas from many sources, shaping them to his needs, but he always insisted that 'the proof of the pudding was in the eating'.

Even in the 1920s, his plays sounded like nobody else's, for Brecht was a poet in love with his craft, who invented a diction easier to recognise than to imitate. The traditional language of the German theatre was more sharply class-inflected even than the British. High German was spoken by tragic heroes and the rustic style, Low German, by clowns. In Gerhart Hauptmann's *The Weavers* (*Die Weber*) (1892), the accents of the Silesian workers were thought to demean their heroic struggle. In his youthful revolt against everything Augsburg, Brecht borrowed jargon from Western low-life thrillers, but this was too exotic from everyday use. He invented a working-class language, terse and direct, with down-to-earth nouns and few ornaments, a decorum of the proletariate, comradely to all things except their class enemies. The austerity tightened his wit and love of paradox; and provided a plain background against which unusual words stood out with a sudden force.

It also sounded Modern, that is, stripped bare of any local, class or historical connections other than those intended. By the mid-1920s in Berlin, Dadaism had given way to a new mood, *die neue Sachlichkeit* or the New Objectivity, one of many Modernist movements in Europe, akin to Italian Futurism; but as Dadaism fed on social collapse, so the New Objectivity gorged reconstruction.

Modernism, as the name implies, treated the past as something to be discarded, at best as early stages in the progress towards the future or at worst as a nostalgic mire of pre-Enlightenment superstition. It was by definition opposed to Classicism and Romanticism, which harked back to the origins of the Folk. It claimed to be non-idealistic and in tune with science, which was why the intellectuals of the New Objectivity despised even those left-wing Expressionists, such as Toller and Kaiser, with whose views they might have been expected to share some sympathy.

The kind of scientific outlook to which the New Objectivity was attuned can be characterised as Newtonian. It assumed that the world was governed by the laws of cause and effect, which could be understood by the rational mind and applied as much to human behaviour as they did to everything else. For serious scientists, Einstein's Theory of Relativity had cast Newtonian physics into doubt, but it was still too abstruse an idea to disturb the Modernists. Their unacknowledged legislator was Charles Darwin, whose theories of evolution (particularly the survival of the fittest) provided the one cohesive philosophy which bound together the various genres which gathered under the banner of Modernism. Evolution was how the Life Force expressed itself through history, not in a straight line but 'cyclically', which meant there might be setbacks, like wars, but when peace returned, a higher level of civilisation ensued.

Modernists could not decide who were 'the fittest' or what conditions

41

best guaranteed their survival, an alarming thought if you wanted to be one of them. In the latter half of the 1920s, the intellectuals associated with the New Objectivity drifted in different directions, which was why the movement gained an unsavoury reputation with Marxist critics like Walter Benjamin. Some embraced a crude form of social Darwinism, based upon race, and veered towards fascism. Some relied upon market forces to determine the power struggles, moderated by reform and democracy.

Others turned towards Marxist-Leninism, at that time the most determinist of all the Modernist creeds, in that it asserted the 'historical inevitability' of its cause and that capitalism would crumble from its 'internal contradictions'. It followed the Enlightenment habit of classifying life according to one of two criteria, environment or heredity. Marxists chose the environment as the determining factor and split up mankind into classes which represented their roles within the economic cycle of production, distribution and exchange of goods. The interests of the classes were not identical. Indeed they were fundamentally at odds. The interests of the owners were opposed to those of the workers, for lower wages meant higher profits. It followed from this analysis that societies would always be in a state of conflict, of which the First World War was one manifestation, until the competing class claims could be brought within a framework of social justice, egalitarianism and common ownership.

This view was shared by Fabian socialists as well as by full-blown revolutionaries. They might differ on incidentals, such as how the class war was to be conducted and the degree to which power needed to be centralised within the hands of an elite, but not on their general aim. The fragility of capitalism, as shown by soaring inflation in the Weimar Republic and in 1929 the Wall Street Crash, convinced socialists and non-socialists alike that governments needed to control their economies and that these measures had to be accompanied by a spreading of wealth. The common fear in the West in the years after the Second World War was that its reforming measures had not gone far enough and that the Soviet Union would overtake the liberal democracies not only in economic terms but by every other index of social advancement.

Even in the inter-war years, however, there were signs that the Marxist programme was not going according to plan. Capitalism was not crumbling, as predicted, and if the Soviet economy had taken its great leap forward, it had not much improved the lives of its citizens. Many Marxist theorists blamed culture, the way in which the Soviet people clung to their old habits of mind, including the church. Zhdanov's Socialist Realism was one attempt to re-educate the masses, but so too was Brecht's Epic Theatre; and most Modernist artists of whatever persuasion considered it their duty to de-mythologise bourgeois culture and to upset the coffee tables on drawing room conversations.

Another explanation for the slowness of the advance towards utopia was provided by Lenin in *Imperialism, The Higher State of Capitalism* (1916). In individual societies, class conflict could be kept to a minimum, simply by displacing it elsewhere. Who cared in London how many Indian peasants were starving to keep low the price of tea? Communism had to be international, if it was to stay true to its own logic, but this drew it into conflict not only with capitalists but also with those like George Kennan who passionately believed in the conscience of the individual.

Marxists stressed that, in this historical phase, the only personal choice which mattered was whether or not to support communism. In the modern world, the individual was part of an exchange network, which delivered materials to factories, which produced goods to raise capital to build more factories, which demanded more materials, and so on *ad infinitum*. Private acts of goodness were of little value, if the system was exploitative. It might even do harm by moderating injustice and thus delaying change. The emphasis in the West upon free will was interpreted not as self-delusion but as a means whereby the ruling classes subjugated the workers by fragmenting their common purpose.

Brecht started to read *Capital (Das Kapital)* in 1926; but he was not at that stage a Marxist, merely drifting in that direction. In 1925, he wrote a play which represented the first steps on his road to Damascus. *Man Equals Man (Mann ist Mann)* is like a New Objectivity response to Pirandello, whose plays, then fashionable in Berlin, demonstrated how little could be known about the human self. In *Man Equals Man*, Brecht took this argument further by asserting that society moulds the individual, not the other way round.

> 'Tonight you are going to see a man re-assembled like a car
> Leaving all his individual components just as they are.'[12]

Brecht told the story of how in British colonial India a harmless Irish docker was turned into a human fighting machine. The moral was that you must reform society, if you want to redeem the man; but since societies are composed of men and women, this argument was circular, unless you could break through the cycle with a supposedly objective and scientific theory like Marxism.

Brecht's India was a literary invention, more Kipling than Curzon, where Queen Victoria was still on the throne in 1925. Similarly, his Soho in *The Threepenny Opera (Die Dreigroschenoper)* (1928) or Chicago in *St Joan of the Stockyards (Die heilige Johanna der Schlachthöfe)* (1931) are oddly unlike the actual places, as a morning's research would have revealed. But Brecht was not interested in particular societies, only with general principles. It mattered only decoratively if the stories took place in Lucknow or Soho, although Brecht derived fun from the parodies. *The Threepenny Opera* was his first success, but still not Marxist. Its mood is cynical rather than didactic. It would be nice to be good if you can afford it: love is a fine thing, but it gets you into deep trouble. Kurt Weill's music was, if anything, too seductive, the potent charm of slumming.

By 1929, the running battles between the communists and the fascists in the streets of Berlin forced Brecht to take sides. Any delay in commitment would have seemed equivocation. From then on, his primary aim in writing plays was the political education of his public, which he never separated from entertainment. He devised a new form of theatre, *Lehrstücke*, which could be staged almost anywhere, in school halls, sports centres or out in the streets. He sought to involve his audiences in a process of analysis, in which he could raise questions which were Marxist in their formulation but not foregone in their conclusions. Brecht was not one who easily toed the party line. In his didactic plays of the time, such as *St Joan of the Stockyards*, the tug of paradox nearly holds its own against the pull of polemic.

By 1931, most political debates in Germany were deemed to be inflammatory. The Weimar government in an effort to preserve its authority banned his plays. After the burning of the Reichstag in 1933, Brecht began his twenty-five years of exile, wandering from Denmark to Sweden, across the north of Russia to the west coast of the United States, where he lived in California from 1941 to 1947, until after testifying before HUAC, where he was thanked for his misleading help, he returned to Europe, staying in Switzerland while contemplating an epic choice. Where should he settle, West or East? Where did the future lie?

Exile hardened his conviction that fascism was the main enemy of mankind and that its seeds lay scattered throughout the West. He made allowances for Stalin's record of barbarism. 'Better socialism by force than no socialism at all.' He ignored Stalin's pact with Hitler on the eve of the war; and turned a deaf ear to the stories of atrocities behind the Iron Curtain. His political principles drew him eastward.

But there were practical problems, not least aesthetic ones. Zhdanov's Socialist Realism was exactly how Brecht did not intend to write plays. He disliked the idea that audiences should be encouraged to identify with a 'positive hero'; and loathed the mixture of naturalism and the well-made play, whose model in the Soviet Union was not Ibsen but Gorki. He hated most of all the low priority in Zhdanov's philosophy given to fun and scepticism. In the Soviet Union, his plays were held in the utmost suspicion. They were accused of being Formalist, which originally meant that form was valued at the expense of content.

Formalism became the general charge directed against anything artistic which did not conform to the principles of Socialist Realism.

From 1935 onwards, Brecht engaged in arcane debates in the West about the direction that socialist writers should follow, knowing that these could not be held in the Soviet Union. The chief fruit of this labour was published in Potsdam in 1949, *A Short Organum for the Theatre* (*Kleines Organon für das Theater*), a terse and witty summary of what he meant by Epic Theatre. The apparent target was Aristotle's *The Poetics*, but the secondary one was Socialist Realism. It was written as a short version of his *Buying Brass* (*Der Messingkauf*), a dramatised play post-mortem, begun in 1937 and not finished.

He started out by stressing that a play's main purpose is entertainment. The theatre 'has no other passport than fun, but this it has got to have'.[13] He then distinguished between higher and lower pleasures, and those most appropriate for a scientific age and concluded that the passive acceptance of things as they are (which was what Aristotelian theatre was supposed to provide) was less pleasurable and less scientific than the recognition that society can and should be changed.

What kind of theatrical pleasure could be derived from the prospect of changing society? The best illustration came not from *A Short Organum* but from a previous essay, *A Street Scene: a Basic Model for an Epic Theatre* (1938), in which he describes how a traffic accident might be handled dramatically. In a classical tragedy, you would be expected to identify with the man behind the wheel; and the flying glass would be a divine retribution for the flaw of driving recklessly. In his Epic Theatre, the story is re-created after the event by witnesses who act out the factors which contributed to the accident. The emphasis moved from simple narrative (what is going to happen next?) to enquiry (why did it happen?). The audience was placed in the position of a jury, considering how to prevent such things from happening again.

From this shift, other techniques derived, such as his way of telling the story in advance and the *Verfremdungseffekt* (the estrangement effect), whereby the actors retain a detachment from their roles to demonstrate them better. Brecht was not so wedded to his theories that he could not break them in practice. The four great plays which he wrote in exile, *Mother Courage* (1941), *The Good Person of Setzuan* (1943), *Galileo* (1943) and *The Caucasian Chalk Circle* (1948), poorly illustrated his principles. It is a subtle distinction which separates Aristotelian empathy from the kind of response which we feel for Mother Courage, She Teh and Galileo. We share their sufferings: we are not detached. By trying to stifle emotions, Brecht damps them down, as in a charcoal burner's fire, to burn the hotter at the core. The *Verfremdungseffekt* can work in a similar way to classical restraint. Nor did these plays analyse disasters so that they may be avoided in future. What choice did Mother Courage have but to drag her wagon around a war zone?

Brecht was revising *Galileo* in California for a possible Broadway production with Charles Laughton when the news came through that the United States had successfully exploded the first atom bomb. 'Overnight,' Brecht recalled, 'the biography of the founder of modern physics read differently.'[14] It could no longer be assumed that the spirit of scientific enquiry had to be defended at all costs. Nuclear warfare was where the buck of evolution stopped. 'See with your eyes!' begged Galileo at his telescope, 'Look at what is out there in the sky! Forget Aristotle! Throw away your books! Trust the evidence of your senses!' But the high priests of Christendom kept their minds on what ought to be rather than on what was and advised the Grand Inquisitor who persuaded Galileo to re-cant by the usual means.

Science particularly could not be trusted in the wrong hands. Correct politics preceded all other value judgements. And what was Brecht expected to do in Switzerland where his plays could be freely performed at the Zurich Schauspielhaus and where half the dictators of the modern world kept their bank accounts? He played for time. He became a citizen of neutral Austria and looked up a few old friends from pre-war days. Word was sent to the East German government that the famous dramatist, Bertolt Brecht, might be tempted back to East Berlin. The East German government considered its options and sought Moscow's advice. Brecht's return would be a propaganda *coup*, but if he did so, they could not immediately charge him with Formalism.

A compromise was struck. He was invited to establish his own company, the Berliner Ensemble, and given a generous subsidy; but they were asked to play at the Deutsches Theater, whose director, Wolfgang Langhoff, was thought to be reliable. This was not what Brecht wanted, but he had been promised that he would eventually receive his own theatre, the Theater am Schiffbauerdamm. He still had to prove that he was no Formalist or troublemaker. His chance to do so came in 1953. When Stalin died in March, Brecht wrote in a private manuscript that 'the oppressed of five continents . . . must have felt their heart stop beating'.

> 'I praise him for many reasons. Above all
> Because under his leadership the murderers were beaten.'[15]

Nor was this quite as absurd as in retrospect it sounds. In Pakistan, Tariq Ali's mother wept at the news.

To admire Stalin as a war leader was one thing. To embrace the effects of Stalinism was another. In June 1953, building workers massed in East Berlin to demonstrate about low pay and living standards. The Soviet commandant, Major-General Dibrova, sent in the tanks; and the extent of the casualty figures is still not known. There were many deaths. Brecht sent a message of support to the East German Communist (SED) Party Secretary, Walter Ulbricht, only part of which was published. It read: 'I feel it necessary at this moment to write to you and express my association with the SED.' In the unpublished part, Brecht pointed out that the government had made some mistakes and that everybody should try to do better in future. In an ironic little poem, much quoted in the West, Brecht wrote to the effect that if the government was dissatisfied with the workers, it should try electing a new lot. But his overall message was clear. He still supported the SED despite the oppression committed in its name.

In 1954, the Berliner Ensemble moved into the Theater am Schiffbauerdamm. It would be unfair to suggest that Brecht got his own theatre because of his support for Ulbricht at this critical time, but he would certainly not have got it if he had opposed him. This incident did Brecht's reputation no good at all among the German theatres of Western Europe. Despite the efforts of Harry Buckwitz in Frankfurt, his plays were shunned and they did not come back into fashion again until 1962, six years after his death, with the appointment of the veteran socialist director, Erwin Piscator, to the Freie Volksbühne in West Berlin.

This was something of a political gesture, for the Berlin Wall had just been built and the West Berlin authorities under blockade wanted to show that its sector was not only more rich and free than the East but more radical in its ideas. During the 1960s many who had trained with the Berliner Ensemble came over to the West to further their careers, even when they remained ideologically attached to the East. The dramatists Peter Weiss, Volker Braun and Heiner Müller were among them. The West German suspicions of Brecht did not entirely go away, however, and in 1966 Günter Grass wrote a savage parody, *The Plebeians Rehearse the Uprising*, in which a Brecht-like director calmly observes a workers' revolt and takes notes for his production of *Coriolanus*.

Grass's play referred to a time in the early 1950s, when Brecht was adapting *Coriolanus* for his own non-Shakespearian purposes. He re-wrote little but he changed the angle of vision, so that audiences would not identify with the play's tragic hero, Coriolanus, but see him from the perspective of the working-class sceptics, the tribunes. Peter Brook, who admired Brecht, saw the results and found them unconvincing. In *The Empty Space* (1968), he described a scene where in Shakespeare Coriolanus gave way to the pleas of his mother, Volumnia, not to attack Rome. Brecht did not want to suggest that history could be altered on an emotional whim. He changed the text to show that Coriolanus must have seen smoke from the Roman war-factories and feared for his defeat.

Brook argued that, however much one might want to believe that there were logical forces at work in history, its course could be changed on occasions by the devotion of a son for his mother. It was dogmatic to think otherwise. But Brecht struggled against a type of theatre, represented by the naturalistic well-made play, in which domestic emotions were more important than anything else. In devising another way of writing which could express (in Devine's words) 'a scientific adjustment of our values', he often became over-schematic, although sometimes, as in the scene where Mother Courage loses her officers' shirts, he did try to balance private emotions with economic logic.

Brecht's socialism stemmed from a determinist philosophy. There are many ways of categorising mankind, if we should wish to do so, other than in economic classes, and many laws other than simple cause-and-effect. What he saw through the framework of his philosophy was sharp and vivid: what he ignored were the blurred edges or that which did not fit, such as Coriolanus' *volte-face*. In Poland, his plays were often staged for the laughs which he did not intend, while in Moscow *The Good Person of Setzuan* created a furore in 1963. In the West, Brecht's impact spread slowly but deeply. It was felt at the Théâtre National Populaire (TNP) at Chaillot, whose director, Jean Vilar, declared that the theatre should provide 'a public service in exactly the same way as gas, water or electricity'. For the new wave of British directors, despite Devine's scepticism, the Berliner Ensemble became a very model of a modern major company.

5

AT THE BACK OF THE MIND

'Let's go.' They do not move.
(From *Waiting for Godot*, 1953)

Among the projects left unfinished by the time of his death was Brecht's retort to Samuel Beckett's *Waiting for Godot*, which he considered to be the last word in social pessimism, an illustration of the state of despair to which capitalism reduces mankind. But he never completed it and what could he have said? That Godot *had* come, in the shape of a Communist Party official from Georgia? That would have risked a few misplaced laughs, not only in Poland.

He could have argued, in the style of *Galileo*, that the two tramps, Vladimir and Estragon, were trapped into doing nothing because they were expecting a saviour. 'Unhappy is the land that has the need for Godots.' But this might have been interpreted as an attack on Stalin's personality cult, which would not have gone down well with Walter Ulbricht either. Or Brecht could have set the play in the West with the tramps as out-of-work dockers waiting for the revolution to save them from their misery. This might have provoked comparisons between the living standards of the two Germanies, for more people were likely to be living on carrots and discarded chicken legs in Dresden than Bonn.

Waiting for Godot was a tempting target for a Marxist writer to attack, but a treacherous one too. It was safer to scorn it from a distance than to grapple with it at close quarters. At a time when gloomy plays from the West were welcomed, the Ministry of Culture in Moscow discouraged *Waiting for Godot*. For thirty years, Beckett's plays were not performed inside the Soviet Union, except rarely in the Baltic republics. Elsewhere in Eastern and Central Europe, Beckett's plays were performed in the little theatres of Prague and Warsaw, influencing the Czech writer, Václav Havel, and the Pole, Tadeusz Różewicz. The drama of the Absurd, to which Beckett's name was attached, became the dissidents' genre, a banner to uphold against Socialist Realism.

Waiting for Godot did not challenge any political system, but it

49

undermined them all by questioning the idea of progress. If it had a target, this might be characterised as scientific optimism. *Waiting for Godot* was not an attacking play, but it offered the idea that European notions of logic and evolution were little more than a massive self-delusion. This was why Brecht hated it, but in its refined scepticism of saviours and causes, *Waiting for Godot* became a more effective political statement than anything which Brecht ever wrote.

It was interpreted differently from place to place. When it was first seen in Britain in 1955, many assumed that it was an anti-Christian play with Godot as a diminutive of the word God; and the tramps in Peter Hall's production were drop-outs from a bourgeois society, represented by Pozzo and Lucky. *Waiting for Godot* was obviously an attack on the British class system. In South Africa during the 1960s, the tramps were played by black actors, with Pozzo and Lucky as their white oppressors, while at San Quentin prison in the United States, *Waiting for Godot* was performed by convicts who knew nothing of Absurdist drama but everything about waiting. There were feminist *Godots*, student *Godots* and Zen *Godots*; and the popularity of a play in which 'nothing happens – twice', amazed everyone, including Beckett.

Some thought that its success reflected a Cold War paralysis, the suppressed panic that somewhere, silently, convoys of trucks were escorting missiles in kit form to their distant silos. In January 1956 the British Ministry of Defence issued instructions as to what we should do in the event of a nuclear attack. Their advice was to stay indoors and wait. Was Godot the bomb?

Waiting for Godot does not mention the Cold War and its references to Christianity cancel themselves out. According to his unofficial biographer Deirdre Bair, Beckett told Roger Blin, who first directed *Waiting for Godot* in 1953, that the name Godot was prompted by the French word for boot, *godillot*.[1] All of the interpretations were wrong, but none completely so, for the key word in the title is waiting; and Beckett left his audiences to decide for what precisely they were waiting.

Beckett's technical problem was how to translate the feeling of waiting into dramatic terms. He did so first by balancing one expectation against another, birth against death, salvation versus damnation, which resulted in an antiphonal prose-poetry:

> *Vladimir*: Astride of a grave and a difficult birth. Down in the hole, lingeringly, the grave-digger puts on the forceps.[2]

Nothing exactly happens in either act, for if it did, the play would not be about waiting, but about something happening. The second device which Beckett used with skill was to toy with audience expectations. Well-made plays were supposed to move logically towards a crisis where all is revealed, but in *Waiting for Godot*, there is movement without logic, an anticipated crisis which never comes. The play ends where it begins – in waiting.

Beckett wrote *Waiting for Godot* quickly, in just under four months, from October 1948 to January 1949; and he found it a relaxing experience, 'to get away from . . . the wildness and rulelessness' of his novels.[3] He had just finished his novel *Malone Dies*, a draining experience, and writing for the stage was a new game, a chance to display his various skills. He was like a juggler who has found the knack of tossing up and catching five clubs. His wit, his scepticism, his fondness for the films of Laurel and Hardy, his visual imagery and his philosophical concerns dropped lightly into his waiting hands. In that sense, *Waiting for Godot* is a young man's play.

Its success drew him from the shadow of James Joyce, with whom he had been friendly for many years. Joyce's 'stream of consciousness' theory influenced his early novels, but as a method rather than a conviction. *Malone Dies* has the outward appearance of a Joyce-inspired novel, being the passing thoughts of an old man dying alone in an empty room; but Beckett felt the need to impose a structure on the rambling reflections (the inventory, the three stories) before untidying it again. Whereas Joyce delighted in memories and private jokes, Beckett resisted them, aspiring towards more universal statements.

Nor was Beckett likely to have been impressed by the stream-of-consciousness idea that you could capture fleeting mental impressions in a work of art. The act of writing down such thoughts destroyed their ephemeral nature. In New York, the students at Strasberg's Actors Workshop were doing their best to express their unconsciousnesses spontaneously, while Jackson Pollock threw paint at canvases to achieve a similar effect. In France, the process was known as *l'écriture automatique*, which meant that the less that the conscious mind interfered with the creation of a work of art the better. Such *avant-garde* movements, from Abstract Expressionism to 'Happenings', were united in their belief that the rational mind, the Freudian Super-ego, destroyed true creativity.

Beckett, however, came from a rigorous discipline of thought. Born in Ireland in 1906, he won a scholarship in Modern Languages from Trinity College in Dublin to study at the Ecole Normale Supérieure in Paris from 1928 to 1930. This higher college was reserved for the prize-winning students of France, the 'crack regiments' according to its Director.[4] There he first came into contact with Jean-Paul Sartre, his senior by a year and much more self-assured. Sartre was already a member of that tough gang of French intellectuals who imposed their ideas in later years, Paul Nizan, Raymond Aron and Simone de Beauvoir.

For the next fifty years, until Sartre's death in April 1980, they lived at a respectful distance from each other, two sides to a see-saw, sharing a pivot but not much more. At first, Beckett was the shy outsider, torn between Dublin and Paris (he settled in the French capital in 1937), nor did he lose that taciturn detachment from the swirling events into which Sartre plunged with so much vigour. As Sartre's intellectual (as opposed to his political) influence declined, Beckett's rose in comparison, never standing higher than in the years immediately preceding his death, in December 1989. They lived in different quarters of Paris, travelled separately to Berlin in the 1930s, published their first novels in 1938, Beckett's *Murphy* and Sartre's *Nausea* (*La Nausée*), played minor roles within the Resistance movement and from time to time, their paths crossed. When Sartre launched his monthly review, *Modern Times* (*Les Temps modernes*), in 1945, Beckett was among his first contributors.

What drew them together, and forced them apart, was their fascination with one classical riddle posed at the Ecole Normale Supérieure as part of the curriculum. Which came first, existence or the image of existence in the mind of God, its Essence? Was there a kind of divine blueprint for the world, of which the world itself was an imperfect copy? Or was the world created haphazardly with no particular pattern in mind but seeking its own essence to perpetuate its existence?

Either answer led on to more riddles. Classical and Christian philosophers tended to assume with Plato that 'essence precedes existence' and that God had a plan for all creation, including man, which Christians could discover through the Bible, the example of Jesus Christ and the teachings of the Church, through faith. Personal morality was ultimately a matter of obedience to the Will of God. But humanists had long argued that if there were such a Plan, human beings knew little about it. Nor could a theory of a benevolent God explain why He could have allowed so much wastage and suffering in the world. The Church's answer that these were caused by acts of disobedience was unconvincing. Those who were being punished were not necessarily those who had committed the offence. Was God unjust as well as cruel?

The alternative was to assert that 'existence preceded essence', the premise of Existentialists. Existence came into being as an infinite range of possibilities, which had gradually shaped itself into the universe that we can perceive today and was continually becoming something else. On the level of personal morality, the pattern to which we aspire is our essence, not the one to which we obediently conform. Existentialism also runs into difficulties, for if there is no pre-determined order for existence, then anything can happen. 'My tongue,' pondered Roquentin in Sartre's *Nausea*, 'can turn into a centipede.'

If existence is simply a process of becoming, with no end in sight, then life itself is pointless, or Absurd. Albert Camus, Sartre's contemporary

52

and friend, formed the opinion that without some kind of essentialist faith, human beings would always seek to test the limits of their freedom, drawing them towards terror and debauchery, the theme of his play, *Caligula* (1938). Sartre tried to answer such objections with his theory of contingency, whereby one moment defines the next through the nature of its proximity, thus preserving a certain continuity.

During the 1930s, he was much influenced by the philosopher Edmund Husserl, who wanted to confine our theories of knowledge to what could be perceived through the senses, cutting out all speculation. We should observe the river without assuming that it was flowing downhill. Husserl's 'phenomenology' was absorbed into the 'new wave' writing of the 1950s, into the novels, plays and films of Nathalie Sarraute, Alain Robbe-Grillet and Marguerite Duras. Moments of tactile experience were recorded in detail, speculations about causes and effects were kept to a minimum and the author refused to 'play god' to his or her characters.

Elsewhere the idea that there might be no inherent order to the universe led to a wild flapping in a storm of possibilities. 'The sky can still fall on our heads,' wrote Antonin Artaud in *The Theatre and its Double* (1938), 'and the theatre exists to remind us of that fact.' After the war, as governments fell by the month and nobody quite knew what was happening in Indo-China, Artaud's opium-induced nightmares were as credible as a statement from the Ministry of Defence. In France, Absurdism never lost its links with the conundrum posed at the Ecole Normale Supérieure. In Eastern Europe, it was more of a protest movement against the intolerable life imposed by an autocratic bureaucracy.

Throughout Europe, Absurdist plays were iconoclastic, non-naturalistic and anti-bourgeois. Martin Esslin in his book on the subject traced their ancestry back to Alfred Jarry's *King Ubu* (*Ubu roi*) in 1896, to Stanislaw Witkiewicz, better known as 'Witkacy' in Poland, to Dadaism and Surrealism, to Artaud, Kafka and Pirandello, a long list of anarchists and speculators. There were, however, some preoccupations which distinguished the French brand of Absurdism from those elsewhere. One was the Pirandello-like fascination with role-playing. Jean Anouilh, whose plays were as popular in London as Paris, employed such devices as the play-within-the-play, actors playing real people playing real actors, although the sentiments expressed through veils of deceit are closer in spirit to Laclos's *Dangerous Liaisons* (*Les Liaisons dangereuses*) than to Pirandello.

Post-war guilt lay behind the many variants of role-playing in the black-box studios of Paris, asking to what extent human beings could be held responsible for their actions. In Arthur Adamov's *Dr Taranne* (*Le Professeur Taranne*) (1953), a doctor is accused of exposing himself indecently. When he cannot prove his innocence, he accepts the verdict of society and thrusts his mackintosh wide open. We are what other people suppose us to be. Such anecdotes could be interpreted in many ways, but the hidden question often concerned collaboration. Should those suspected of collaborating with Nazis be presumed guilty or given the benefit of any doubt?

In Eugène Ionesco's *Amédée* or *How to Get Rid of It* (1954), a respectable suburban couple have a corpse in their bedroom which swells at an alarming rate, spreading mushrooms and other signs of decay as it does so. In the United States, *Amédée* was interpreted as a Freudian nightmare, while in Britain it was a domestic farce. In France, the corpse was thought to be a wartime secret, a collective guilt from which Frenchmen suffered. Apart from *The Bald Prima-Donna* (*La Cantatrice chauve*) (1950), Ionesco's most successful play was *Rhinoceros* (1960), an Absurdist parable which did not need to be explained to anyone who had lived under the Nazis.

An ordinary man, Berenger, finds himself in a world where other human beings are turning into rhinoceroses, until only he is left, defending his humanity among horned beasts. In an interview with *Figaro Littéraire*, Ionesco made clear that his story applied to all political fanaticism, left or right;[5] but Jean-Louis Barrault's version at the Théâtre de France brought out more Nazi than Stalinist parallels. It was a triumph for Barrault, an exemplary blend of mime and meaning.

As war-time memories began to fade, the underlying questions asserted themselves. Do we create or are we creatures of our societies? If the bourgeoisie persists in treating those who do not belong to it as criminals, are the outcasts entitled to behave in a criminal way? Jean Genet was one such example, homosexual prostitute, a thief, a murderer, who spent much time in jail. Sartre canonised him in *Saint Genet* (1952) for the way in which he had accepted all that the French courts could throw at him and converted his shame into 'sanctity'. Genet's advice to all outcasts was that they should be proud of their debasement. Blacks should not pretend not to be black. They should 'negrify themselves' by rubbing black boot polish into their skins.

The purpose of role-playing was to heighten one's image in the eyes of other people, a function akin to art. In Genet's case, it *was* an art, in that his personal humiliation had been converted into literature. 'Ma victoire,' Genet wrote in *The Thief's Journal* (*Le Journal du voleur*) (1948), 'c'est verbale' ['my victory is in language']. His plays, which seem so over-written in English, provided a strange new context for French classical rhetoric. At a time when in Germany and Britain, the high style was giving way to the low, in France low-life poets like Genet were aspiring to top the high. Genet's vision of role-playing stretched across the span of human behaviour, from masturbation to Church rituals.

His play, *The Balcony* (*Le Balcon*) (1956) connected brothel fantasies with state institutions. He could not understand what socialism meant. Egalitarianism was against human nature. All revolutions adopted and then modified the ritualistic displays of the regimes they displaced.

To many such questions, Sartre's Existentialism offered instant answers, which was why it became popular after the war. To the Pirandello-like obsession with the unknowability of self, Sartre replied that there was nothing there to know. 'The Self,' he wrote in *Being and Nothingness* (*L'Etre et le néant*) (1943), 'is the hole in being, the being through which nothingness enters the world', which, roughly interpreted, meant that human awareness has no characteristic other than its freedom.

A tension is then created between the freedom of the Self, 'pour-soi', and the thing-ness, or lack of freedom, in the outside world, 'en-soi'. Individuals could pretend not to be free. In *The Flies* (*Les Mouches*) (1943), based on the Orestes legend, Sartre blamed the people of Argos for letting the tyrant Zeus punish them with a plague of flies and Orestes kills Zeus by behaving as a free man. In occupied Paris, this amounted to a call to join the Resistance, to *commit* oneself to freedom, from which Sartre's post-war stress on commitment derived.

To attempt to give up freedom was for Sartre the supreme act of 'bad faith', which became his all-purpose term of disapproval. In *No Exit* (*Huis Clos*) (1944), where 'hell is other people', each of the three mutual torturers are guilty of acts of bad faith, which is why they torment each other. Bad faith also meant the denial to others of a freedom that you were claiming for yourself; and the Sartrean Existentialist extended the use of the word 'sado-masochism' to apply to practices which had little to do with sex.

The sadist was someone who tried to transform another person into a mere object of his or her will. The masochist submitted to this domination. They were both guilty of bad faith, for a human being could not give up freedom without ceasing to be human. This was why the sadist felt drawn towards killing his victim, and yet in the moment of death, the battle was lost. It was the freedom that the sadist wished to control, not an unfree dead body. Sado-masochism was the charge levelled against Nazism and extended to apply to capitalism and all class-bound societies.

In his play *The Condemned of Altona* (*Les Séquestrés d'Altona*) (1959), Sartre portrayed a family of ex-Nazis living in Hamburg after the war. Sado-masochism was part of their daily life, in their rituals defining levels of authority. 'Never look at a man in the eyes,' the dying Herr von Gerlach instructed his son, Werner, to whom he hands over the control of his industrial empire, 'Only at the bone in his forehead!' Werner's elder brother, Franz, a former SS officer accused of wartime atrocities, is kept alive and in hiding in the family attic. Franz shares a *folie à deux* with Werner's wife, Johanna, because they have a similar outlook. She has committed no acts of cruelty, but as a film star, she delighted in dominating others through her screen image. When her beauty faded, she resigned herself to becoming an object of someone else's will. In Sartre's terms, she too was a sado-masochist.

Sado-masochism like bad faith could be used to damn almost anything, all authority, all class distinctions, all honours and titles. Marriages were inherently sado-masochistic, particularly if the wife took the husband's name. Only an egalitarian society where everyone was free to behave as he or she liked, but refused to boss or be bossed, could be acquitted from the charge. Sartre, like Brecht, was drawn towards Marxism as much from his hatred of bourgeoisie as from his dreams of utopia. He found it hard to reconcile his idea of freedom with the determinism of communist thinking. He tried to bring together a third force in politics, the Rassemblement Démocratique Révolutionnaire (RDR). When that effort collapsed, and the Cold War intensified, and colonial wars demanded French blood, he threw in his lot with the communists.

In 1952, Sartre went to a World Peace Movement conference in Vienna, organised mainly to discredit the West. He was greatly affected by it and compared it to the Liberation. *Modern Times* started to publish long articles in praise of the Soviet Union. Camus could not understand how he could be so blind to Stalinism and Sartre defended himself by pointing out that Stalin's crimes were committed in a good cause, whereas those of capitalism were part of the system. In July 1953, while the tanks were cooling in East Berlin, Sartre was invited to the Soviet Union and had a marvellous time. On his return, he wrote euphoric articles for *Libération* and *France–URSS*. Of course, there was free speech in the Soviet Union, but they knew how to criticise constructively. Of course, Soviet citizens could travel, but they did not feel like doing so because it was so exciting where they were.

Sartre redefined his theories of Existentialist freedom. Of course, human beings were free, but in that freedom, they were morally bound to commit themselves to communism as the only political philosophy compatible with Existentialism. Class conflict was the great enemy of freedom. Alternatively, human beings could only enjoy the benefits of their freedom if they lived in a free society, such as the Soviet Union.

It took about four years for this glow to fade, during which time Sartre travelled widely in the Eastern bloc, met Brecht, went to Czechoslovakia and Hungary, wrote a polemical play *Nekrassov* (1955) and many pro-Soviet articles in which it is possible to detect a new caution or a more complicated re-interpretation of what Sartre thought he may have once meant.

In 1956, his love affair finally collapsed; and from then on, he attacked the Soviet Union with almost as much venom as he did the United States. Perhaps he was disillusioned by Kruschev's denunciation of Stalin in March, or by the suppression of the bread riots in Poznan in Poland, or by the Soviet invasion of Hungary, or by the new Soviet policy of 'peaceful co-existence' with the West; but his re-conversion, when it came, was total.

His loss of faith in Moscow did not lessen his revolutionary fervour, which was transferred to other causes and eventually altered the public perception as to what was meant by class warfare. Previously, the notion of 'class' had been defined in economic terms, with the struggle primarily being between the workers and the bosses. The workers of the world were the ones who were supposed to unite to cast off their chains. Without losing contact with this definition, Sartre extended it to apply to forms of oppression which were not necessarily economic at all. He brought his ideas about sado-masochism into the debate, so that the true test of class warfare became whether one social group had transformed another into an object of its will. Class warfare then applied as much to sexual injustice and racial discrimination as it did within factories and the marketplace.

This formula solved many problems for those who, like Sartre, had come reluctantly to the conclusion that there was little to choose between the United States and the Soviet Union in terms of class oppression, but who wanted to keep the revolutionary spirit alive. Why was it that countries exploited under colonial rule showed few signs of economic recovery when they were independent? The answer was that they were still being subjected to cultural oppression, which might be symbolised by the way in which Britain bequeathed parliament buildings to its former colonies, but also by how their boundaries were drawn according to Western maps, by their state languages and by how some newly independent countries became non-places, ignored by traders and the world's press.

Egalitarianism had to be extended to the world's cultures as well, so that all were considered equal, and the implications of Sartre's existentialist socialism did not end there. They also applied to sexual politics. In 1949, his long-lasting companion-in-arms, Simone de Beauvoir, had written a persuasive book, *The Second Sex* (*Le Deuxième Sexe*), in which she argued that a woman's biological needs tempted her into losing her independence and individuality in her relationships with the more aggressive and self-sufficient male. After 1956, the emphasis shifted so that male-dominated cultures were blamed for exploiting women's biological needs.

Sartre's impact on left-wing thought was considerable, but he did not attempt to shift the primary antagonisms on which class warfare was based. The target was still the Western bourgeoisie with its Christian-Classical habits of mind. Race discrimination was something which whites did to blacks, not whites to whites, blacks to blacks or blacks to whites. If women were sometimes in a position to exploit men, and took advantage of it, this could be regarded as a laudable revenge for centuries of oppression. He extended the dimensions of what was thought to be class warfare but he may have lessened its effectiveness as practical politics. It is easier to organise a factory strike than to assemble a rainbow alliance of blacks, unmarried mothers, students and gays.

The double-edged value of left-wing Existentialism was that it could be applied to most grievances. Sartre sometimes got himself into trouble by supporting the Israelis against the Palestinians on one occasion and the Palestinians against the Israelis on another. But he became a hero-philosopher and in 1960, when his support for the Front de Libération Nationale (FLN) in Algeria led to calls for his arrest, General de Gaulle refused, saying 'You do not imprison Voltaire'.[6]

The *événements de mai* in 1968 came too late for his active participation, to his regret for the students had embraced so many of his ideas. He wrote voluminously, travelled constantly and kept himself going by smoking, drinking and popping pills. He adapted *The Crucible* into the film *The Witches of Salem*, started a screenplay for John Huston on the life of Freud, in which he wanted Monroe to star, and began, but never completed, a biography of Flaubert. His relentless energy could be interpreted as the attempt to assert the freedom of his will over the thing-ness of his body. To the end of his life, he tried to cheat death and when he went blind, he sought a new career in television.

In contrast, Samuel Beckett stayed with the paradox that Existentialism originally posed, of the free mind trapped inside an unfree body. It was a bleak but fundamental vision. Whatever we may want to be, whatever we may want to do, we are confined within the limits of our mortality. Our hearts tick through the remaining seconds of our existence, although our minds protest.

This was why his characters are often so old. They have reached a point where they can fool themselves no longer or if they try, their self-deception is obvious. Winnie in *Happy Days* (1961) cheers herself up by keeping track of her possessions, including her husband, while the sands pile high around her neck. Krapp in *Krapp's Last Tape* (1958) replays memories of his youth to while away the time but is disgusted by his old optimism.

The limits are psychological as well as physical. Hamm in *Endgame* (1957) was tormented by his dead parents, stuffed into dustbins, who refused to rot or get themselves collected. In *Play* (1963), Beckett borrowed a plot from almost any boulevard drama and transformed it into his own terms. Two women and one man, transfixed in separate urns, quarrel over who possesses whom. Beckett peeled off layer after layer of surface concerns – jealousies, traumas and political commitments – in order to arrive at the underlying states of feeling. One of his plays, *Breath* (1969), lasted for less than a minute. The audience was simply invited to hear and watch an old man breathing. It was first performed as the opening sketch to the New York production of *Oh! Calcutta!*, a daring way to start Tynan's 'civilized erotic entertainment', the ultimate strip for an evening of strip.

Once, a member of the audience met Beckett on the steps of the Royal Court Theatre after a performance of *Happy Days* and said, 'That was a very boring evening!' Beckett replied, 'Not nearly boring enough.' Beckett's plays may seem boring, for there can be no progress. The circle is complete when the play begins. Those who admire Beckett find this lack of progress refreshing, a reminder that time passes without necessarily going anywhere. His plays may be static, but they do not lack emotional range, variety or theatrical delights. The strange popularity of *Waiting for Godot* is explained by examining the text. It is entertaining because Beckett struggled so hard to keep us amused. In his later work, he refined the metaphors, intensified the emotions, relied less on words and more on imagery, and distilled the despair.

Nobody has successfully managed to imitate Beckett, although many have tried. This is because the feelings which he expressed in theatrical terms seem so elusive, so much at the back of the mind, buried, hidden, almost beyond reach. How, for example, do you express the sensation of hearing yourself speak in words that are not quite your own and in a voice both familiar and strange? It is a common experience, but hard to express. Beckett did so in *Not I* by placing a disembodied mouth, in a tight spotlight, high up on a darkened stage. Elsewhere there was a large shadowy figure, cowled like a monk. For twenty minutes, meaningless words poured out of the mouth, until the lips were stifled by their activity. The cowled figure turned away.

The precision of Beckett's stagecraft, his artistry, made its impact elsewhere. Within many post-war Modernist theories, there ran a vein of philistinism, a preference for useful and committed art, a fondness for proletarian roughness. Its effects can be seen in the concrete cities across Europe. Sartre was once offended when someone admired the beauty of his prose. 'I am not a flute-player,' he replied. Sartre had two writing styles, one carefully contrived for its literary effect and the other untidy, impassioned and spontaneous, always unfinished; and it was this latter style which prevailed in his later years, as he plunged himself into political activities. He scorned the purity of Flaubert's literary style as a class affectation.

During the early 1960s, however, Existentialism became unfashionable among Paris intellectuals, because the debate about whether essence preceded existence or not was perceived to be a language trap, an example of the binary logic which, according to the Structuralists, bedevilled Western thought. Roland Barthes, Claude Lévi-Strauss and Michel Foucault criticised Sartre more for his loose use of language than for his political opinions, which they tended to share. This did not affect the charisma of his name, but it chipped away at his arguments. Words and phrases associated with Sartre (bad faith, commitment, 'en-soi' and 'pour-soi') entered the popular vocabulary, but lost their precision. Existentialism itself became a rough way of life rather than a philosophy, welcomed around the world as a good excuse for sexual promiscuity, drug-taking and terrorism.

In contrast, Beckett's plays retained their precision though they could be interpreted so variously. Godot can be whatever we are waiting for, but the play focuses our attention on what it is like to wait and it can mean nothing else. Beckett fulfilled what W.H. Auden described as the duty of a poet, the purification of language, and in the years to come, his plays stood as a reminder that the function of art was to provide patterns which help us to concentrate upon our experiences, and not to divert us from them, however entertainingly.

6

OLIVIER PASSES THE BATON

'I have done the state some service, and they know't;
No more of that.'

(From *Othello*)

The chief pioneer for French Absurdist drama in London was the English Stage Company under George Devine, but the box-office figures at the Royal Court make gloomy reading: 28 per cent for Beckett's *End Game* and *Krapp's Last Tape* in 1958; 20 per cent for Ionesco's *Jacques* and 30 per cent for Genet's *The Blacks* in 1961.[1] British Absurdist drama did better and N.F. Simpson's *One Way Pendulum* (1959) achieved 87 per cent of maximum box-office income, but to compare Simpson's plays with those of Ionesco and Genet is to measure the unnatural width of the Channel. Simpson's Kirby Groomkirby in *One Way Pendulum* taught 500 Speak-Your-Weight Machines to sing the Hallelujah Chorus, but this nonsense was quite different from the corpse in Amédée's bedroom. 'There is about Simpson,' said the US director, Charles Marowitz, 'the odour of civil service levity.'[2]

The tramps in the British *Waiting for Godot* were so lovable that they were picked up by television in *The Arthur Haynes Show*. Simpson parodied them in *A Resounding Tinkle* (1956), where two comics, after playing with socks and shoes, try profundity:

First Comedian: The stars are a long way off tonight.
Second Comedian: The planets are not much nearer.

Such imitation was the sincerest form of snubbing.

There was one exception to the ESC's string of box-office failures with French Absurdist drama. Ionesco's *Rhinoceros* played to capacity houses in 1960 and transferred for a West End run. The reason for its success was the presence in the cast of Sir Laurence Olivier, who played Berenger. His name was a great attraction, but not enough in itself to ensure success. He failed badly as Fred Midway in David Turner's *Semi-Detached* (1962) in which the comic actor Leonard Rossiter made his name.

Berenger was not one of Olivier's spectacular roles, no giant leaps, no howls of anguish, but an accumulation of details which mounted to an assertion of humanity against the odds. At first, his effects seemed too calculated, the drooping shoulders, the walrus moustache, the way of sitting slumped in a chair, not quite listening to what was being said around him. As Coriolanus in the 1959 Stratford production, Olivier seemed to be the most athletic man on stage. As Berenger, he was below average height and prone to ailments. He was the last person to react to the news that in some parts of the country human beings were turning into rhinoceroses. While others were scandalised or amused, he peered at the newspaper held before his eyes by his managing director, Mr Butterfly (Miles Malleson), and furrowed his brows. As the epidemic came nearer, his habitual wariness became fear and then a panic, expressed through a paralysed stillness. He wrapped his clerkish habits around him to keep the world at bay. From that cocoon, anything could emerge.

A Polish Jew, who had spent her childhood escaping from the Nazis, saw his performance and could not speak from emotion for an hour afterwards. She said that she had just seen her father.

As a whole, the production was disappointing. One critic wrote that its director, Orson Welles, had reduced 'a Champs Elysées satire to a Whitehall farce'.[3] Welles did not even like the play. It was too much like a cartoon. 'I only did it,' he later explained, 'for Larry.'[4] Welles had a trans-atlantic reputation as an imaginative director, good at symbolism (*Citizen Kane*) and science fiction (*The War of the Worlds*), which was why Olivier asked him to direct; but in rehearsal, Welles seemed more perplexed by the problem of getting his actors to behave like rhinoceroses than with what such transformations might mean.

In Paris, Jean-Louis Barrault, the French Olivier (but younger), had studied mime with Etienne Decroux before the war and knew exactly how to instruct his actors. He understood the play as someone who had survived in occupied France and was prepared to introduce chilling details of physical barbarism. The British actors had little mime training but a good sense of fun, and turned in their revue acts. Olivier behaved well during rehearsals but gave colleagues the benefit of his advice off-stage. Welles said that 'he got them off in little groups and had quiet little rehearsals having nothing to do with me'.[5]

Four days before the opening night, Olivier asked Welles to stay away from the rehearsals altogether. 'He had to destroy me in some way,' Welles said, 'He doesn't want anybody else up there. He's like Chaplin . . . a real fighting star.' Olivier was 'the leader of the English stage. *He*'s playing the leading role and directing all the time. What was *I* going to do?'[6] Others had similar experiences. Olivier asked Gielgud, who could be an indecisive director, to stay away from the last rehearsals of the 1955 Stratford *Twelfth Night*.[7] What made such interventions more galling was that they came with the best motives, not to protect his role but to save the production. A great man can be forgiven everything but for being right.

During the Stratford run of *Coriolanus*, Olivier took its director, Peter Hall, to lunch and said, 'I'm going to have a go at making the National Theatre. Will you join me as Number Two?' Hall, then 29, replied, 'I'm very flattered, Larry, I'd love to . . . But I'm going to make my own as Number One.'[8] Years later, Hall confessed to the fear that if he had joined forces with Olivier at this stage, Olivier would 'have trampled me into the ground'. Hall's decision had consequences for British theatre for it led to the establishment of two national theatres where there was previously none and destroyed a plan to have one national theatre with centres in London and Stratford. It also provoked a rivalry between the Royal Shakespeare Company (RSC) and the National Theatre (NT) which lasted until Hall took over from Olivier as the NT's Director in 1973.

Other young directors and actors had mixed feelings about the way in which Olivier was adapting to the demands of the new age. It was gratifying that he should want to do so, but they did not trust him. Was he really a Tory playing at socialism? Was he trying to hijack their revolution? On his part, Olivier groomed himself for the role in which he had been cast by Lyttelton at Notley Abbey. Berenger, his first and only attempt at playing French Absurdist drama, was part of the process. He tried out his singing voice in a screen musical, John Gay's *The Beggar's Opera* (1728). He lost money on an Ulster play, Sam Thompson's *Over the Bridge* (1960), banned in Belfast, which deserved a better fate in London. In 1962, he became the first Director of the Chichester Festival Theatre, as a preliminary towards forming the NT company, which took up lodgings at the Old Vic in 1963.

At Chichester, he had his first experience of directing and acting on a Tyrone–Guthrie style 'open stage', with the audience on three sides. He was not sure how it could work. As an actor, he was used to controlling the audience 'with his eyes', which was easier when they sat in one block, out front. He forced himself to attend committee meetings, where he behaved more like Berenger than Coriolanus, and to be civil to Kenneth Tynan. He tried to build a bridge between the pre-war acting traditions to which he belonged and the post-war Method actors, Oxbridge directors and angry playwrights. The gulf between them was wider than he had imagined. He could overcome some prejudices, against, for example, his film of *Hamlet* which won four Oscars and his habit of calling his colleagues, 'Dear boy', but others were harder to control, such as his wary respect for public money.

Olivier took a long time to get adjusted to the rights and wrongs of state subsidies. His background was in the commercial theatre and private charitable ventures, such as the Old Vic, but he had acted in war-time films where the national interest was self-evident. What was the purpose of a national theatre in peacetime? He had some texts to guide him, among them an essay by the Victorian critic Matthew Arnold, *The French Theatre* (1880), and a detailed study prepared by the critic William Archer and the actor-director Harley Granville Barker in 1904.

These presented slightly different emphases. For Arnold, who was impressed by the Comédie Française, a national theatre should provide a repertoire of great plays from the past in productions which aspired to high excellence and offered to the public at ticket prices reduced by subsidy. National theatres on the continent were often patriotic institutions, brought into being when monarchies became republics and court theatres were handed over to the state. They specialised in national repertoires, with some famous plays from other countries, such as Shakespeare's. Arnold was patriotic too but in a liberal way. He favoured a broader European repertoire, starting with Aeschylus, and his purpose for a national theatre was not to wave flags but to educate. It was to bring the public into contact with what great minds of the past had written and created.

Archer and Barker shared this aim, but whereas Arnold seemed to think that you could get in touch with what Aeschylus meant by using a national theatre as a kind of ouija board, they were more cautious. A national theatre should be a research centre to seek out the original meanings of plays and how they might have been staged. The educative process started with the company. They wanted the national theatre to be a place where the experience of eminent theatre professionals could be handed down to the next generation. This Archer–Barker model motivated Olivier's first attempt to establish a national theatre with the Old Vic company in 1945/6, which had a theatre school attached, a young people's theatre company, and an experimental stage.

Archer and Barker, but not Arnold, hoped that the repertoire would include revivals of modern plays of merit, denied a fair hearing by West End managements; but all three were agreed that a national theatre should not put on commercial plays nor *avant-garde* ones. This was for practical and philosophical reasons. They did not want to alarm the commercial theatre by proposing that a large rival should be established in its midst financed by public money. More significantly, they considered that a national theatre should be separated from passing fashions by providing a 'touchstone of excellence'. In classical theory, if a work of art had lasted a long time, it was more likely to be excellent. Bernard Shaw, a lifelong NT campaigner, was convinced that his plays would not be performed there until after his death.

Olivier was bringing the NT into being at a time when the commercial sector was in trouble and the Modernist spirit was disparaging everything old-fashioned. It could be difficult to detach the idea of excellence, in which everyone believed, from that of class, which was contentious. Brecht was one of those who asserted that plays could not retain their original meaning, as Arnold envisaged. Plays were products of their societies. The aim in a Shakespeare production should not be to mimic what an Elizabethan audience may have seen, which was guesswork, but to respond as modern minds to the stimuli of an old text.

Olivier had the instincts of an actor-manager and one of his ambitions was to preserve the centrality of the actor in the NT. This was not a matter of egoism but conviction. Only the actor could control to some degree what was happening in a theatre, not the writer or director. He alone could sense whether the audience was sitting in awed, or merely bored, silence. The rest was theory. But were actors the right people to run major companies? They had to concentrate too much on remembering their lines. Elsewhere in Europe, there was a rivalry between the old actor-managers and the new Intendants, who could be actors, directors or even critics, but whose purpose, like that of a football manager, was to harness the talents of others.

There was also a European tradition of the Grand Director, a puppet-master to his marionette actors, as recommended by the British prophet, Edward Gordon Craig, whose vision was supposed to encompass every detail of a performance from the placing of a chair to the blink of an eyelid. Max Reinhart was one example, but after the war there were many others – Konrad Swinarski who first directed Peter Weiss's *The Marat/Sade* in 1963, Andrzej Wajda in Cracow, Peter Zadek at Bremen and Yuri Lyubimov in Moscow. By British standards, their behaviour in rehearsals verged on the dictatorial, but their productions had the merit of being 'through composed'. When Peter Daubeny brought their companies over to London in the 1960s as part of his World Theatre seasons, British critics were usually much impressed.

Peter Hall was closer to the continental model. He was no actor and his strengths lay elsewhere, in handling committees, in explaining the latest theories and putting them into action. When he took over as the Director of the Shakespeare Memorial Theatre in 1959, he arrived with a grand plan. 'Suddenly,' Peter Brook recalled, 'the vast company, the immense repertoire, the excitement, the disasters, the strain all came into being.'[9]

Hall persuaded his board to lease the Aldwych Theatre in London to which Stratford productions could transfer and which enabled him to present contemporary plays. These could not be performed at Stratford within the theatre's aims as a charity. It was a considerable gamble. The reserves of the company were put at stake, some £100,000. Hall calculated that the days of state subsidy had arrived when assets in the bank would prove to be a disadvantage. He changed the name from the Shakespeare Memorial Company to the Royal Shakespeare Company, a title which had 'practically everything going for it except God'.[10]

This move also took the wind from the NT's sails. By the time the NT came into existence at the Old Vic in 1963, the RSC already had two major theatres and a lease on the Arts Theatre Club for try-outs, and behaved like a national theatre although the government explained that it was not one. There was also a party-political dimension. The NT was brought into being during the years of Macmillan's time as Prime Minister, whereas the RSC was more in tune with the socialism of Harold Wilson.

Wilson became Prime Minister in October 1964, after narrowly defeating Macmillan's successor, Alec Douglas-Home, who renounced his title as the fourteenth Earl of Home to lead the Conservative Party. Wilson could be described as a Modernist politician. At the Labour Party Conference in 1963, he promised to re-define 'socialism in terms of the scientific revolution'. Like Hall, Wilson came into office with a grand plan in his mind – suddenly, a Five Year economic plan, suddenly a Department for Economic Affairs, suddenly a Ministry of Technology and fairly suddenly, well down on his list, a new policy for the arts.

This shifted the responsibility for funding the Arts Council of Great Britain (ACGB) from the Chancellor of the Exchequer to the Department of Education and Science, where one Joint Under-Secretary was Jennie Lee MP, the widow of Aneurin Bevan who, as a member of Attlee's post-war government, had introduced the National Health Service. She became known as Britain's first Minister for the Arts and in February 1965 introduced a white paper, *A Policy for the Arts*, which envisaged a national arts service not unlike, as a model, the National Health Service. It had three main aims – to raise the standards of the arts, to improve public accessibility to the arts and to enter into a partnership with the local and regional councils, which were also encouraged to provide subsidies.

It promised that more public money would be spent on the arts and this was to some extent fulfilled. In 1964/5, the ACGB received £3,205,000 from the Treasury. In 1969/70, it received £8,200,000 and its annual report spoke glowingly of how Jennie Lee's White Paper had been implemented. It had a long list of clients and 'more than 100 new or radically re-constructed buildings were completed or in the process of completion'.[11] This did not provide the complete picture. While the public sector was growing, the private sector was in decline. The touring circuits of Beaumont's heyday no longer existed.

Whether grants had raised the artistic standards of British theatre was another matter. Most critics believed that they had and it would have been surprising if this were not the case for the theatre seemed to be better financed. Entertainments tax had been abolished in 1958, a Treasury gift to the arts, and within ten years, British theatre had moved from a situation where it was being unfairly taxed to one where it was being subsidised. But the old commercial system did have some advantages. A play which received a moderately successful West End run could expect to tour the regions for a year or more. The loss of the touring circuits prevented this from happening. Some actors welcomed this change on the grounds that long runs made them feel stale. Others chose their plays carefully and used the opportunity to perfect their performances. The Lunts (Alfred Lunt and Lynn Fontaine) were one example. In Friedrich Dürrenmatt's *The Visit*, Lunt agonised as to whether he should drop one pebble or two from a shoe. He was right to do so. It altered the dramatic effect.

Whether grants raised artistic standards or not, it certainly changed them. The new reps received most benefit, basing their programmes on the library principle of offering a selection of plays, 'each good of their kind', in monthly or three-weekly runs. This system was not best suited to new plays, which came to be staged in attached studios, for musicals or for directors with a concentrated vision from which they did not want to be diverted. Another effect of grants was to bring a younger generation of producers to the theatre, who could not, unlike Beaumont, raise money from angels in the City. Its impact favoured pluralism, new ideas, new accents, none cut-glass.

In its reconstituted form under Jennie Lee, the ACGB was a 'quango', a 'quasi-autonomous non-governmental organisation'. Wilson's government had a lot of them, each with a board of the good and the great, and appointments to quangos amounted to a secondary system of government patronage. Quangos were devised as a compromise between the command economies of the East and the liberalism of the West. Through them, the government maintained a measure of control while not interfering with detailed decisions. The quango system commanded much cross-party support and was a feature of 'Butskellism', a word which combined the names of the moderate Tory, R.A. Butler MP, and the moderate former leader of the Labour Party, Hugh Gaitskell. Under Wilson, the quango boards were balanced between lefts and rights, excluded trouble-makers and provided jobs for Classical guardians in a Modernist world.

The ACGB was supposed to be 'at arm's length' from the government, which determined the amount of money at the ACGB's disposal. This block grant was calculated by assessing the needs of those arts ventures approved by the ACGB and the Ministry; and then, according to sceptics, divided in half by the Treasury. Wilson wanted to avoid giving the impression that his government was creating anything like Zhdanov's Ministry of Culture. Jennie Lee's mandate did not extend to broadcasting (handled by the Postmaster General) or to films (overlooked by the Department of Trade and Industry). The government's definition of the arts may have been limited, but the principle of free speech was upheld by having several ministries helping the arts instead of just one, each supported by quangos whose members might very well not have gone to the same Oxbridge colleges.

The acknowledged flagships of British theatre were the NT and the RSC, which received the largest grants. Although it was still not supposed to be a national theatre, the RSC provided a better illustration of how at the time a major subsidised theatre was supposed to behave. It had a substantial repertoire of classical plays, some modernised to make them more relevant. It promoted new plays, disparaged the commercial theatre and proved its independence from government by attacking those British sacred cows, many of which Harold Wilson wanted in any case to be slaughtered.

In 1963, the RSC launched a 'Theatre of Cruelty' season in a studio attached to the London Academy of Music and Dramatic Art (LAMDA). It was brought together by Charles Marowitz and Peter Brook; and its title came from Antonin Artaud, whose short play, *A Spurt of Blood*, was part of the programme. It provided a quick guide to everything then considered to be *avant-garde*: an extract from Genet, a spot of Bard-abuse (*Hamlet* reduced to an Oedipal playlet), some political satire. In one sketch, Glenda Jackson as Christine Keeler, a call-girl mixed up in a recent Tory scandal, stepped into a prison bath, naked, and emerged as Jackie Kennedy, recently widowed by the murder of President Kennedy. It was a triumph of tacky taste and performed, of course, in a club, away from the Lord Chamberlain. The significance of the season lay not so much in its technical innovations or its themes, which were half-baked, but in the way in which it marched so boldly and on such a wide front on the perceived faults of British culture, its inhibitions, its snobbery, Eng. Lit., racism and false decorum. An analyst might add that we were trying to murder our parents.

Naturally it had a liberating effect. Fringe theatres pursued ideas stimulated at LAMDA throughout the 1960s and Brook used the gleaned knowledge in two major RSC productions, *The Marat/Sade* (1964) and *US* (1966). The season could not have taken place without Hall's background support. It was too controversial. It alienated members of the RSC Board, including the impresario Emile Littler, who accused Hall of sponsoring 'dirty plays'. They also had in mind *The Marat/Sade*, Harold Pinter's *The Homecoming* and a Dadaist play by Roger Vitrac, *Victor*, which took the bourgeois society to task for being disgracefully bourgeois.

Hall fought back and the ensuing 'dirty plays' controversy in 1965, which he won, was a major turning point in British theatre, where the radicals glimpsed sight of their eventual victory. It could be interpreted as a triumph of Modernism over Classicism. It was also exactly how, according to Archer and Barker, a national theatre should not behave.

Olivier meanwhile was trying to run with the hares and hunt with the hounds. He kept away from rivalry with the West End by only producing those new plays, such as Peter Shaffer's *The Royal Hunt of the Sun*, whose scale would have deterred commercial managements. He brought a young team together to run the NT, two directors from the Royal Court, John Dexter and William Gaskill, together with Kenneth Tynan as his literary manager. His company also included young ESC actors, Frank Finlay, Colin Blakeley, Joan Plowright (whom he married in 1961), Maggie Smith and Robert Stephens. With actors of his own generation, he was less successful. Michael Redgrave joined the company, but Gielgud and Richardson kept their distance. Some thought that this was Olivier's way of warding off rivals, but one such actor said, 'The National Theatre? I thought it was Larry's mid-life crisis!'

Some actors were wary of appearing on the stage with him. He could be so mesmeric. He was not a selfish actor and often a generous one, but when he was on form, the audience could not keep their eyes from him. His physical transformations were astonishing, so gnarled as Titus, so slight as Shallow. Welles confided to Tynan that Olivier could never play Othello. 'Larry's a natural tenor and Othello's a natural bass',[12] but he trained his voice and when he prowled on to the stage as Othello in 1964, his voice was an octave lower than anyone had heard it before.

Such disguises were attributed to his technique, sometimes a way of damning with faint praise. 'Olivier,' said Gielgud, 'is a great impersonator. I am always myself.'[13] 'Acting,' said Hall, 'is not imitation but a revelation of the inner self.'[14] The critic, Harold Hobson, used a French distinction between an *acteur*, a Gielgud, who always played himself, and a *comédien*, an Olivier, who imitated other people. Olivier said that he never wanted to 'express himself', adding over-modestly that 'I have never been conscious of any need other than to show off'.[15]

He never liked to talk much about his craft, but in 1962, he said that the actor must be 'a great understander. He must . . . love the person he is portraying, no matter how unsympathetic . . . he must make the subject real and understandable to his audience, not by any means playing *for* sympathy, but *with* sympathy, or at least, with empathy.'[16] This was another point of difference with the new wave, which liked hard outlines, akin to satire, not only of an individual person but of whole societies.

Olivier built up his portraits detail by detail, revealing no more to the audience than they needed to know at the time. He would start with the physical shape, the character's size and bulk, and add such broad details

69

as an accent or a way of walking. Jonathan Miller, who directed him in *The Merchant of Venice*, was amused by his fondness for nose putty and such tricks of an old pro's trade, but this was the way in which Olivier searched for the vocabulary of his performance.

Olivier never claimed to be an intellectual, but he was an exceptionally thoughtful and well-organised actor. He needed to understand what the play was about, which was why he succeeded as Berenger while all around him failed. He had seen the rise of Nazism and visited Belsen just after the war. Nine-tenths of his performance was calculated in advance. On films or television, he often seemed contrived. The tenth part, however, he reserved for his theatre audiences and it was that for which they waited.

Olivier seemed to wind himself into a role, so that each detail tightened the screw of his, and their, concentration. There came a point when the tension was hard to take, but he would still turn, and his public could not move for watching, and he would still turn, and they could not breathe for listening, and he would still turn. Then it seemed as if his pent-up energy would flood out in one torrent, as if he had penetrated to some liquid core. Many have tried to describe the power that he could generate on these occasions, Tynan better than most. The word, volcanic, recurs in reviews, with 'leonine' and 'animality'.

Olivier knew that he could achieve this intensity, but he did not know how or why. Once after a memorable Othello, his fellow actors applauded him to his dressing room; but he swept past and Frank Finlay asked him quietly, 'What's wrong, Larry? That was great.' He replied, 'I know it was great, dammit, but I don't know how I did it. How can I be sure of doing it again?'[17] Before his Richard III in 1944, as before his James Tyrone in O'Neill's *Long Day's Journey into Night* in 1971, he sat in his dressing room, convinced that he was heading for disaster. His power, but not his competence, was unpredictable. It took his old friend, Ralph Richardson, by surprise, who on one occasion whispered to him appalled, 'Steady on, old chap, steady on!'

There could indeed be something shocking about the emotional strength of an Olivier performance, an unexpected nakedness in a public place. He had the habit of slightly tilting his head so that the lights caught his eyes and when he did so, members of the audience thought that he was looking at them individually. His Othello provoked extreme reactions, for and against. He chose to play him as a swaggering black general, a born fighter like Mohammed Ali, formidable and sensuous. Alan Brien described it as 'the kind of bad performance of which only great actors are capable. . . . His hips oscillate, his palms rotate, his voice skids and slides'.[18] At a time when the US civil rights movement was gaining ground and Britain was escaping from her colonial past, some thought that he was making a racist statement. That was most unlikely, but he may have been providing a motive for the white man's fear of a black usurper, which is in Shakespeare.

Few reviews did more than mention Finlay's Iago, which shows the difficulty of playing with Olivier. It was also Olivier's problem in bringing together his company. He wanted to assemble a team of equals but nobody could doubt who was the real star of the show. He did his best. He played small roles, where needed, and joined Gaskill's improvisations for *The Recruiting Officer* (1963), where Gaskill followed Brecht's example by asking his cast 'Who *owns* whom?' He ensured that salary levels were kept within a narrow band, so that the stars, including himself, never earned more than four times the amount of a raw recruit.

After three years, Dexter left, as did Gaskill, seeking a more overtly socialist company. In 1966, Tynan, wary that the RSC might steal the march on radicalism, came into Olivier's office with a script, *Soldiers*, by the Swiss writer, Rolf Hochhuth. 'This is the most imposing play I have ever read', he said.[19] *Soldiers* blamed Churchill for sanctioning the killing of the Polish general, Sikorski, and for bombing Dresden. Lyttelton, who as Lord Chandos was now chairman of the NT's Board, demanded to know what evidence Hochhuth had to support his assertions. It was locked up in a Swiss bank. Olivier stood by his literary manager, although he did not like the play, and saved him from dismissal. The play was not performed at the NT and after 1967, Tynan's influence declined. The team which had successfully steered the NT through its early years was thus disbanded.

Olivier brought in a no less talented team of Jonathan Miller, Frank Dunlop and Michael Blakemore, but rumours spread that he was out of touch with the new world of British theatre. In 1968, he invited Brook to direct Seneca's *Oedipus* and Brook planned a finale in which the company danced around a flagpole with a Union Jack, mangling the National Anthem. Olivier thought it inappropriate for a national theatre. Brook substituted a gold phallus for the flagpole, asking his cast to sing 'Yes, we have no bananas'. Olivier hated the dress rehearsal but resigned himself to the fact that he could do nothing about it.

He became plagued with ill-health due to cancer, but recovered and stuck to his duties. He wanted above all to lead his company into their promised new building on the South Bank, which in 1970 had not risen above its foundation stone. Only its costs were rising. In 1968, Jennie Lee had announced that the government would provide £7,500,000 to build the place. If it cost more, they should 'jump in the river'. It did and they didn't.

By 1973, it had still not been built. The new chairman of the Board, Sir Max Rayne, decided to appoint Peter Hall as Olivier's successor. Olivier was not consulted nor did he hear about the offer until months after it had been made. His pride was hurt, of course, near mortally, but not exactly his vanity. It angered him that a director's theatre should replace an actor's one and that his chairman did not seem to know the difference. What upset him most of all was that he had tried to defend (if not the British way of life) the best traditions of British theatre, as he interpreted them. His reward was to see the prize to which he had devoted his life go to those who wanted to subvert them. It offended his whole scheme of values, what was done, how it was done, why it was done. He may have taken it too much to heart, but it was rare to find in the following years an actor who worried neurotically about whether one pebble or two should drop from his shoe or who could control an audience with his eyes.

7

THE VELVET PRISON

Irina (alone in her misery): 'To Moscow! Moscow! Moscow!'
(From *The Three Sisters*)

The first night of Olivier's *Othello* in Moscow on 7 September 1965, could easily have been mistaken for an historic occasion. It was the NT's first visit abroad, the first by any foreign company to the Kremlin Theatre, built by Stalin inside the walls of the palace to avoid the risks of the open streets; and the first public manifestation of a cultural exchange agreement signed by two new governments, each wanting for their own reasons to show their willingness to bring the Cold War to an end.

The NT's reception, according to the theatre critic Felix Barker, made 'enthusiasm a pale word'. 'The audience from the back of the theatre swept down the central gangway in a great human tide. They stood three-deep in the front of the stage, hurling flowers and clapping . . .'.[1] Olivier thought that the performance had 'that little extra something',[2] although Barker felt that on this occasion he 'overdid it'.[3]

Whatever its merits, the event was a triumph of cultural diplomacy. In Moscow, it was heralded with a huge relief, as if decades of isolation were drawing to a close. Barker noticed one woman in black who could not stir from her seat for sobbing; while the Soviet critic Aleksander Anikst said twenty years later that he kept 'a private film' of the occasion in his mind, to re-play in moments of despair. In London, it strengthened the hand of the Minister of the Arts who signed the agreement, Jennie Lee, and it came at the right time for the British government.

Harold Wilson and the new collective leadership of the Soviet Communist Party came to power on almost exactly the same day, 14/15 October 1964. Their positions were almost equally tenuous. Wilson's majority in the House of Commons was only four, while the *coup d'état* which deposed Kruschev left a power struggle in the Kremlin in which it was still unsure who would emerge as the eventual leader. There were four contenders, the new head of the Soviet Communist Party

73

Leonid Brezhnev, the Prime Minister Alexei Kosygin, N.V.Podgorny and Mikhail Suslov, the ideological purist who denounced Kruschev.

Wilson, facing the prospect of another general election, wanted to present himself to the British people as a kind of honest broker between East and West, a better man to talk to the Russians than the fourteenth Earl of Home. In June 1965 he tried to organise a Commonwealth peace-keeping mission to Vietnam, which failed because all the major powers concerned were supposed to be keeping the peace. Nor was Wilson in any position to conduct any independent diplomacy. The new Labour government was as much tied to NATO as its Tory predecessors; it retained the British claim to an independent nuclear deterrent and in the House of Commons, Wilson stoutly defended the US peace-keeping mission in Vietnam, which might otherwise have been mistaken for bullying. Bertrand Russell tore up his Labour membership card.

The NT's Moscow visit had the diplomatic subtlety of a man who sends flowers to his wife to avoid a cross-examination about last weekend and it was received in much the same spirit. The collective leadership wanted to assure the West that Kruschev's departure did not mean a return to Stalinism or an end to his policy of 'peaceful co-existence'. At the same time, the Soviet leaders had little intention of continuing with those policies thought to be liberal in the West. Their main aim was to restore the Soviet Communist Party's authority and, in particular, its leadership of the communist world. They were alarmed by the challenge from Mao's China, for the Sino-Soviet split had plunged to new depths in the last months of Kruschev's regime.

Mao Tse-Tung had accused the Soviets of giving way before imperialism, over the Cuban missile crisis among other matters. Kruschev retorted by calling Mao a second Stalin and insisted that the Chinese did not know the risks of modern war. In 1964, China became a nuclear power and after Kruschev's downfall, the Soviet leaders invited the Chinese leaders to Moscow to see if their differences could be reconciled. If this peace-making had been successful, the NT's visit would probably not have taken place, but it failed. The Soviet leaders had to show a friendly spirit towards the West, while tightening their grip at home.

This was one role of Cold War cultural exchange programmes, not only to offer the hand of friendship, but to distract the attention away from what the other hand was doing. The motives were not entirely cynical. In theory, most European governments held the arts in high esteem, but they tended to define them narrowly and to invest what remained with some immense dreams. The arts were expected to provide a sense of national identity. You were lucky if you were not confronted at some point in a cultural exchange programme by folk dancing. They were also expected to offer a vision of 'heritage' and to raise the mind towards the 'higher things in life', behind which foggy phrase could be detected some neo-Platonism and a yearning for absolute values.

Such criteria cut out the day-to-day arts of advertising, pop music and architecture. The arts were not exactly useful, which dispensed with commercial and industrial design, and although they were uplifting, they did not help with decisions which you might meet in ordinary life. In the Soviet Union, there were state-subsidised colonies of poster artists, whose work was never seen in the streets, only in international exhibitions. It was taken for granted that the arts were good for you, the most question-begging assumption of all, for the state decided which which were good for you and which were not.

The NT's programme in Moscow consisted of *Othello*, Congreve's *Love for Love* and Brighouse's *Hobson's Choice*; and was the sort of thing that most national theatres were expected to provide on state occasions. The objection to such packages was not that they were trivial, but that they were bland. They asked no questions and were told no lies. The king was in charge of the mousetrap.

Jennie Lee's opposite number in the Soviet Union, Mme Furtseva, had inherited a definition as to what the arts were supposed to do. Their purpose was to 'raise the consciousness of the people'. As Konstantin Chernenko pithily expressed it: 'the real extent of the influence that literature and art on the whole exert on the moulding of the ideological and moral frame of the people's mind is the most precise criterion of their success.'[4]

In Stalin's day, this meant state propaganda, but Mme Furtseva was Minister at a delicate time when Stalinism was giving way to post-Stalinism and, after Kruschev's fall, vice-versa. In his campaign against Stalinism, Kruschev had admitted the possibility that raising the consciousness of the people might mean some criticism of the state. The question which confronted Mme Furtseva was 'How far could this go?' The precedents from Kruschev's time were unreliable. Boris Pasternak had not been sent to a labour camp for publishing *Dr Zhivago* abroad in 1957, but he had been denounced as 'a pig who fouled his own sty'.[5] *Dr Zhivago* did not attack the Communist Party directly, but it did describe the destructive impact of the Revolution on the lives of Soviet citizens and in language which hauntingly evoked a sense of loss, of wasted lives and hopes.

In Kruschev's last years, there were signs of a new tolerance everywhere. In 1960, following the death of Pasternak, a group of young poets gathered around Mayakowsky's monument in Moscow to distribute satirical poems in typewritten sheets, crudely carbon-copied. It was the start of what came to be known as *samizdat*, or self-publishing, and it was several days before they were beaten up formally. The incident which caused most controversy was the publication in 1962 of *One Day in the Life of Ivan Denisovich* by an unknown schoolmaster, Alexander Solzhenitsin, in *Novyi Mir*, a cultural magazine, subsidised by the state. It was an account of what one inmate of a labour camp had to endure without any hint that his punishment could be morally justified. Kruschev, who authorised it himself, must have hoped that readers would use it to compare favourably the tolerance of his regime with that of Stalin's; but it provoked an outpouring of similar stories, some even more horrific, calling the whole history of the Revolution into question. The misery of the Soviet people became apparent.

These accounts could not be published. In two hastily summoned meetings of the Soviet Writers' Union in December 1962 and March 1963, Kruschev and Ilyichev, the head of a newly formed Ideological Commission, tried to lay down guidelines as to the limits of the permissible. The writers received a somewhat different message. They formed the opinion that the authorities were reluctant to use force, unless provoked to do so, and that they needed to be more subtle in criticising the state. As a result, there was a wave of concealed attacks on communism, buried in fantasies, fairy tales and interpretations of classics. It spread through Eastern Europe, to Budapest, Prague and Warsaw, where writers could also be subtle, angry and speak in foreign tongues.

Kruschev's liberalism similarly affected the theatre. In 1963, an actor who had trained with the Moscow Art Theatre, Yuri Lyubimov, tried out a play by Brecht, *The Good Person of Setzuan*, with third-year students at the Vakhtangov Institute. Its style was far removed from Socialist Realism. The gods had bowler hats, green ties and carnations in their button-holes. It did not preach or indulge in sentimental gestures. The acting was sharp and lively, demonstrating in Brecht's manner and not seeking an internal identification with their roles as Stanislavski taught. It was visually attractive and the mimed cartoons were subverted by ironic tunes plucked on guitars. The audience went wild and Lyubimov had to climb from the lighting box to calm them down. The Institute's director promptly cancelled the next performance, but a leading critic, Konstantin Simonov, wrote an article in *Pravda*, praising this 'gust of fresh air'. In 1964, Lyubimov was offered his own theatre, the near-derelict Taganka.

Aleksander Anikst explained this triumph by pointing out that it was not only fresh and original, but nostalgic. For older members of the audience, it harked back to the days before Socialist Realism when such Soviet directors as Meyerhold and Tairov excelled in Expressionism. For Kruschev, it provided a vivid example for its Moscow public of what had been lost under Stalin. Lyubimov became a symbol of post-Stalinism. He had the right credentials. His grandfather had been a persecuted kulak, his parents were jailed in 1925 when he was only 8, he had trained as an electrical engineer and fought with the Soviet army to protect Moscow in December 1941. His career as an actor with the Vakhtangov Theatre before and after the war had won him the Stalin Prize in 1951, but he did not become a member of the Soviet Communist Party until 1953, immediately after Stalin's death.

Lyubimov was aware of his value to the regime. Before taking on the task of restoring the Taganka, he sent a letter to the Ministry of Culture with thirteen conditions, which included throwing out the old Socialist Realist plays and bringing in the actors whom he had trained at the Vakhtangov Institute. These provided the legal basis for his life as a licensed rebel, but he would not have lasted for the next twenty years at the Taganka, if he had not proved his political worth as an example of a major artist who spoke out with apparent freedom and was showered with honours by a broadminded, post-Stalinist government.

While Lyubimov was clearing out the dry rot from the Taganka and the collective leadership was playing host to the NT company, steps were being taken to crack down on dissidents. Evidence was gathered in the autumn of 1965 to stage show trials in the spring of two writers, Andrei Sinyavsky and Yuli Daniel, who had stepped over the boundaries of constructive criticism. In February 1966, they were sentenced to seven years and five years respectively in labour camps for spreading anti-Soviet propaganda. In Stalinist terms, these punishments were light, but enough to remind anyone who planned to follow their examples that the bear could still bite.

In general, the collective leadership preferred to adopt post-Stalinist methods of censorship, which the Hungarian writer, Miklosz Haraszti, has described in his book, *The Velvet Prison*. The post-Stalinist state, instead of bullying intellectuals, entered into a conspiracy with them. It offered them job security and the chance to travel. It reminded them flatteringly of the vital role that culture plays somewhere and that the future depended upon sound intellectual leadership. It even allowed them some freedom to dissent. A little controversy did the post-Stalinist state no harm at all. It reminded sceptics of how far the state had travelled since the bad old days of Stalinism, how enlightened it was now, how 'soft' as opposed to 'hard'.

This is what Miklosz Haraszti, writing about Hungary, called 'the velvet prison'. It was a prison because the government still controlled the media, it set the agenda and determined the form as well as the substance of the public debate. Unlike most prisons, it was a pleasant place in which to live, privileged but not *so* privileged that it aroused feelings of guilt. More people battled to get in than get out; and the state regulated entry. Its main weapon was not the threat of the labour camp, but the promise of more subsidy.

Nor were its inmates negligible or naive. They included academicians of world renown and licensed rebels like Lyubimov, liberal scientists like Andrei Sakharov, who was not finally disgraced and placed under house arrest until 1980, as well as the broad mass of those who worked in the arts and the media. The velvet prisoners were under considerable pressure to conform or to moderate their lack of conformity. Thus, post-Stalinist censorship penetrated deeply intellectual orthodoxies, unlike Stalinism which buried dissent without poisoning it first.

One such velvet prisoner was Aleksander Anikst, whom Olivier met in Moscow and found 'extremely erudite',[6] as he was. He was a friend of Pasternak, whose Shakespearian translations he edited, and the man to whom Soviet directors turned for advice about shades of Shakespearian meanings. He was the Chairman of the Soviet Shakespeare Commission, a difficult, unpaid chore, for Shakespeare was one battleground where the war between the dissidents and the establishment was raging.

The collection of essays, published in Warsaw in 1961, by a professor of comparative literature, Jan Kott, contained in its cunning title, *Shakespeare Our Contemporary*, hidden messages for the Eastern bloc. On one level, nobody could complain about it. For two hundred years, critics had talked of Shakespeare's *universality*, the interest of his plays for all times and all men, and if Shakespeare was so immortal, he must be contemporary too. By stressing the word contemporary, Kott hinted to directors that Shakespeare's plays could comment on current affairs without fear of censorship. Such connections had been made before. The critic Anna Földes attended in 1955 the first night of a *Richard III* in Budapest. 'I can remember the scene where the scrivener announced the tragic death of Hastings to fantastic and unusual applause. The sentence without trial, a public murder through accusation and without any real investigation, had a special political message for those times, when the Rajk trial was still in our minds and not openly discussed.'[7]

Kott turned the accidental into the deliberate, demonstrating that the classics could be used as a metaphorical language to describe the present. '*Hamlet*,' wrote Kott, 'is like a sponge. Unless produced in a stylized or antiquarian fashion, it immediately absorbs the problems of our time.'[8]

The effect was immediate, challenging and, so far as the cultural authorities of Eastern Europe were concerned, alarming. They could not ban Shakespeare without seeming to be philistine. They could try to vet the directors, more difficult than it sounds, for directors were not always in control of their actors and a detail, such as an Uncle Joe moustache on Richard III, spoke volumes. They could bring pressure on theatre critics to give poor reviews to subversive productions; but critics learnt a double-speak, whereby, in blaming something for not being authentic, they offered reasons why the public should see it.

Finally, they could turn to an authority like Anikst to provide a single definition as to what a particular Shakespearian play was supposed to be about, but Anikst had too subtle a mind to be caught in this particular trap. To his death in December 1989, Anikst insisted that he was a Marxist, but his beliefs were shot through with a liberal humanism which many in the West would have deemed an unsustainable paradox. His parents were personal friends of Lenin, in exile together in Zurich and returning with him to Moscow in 1917. As a young man, Anikst had watched at close quarters the intrigues of the Soviet Communist Party, the rise of Stalin and the fall of Trotsky. In 1938, his father was shot, arbitrarily, without trial, by one of Stalin's gangs. His mother was sent to a labour camp and he was denounced as a 'cosmopolitan', hence, a dangerous Jew and a subversive.

During those years, until Kruschev allowed him once more to work within a university, Anikst kept a copy of Shakespeare at his side, in English, hiding it away from the KGB who might have seized it as further proof of his cosmopolitanism, together with tattered editions of Aeschylus, Sophocles and Euripides. These reminded him that the bloodthirsty events which he had witnessed in his own times were not historically unusual and that there was still hope for salvation. In that sense, Anikst was an optimist, a pragmatist and someone who, while seeing Kott's view, would not allow himself to be drawn into wilfully distorting Shakespeare's text or the condemnation of Marxism itself.

Points of interpretation remained, some contentious, among them, what happens in *Hamlet*. In the traditional Soviet view, Hamlet was an ineffectual man, a social democrat at heart, whose conscience creates havoc in the fascist Danish court, which collapses from its internal contradictions. A proletarian leader from Norway, Fortinbras, restores law and order. *Hamlet* was thus a parable for Soviet intervention in East Europe, as the Soviets saw it. Under Kott's influence, a different version emerged, whereby Denmark was a small country, under threat from its larger neighbour, Norway, with whom old Hamlet tried to arrange a peace pact. The usurping Claudius, a strong leader, tears up this deal to secure Denmark's independence, but his authority is undermined by an immature Hamlet, fretful of his mother's marriage. Denmark, divided against itself, falls victim to the invading army of Fortinbras, another parable for our times, as the Poles saw it.

Which was 'right'? The case for either could be argued from Shakespeare's text, but the choice might affect how characters were interpreted, the sense of the verse and such staging details as the trumpets which announce Fortinbras's arrival. Brecht would have argued in his later years that the only right answer was the politically correct one and that we had no choice other than to interpret Shakespeare in the light of modern knowledge. Brecht may well have chosen the

Polish version, for his brief telling of the story put the idea into Kott's mind.

Anikst was more subtle than Brecht. While he conceded that we had no option other than to approach Shakespeare in the light of our modern experience, for we were not Elizabethans, he went on to argue that the accurate study of his plays was more rewarding than finding contemporary parallels, precisely because we were modern. If we superimposed our current concerns on Shakespeare, we would find our limitations reflected from a mangled text, which was satisfactory neither as an approach to Shakespeare nor to our problems. Anikst pleaded for 'open' interpretations, ones which preserved the ambiguities of the text, and he saw no reason why a production of *Hamlet* should not contain both the Soviet and the Polish views. Fortinbras's arrival was an act of invasion for the Danes, of liberation for the Norwegians. He admired Olivier for not trying to duck the charge of racism by presenting an off-white Othello but not veering into bigotry either.

In ways which did not conflict with his probity, Anikst steered directors from too bold a confrontation with the state by offering, say, a Brezhnev look-alike as Richard III. He said that he was trying not to narrow the range of Shakespeare's possible meanings. In the Years of Stagnation under Brezhnev, who emerged as the boss of the collective leadership, Shakespeare's plays were performed more often in the Soviet Union than those of any other writer, including Gogol, Gorki or Chekhov. Regional Shakespeares were often rather old-fashioned, where middle-aged actors wore blonde wigs for Hamlet, black curly ones for Romeo and dressed in doublet and hose; but in the main cities, where directors listened to Anikst and read Kott, Shakespeare did absorb the problems of the time 'like a sponge'.

Nor was it only Shakespeare who became a contemporary, but other eminent and dead dramatists. Molière's *Tartuffe* was popular with Tartuffe as a neighbourhood *apparatchik*. The big laugh came at the end where the state intervened to save Orgon's family from dispossession. Yevgeny Schwartz's *The Dragon*, a satirical fairy tale, written to attack Nazism in the 1930s, was played in modern dress, to remind us, as one Soviet director blandly remarked, that fascism was still a world threat. The public saw the dragon dressed as a party official and drew their own conclusions. To commemorate the fiftieth anniversary of the October Revolution, the National Theatre in Warsaw staged Adam Mickiewicz's nineteenth-century romantic epic, *Forefathers' Eve*, in November 1967. The Ministry of Culture approved. It demonstrated the connection between the revolutionaries of Poland and their Soviet comrades, who stormed the Winter Palace. But the play contains such lines as 'Moscow only sends rogues to Poland' and the First Secretary of the Polish Communist Party, Władyslaw

Gomulka, had to send in the troops to suppress the riots which followed.[9]

To make life even more difficult for the authorities, they could no longer complain about Expressionism, with Lyubimov clinging on at the Taganka like a cowboy on a bucking bronco. With Socialist Realism, they knew where they were. If a play had an ideologically correct message, there was little chance that it would be contradicted by the acting or staging, which had to be naturalistic. Under Stalinism, according to Haraszti, 'ambiguity was betrayal'. Post-Stalinist Expressionism on the other hand revelled in ambiguity. A line which looked innocent when read by the censors in Moscow took on a different meaning when played against a lighting change which turned the set blood red. The Soviet Ministry of Culture sent representatives to watch the dress rehearsals of Moscow productions before certifying them fit for public performance, but they could not be equally diligent for all the 625 theatres throughout the Soviet Union. They had to rely on their local officials who could be more repressive or more lax and unsophisticated. The further from Moscow, the more arbitrary the rules, and in some outlying states, such as the Baltic republics, it might even be said that the censors were sometimes on the side of the censored.

The Ministries of Culture in the buffer countries of Central Europe faced a similar problem. 'Look at it this way,' the censor wearily remarked in Tadeusz Kowícki's *samizdat* novel, *A Small Apocalypse*, 'my job is basically to increase the allusiveness of Polish literature!' It was a typical Polish joke, bizarrely apt, as if in Britain a detective conducting an interrogation in a lonely cell had quoted William Empson's *Seven Types of Ambiguity* before applying the boot to the prisoner's groin.

Polish theatre was proud of its allusiveness. With each attempt at repression, the layers of irony went one step deeper, so that the surface meaning was contradicted by a secondary one and then at a tertiary level. It constituted a kind of meta-language, which only Poles could understand. It stemmed from the writings of Stanislaw Witkiewicz, 'Witkacy', a painter, dramatist and Polish father of the Absurd, who committed suicide at 54 on the eve of the Second World War. Witkacy's *Pure Form in Theatre* (1920) dispensed with story-telling and substituted an associative logic in which visual and aural symbolism played as much part as words themselves. His influence could be felt in the imagery and layering of Andrzej Wajda's Cracow productions and in the work of such Absurdist dramatists as Tadeusz Rożiewicz, Slavomir Mrożek and Witold Gombrowicz.

Two directors in particular, Josef Szajna and Tadeusz Kantor, polished Witkacy's ideas into a rich theatrical language. Both had trained (like Witkacy) as architects, both preferred empty rooms to formal theatres, both sought a total theatre where sounds and images absorbed words for their sensuous effects and both treated actors like puppets in the style of Edward Gordon Craig. There the similarities end. Szajna was haunted by his experiences in a concentration camp during the war and in his versions of the holocaust, *Replica*, the world is destroyed again and again, struggling back to life as a fragile egg.

Kantor ran an underground theatre during the war and in the mid-1950s, having designed sets for Cracow's Stary Theatre, he broke away to found what amounted to a painter's theatre, Cricot 2, in 1956. During the 1960s, often using texts by Witkacy, such as *The Water Hen* (1968), he developed a surreal theatre in which bizarre but evocative images swirled into view and receded, a *pavane* of the unexpected. Later, the 1920s irreverence, Witkacy's contribution, gave way to a unique performance art, which Kantor termed 'the Theatre of Death', where he conducted a séance of ghosts from Poland's past, as in *The Dead Class* (1975).

A dangerous feature of these developments, from the point of view of the communist authorities, was that they travelled well, could take place almost anywhere and required little in the way of official support. Kantor used amateur actors, while the young Polish director, Jerzy Grotowski, wanted to get rid of theatres altogether, concentrating on the actor's relationship with a small audience in a bare room. He talked of it as a new science and started a 'laboratory' near Wrocław for his research. In Prague, Pavel Kahout took his plays into private flats if they seemed too subversive even for the little theatres which had mushroomed up in the mid-1960s, the Balustrade, the Gate and the Semaphor. Dissidents denied entrance to the velvet prison, like Milan Kundera and Václav Havel, wrote heavily ironic plays for them which bordered on the permissible. Havel had a Czech knack of making the state seem not only sinister but ridiculous. Who took seriously his idea in *The Memorandum* (1966) that the state might introduce a language, Ptydepe, planned so that the words used most often had the fewest letters? Everyone knew that in official papers the words used most often had the most letters.

Prague had a National Theatre with a golden roof, a classical repertoire with sets by Josef Svoboda and a nineteenth-century slogan above its proscenium arch, 'A nation's gift to itself'. It was a glory of Central Europe, but the Czech plays published in the West were by Havel and Kahout, which left the impression that life under communism was a chaotic, corrupt and vicious mess.

When in April 1966 Brezhnev emerged as the single leader of the Soviet Union, he was determined to stop to this nonsense. A test of his resolution came in the following year when the pro-Moscow leader of the Czech Communist Party, Antonin Novotny, was challenged by a soft-liner, Alexander Dubček. Dubček won and in January 1968 the 'Prague Spring' began, and lasted for six months. Everything seemed possible then, a free press, open political debates, a general release from tyranny, and Dubček was convinced that the spring would last into high summer. The Soviet Union would not risk its post-Stalinist reforms by invading a friendly neighbour, as it had done twelve years before in Hungary. When the news came to the Praesidium in Prague that the Russian tanks were rolling, Dubček was stunned. 'How could they do this to me?' he said, 'This is a profound personal tragedy!'[10]

There was fighting in the streets and many acts of individual heroism. On 26 January 1969, a student, Jan Palach, set himself alight in Wenceslas Square and died two days later. An uneasy silence descended on Prague, which lasted for twenty years.

The Years of Stagnation began with tighter censorship. In Moscow even the Taganka was vetted at the highest level. In March 1969 Mme Furtseva herself came along to see a preview of a new play, Boris Mozhayev's *The Man Alive*. It concerned a farm worker, Kuzhkin, who battled to scrape a living for his family against the corruption of the local party and the collective farm for which he worked. It had a happy ending. Kuzhkin's appeal to a higher authority was heard, his wrongs eventually righted.

A Taganka actor, Valerie Zolotuchin, described its reception. The theatre was cold and empty. Mme Furtseva sat at the back, wearing a fur coat, with her officials. Zolotuchin noticed how Lyubimov made the sign of the cross secretly in front of one of the birch trees which constituted the set, 'a communist seeking a Christian blessing to save *The Man Alive* from the Ministry of Culture'. When it was over Mme Furtseva turned to Boris Mozhayev and said, 'I suppose you think this is brave. It is not bravery. It is anti-Soviet. It is disgusting.' Mozhayev replied, 'I have written a comedy about our bad collective farms. . . .' 'Is this a comedy?' said Mme Furtseva, 'It is a tragedy. People will come out and ask, "Is this what we have built our revolution for?" The head of the collective farm is an alcoholic, the chief of the team is an alcoholic, the chairman of the executive is a rascal! And you, comrade Lyubimov, we can see in which direction you are taking your collective!'

'Don't frighten me,' said Lyubimov, 'I have been thrown out of this job many times and many respected people have defended me, many academicians!' 'I am the one in this country,' said Mme Furtseva, 'who is responsible for art in this country, not any academician. And nobody will support you.'

A leading poet, Andrei Voznesenski, said quietly, 'I liked it. I have seen four rehearsals and it is deeply Russian and not anti-party, whatever party officials may think.' He was ruled out of order. Vladekin from the Ministry's Commission of Acceptance summed up, 'Today's performance,' he said to Lyubimov, 'is an apotheosis of all your bad tendencies. What I have seen today is political vulgarity. And where, Comrade Mozhayev, does this Kuzhkin get such ideas about happiness?' 'I must refer you to page 78 in *Novyi Mir* in 1962,' said Mozhayev, meaning *A Day in the Life of Ivan Denisovich*. 'Have you read today's *Pravda* about *Novyi Mir*?' retorted Mme Furtseva, 'From such things, the events in Prague began . . .'[11]

The Man Alive was not seen for twenty years. When it was finally presented at the Taganka, it seemed old-fashioned. It was like a Soviet *Woyzeck* in showing how a man and his family could be degraded by poverty and oppression, but there was a higher authority to which Kuzhkin could turn. The system itself was not rotten. The optimism, not the pessimism, had dated. A thin line of cheap hopefulness scarred the surface of its despair. Not the least ill-effect of post-Stalinist censorship was to turn such attempts at honesty into something little better than *kitsch*.

8

THE SECULAR BAPTIST

'Sire, they come from *another world*!'
(From *Rabelais*, 1968)

Few in the West had heard of Jerzy Grotowski before 1966, when his Laboratory Theatre from Wrocław came over to Paris to present *The Constant Prince* at the Théâtre des Nations, but his influence spread quickly. It could be felt at the Edinburgh Fringe Festival before 1968, when his company first appeared at the Traverse, and in the United States, where it turned socialist collectives into religious communes. Grotowski prompted Richard Schechner to set up the Performance Group above a New York garage. His was the hidden hand which beckoned Brook towards the Sahara desert and the Italian director, Eugenio Barba, to the cold North, Oslo. He held workshops in North American universities, displaying the bravery of a missionary seeking discourse with cannibals. He even looked like a prophet, with a round face and whispy traces of beard, moon eyes, going through life, it seemed, in the wrong direction, from death to birth, prematurely young.

The Constant Prince was an historical epic by the seventeenth-century Spanish dramatist, Calderón de la Barca, translated by the nineteenth-century Polish Romantic, Juliusz Słowacki, and cut by Grotowski into three parts, with most of the history removed. Two-thirds of the text went, the Polish liturgy was introduced and the fourteen parts were reduced to seven, played by six actors. This compression resulted in a structure not dissimilar to ancient Greek tragedy with a protagonist, the Prince, and five actors who played individual roles but combined into a Chorus.

In the first phase, a prisoner, 'Don Enrique', was subjected to torture and sexual domination, but his suffering became part of a sado-masochistic game. After his castration, he joined his persecutors to torment the second prisoner, the Prince, who offered to his tormentors 'only passivity and kindness, referring to a higher spiritual order'.[1] The second phase dwelt on the Prince's suffering, freely endured, which became the means of his redemption, not only for himself but apparently for others, who fed from his flesh and worshipped him as a Saviour.

In the third phase, this Christ-like behaviour was turned into an un-Christ-like message for, after his death, the Prince laughed at his enemies whom he had lured to their destruction. Martyrdom brought a subtle revenge, which was more than could be said for persecution. 'The effect', wrote Christopher Innes, 'was intellectually confusing',[2] but Grotowski made breakfast by scrambling the brains. He intended to break up the framework of assumptions in which societies conducted their affairs and to free the log-jam of ideologies which characterised the Cold War.

The Constant Prince could be interpreted as a Christian or as an anti-Christian play, although it was neither. Its anti-Christian message might have run like this. The crucifixion was an act of barbarism, which over the centuries had released a chain-reaction of further atrocities. Far from being a symbol of peace and Divine Love, it had become a provocation for slaughter.

Everybody talked about peace but plotted for war. 'Peaceful co-existence' was the kind of euphemism a hangman might relish, a quiet night playing cards, a good breakfast, a quick drop. It meant stalemate in Europe, famine in Africa and blood in Vietnam.

The first and lasting impression of *The Constant Prince* was of extreme emotional intensity, personified by Ryszard Cieslak's Prince, whose ecstacy under torture can be glimpsed from the stage directions: '. . . with closed eyes he hits himself in the stomach with his bunched up shirt. He rubs his head on the floor, one hand tearing at his hair'.[3] His cries set the rhythm for a macabre polka, and then the intonations of a church service, at which point his sufferings became sacramental.

The Swiss psychiatrist Carl Jung wrote that 'the primitive mentality does not *invent* myths, it *experiences* them,'[4] a distinction which begged the question as to what was meant by primitive. Grotowski took the view that modern man was subject to myths which he had lost the capacity to experience. They were buried in the mind, like lumps of primeval oak, covered by layers of social convention. He wanted to bring these fossils back to the surface and breathe new life into them, except that they were not dead, but always stirring unnoticed in the unconscious.

In this, Grotowski had much in common with Artaud, whose theories *The Constant Prince* was held to exemplify, but he did not read Artaud's *The Theatre and its Double* until 1964, five years after his Theatre Laboratory was formed at Opole, a town in south-west Poland. It moved to Wrocław in 1965. As its name suggests, his Theatre Laboratory was not really a theatre at all. It was too small – '13-Rows' – and did not give regular performances. It got its grants as a research project into the nature of acting and was part of the trend to place the arts within some scientific framework. The audience was the raw material upon which the actor worked, not just there to be entertained or to buy tickets.

The object of his research might be described as an enquiry into the nature of the theatrical language, derived at several removes from Saussure. It assumed that language was a structure of signs inserted into the mind, rather like software into a computer, which shaped our perceptions of the world and helped us to communicate with others. The question then arose as to how deeply language penetrated the mind. Was it something which we learnt as children from our parents and at school? – in which case it was the result of social conditioning. Or was there a human propensity to seek out language in an effort to cope with the problems of survival? – in which case it was partly innate.

In the United States, Noam Chomsky argued in *Syntactic Structures* (1957) that the speed at which very young children could pick up simple grammatical structures indicated that they were born with the aptitude to do so. He demonstrated that most languages were constructed along similar lines, which suggested that the capacity to use words and grammar could not be explained through sociology alone, but required a biological cause as well. Was language built into our genes? The French anthropologist Claude Lévi-Strauss went a step further by describing in *Structural Anthropology* (1957–73) and *The Savage Mind* (1962) how certain myths were shared by tribes around the world which could not claim a common ancestry. Did story-telling derive from the way in which primitive clans defended themselves against in-breeding, blood feuds and other kinds of anti-social behaviour?

Grotowski's experiments were intended to break through the surface sign systems of modern societies to reach the primitive building blocks from which all languages are made. He had two motives, which he shared with other behavioural scientists who did not want to call themselves artists. If it could be proved that there were behavioural patterns common to all mankind, these might provide the basis for a new world order, a global harmony perhaps. Such structures could be likened to the Absolute Values of Classicism. They provided a common standard against which the transitory world of daily experience could be measured.

Most Structuralists would have disliked that comparison. Plato *invented* his Ideal World of which the real but imperfect one was a copy. It was a figment of his imagination. The Structuralists set out to prove that such behavioural patterns existed, which they would not have called values. Lévi-Strauss, who for an anthropologist was not noted for his field-work, sat in his study sifting through masses of myths from all over the world to prove that essentially they were very similar.

They also wanted to prove that modern civilisation was a corruption of the impulses of primitive man. All modernity was not equally blamed. The prime targets were capitalism and the consumer society; but secondary ones included the cult of the individual and such concepts as free speech and democracy. The symbol of them all was the United States, whose dedication to freedom was being demonstrated in Vietnam, but if anyone had complained that the Soviet Union was even worse, Grotowski as a Pole would not have disagreed. What was needed was a purified socialism, shorn of its determinism, but based on the scientific recognition that all humanity came from a common stock.

Chomsky and Lévi-Strauss were unorthodox Marxists, but Grotowski's research also had something in common with the theories of the Austro-American psycho-analyst, Wilhelm Reich, who died in 1957, a forgotten and discredited man. Reich lost his reputation with his invention of the Orgone Box, supposed to attract particles of cosmic dust for the benefit of his patients. He regained it after his death through the simplicity of his ideas and the devotion of his disciples. Reich argued that the injustices of a capitalist society frustrated the individual's quest for self-fulfilment, which he described almost wholly in erotic terms. To keep the workers obedient, the ruling classes encouraged them to feel sexually guilty; and these inhibitions, which he called 'armouring', led to a pent-up emotionalism which sought an alternative release in aggression. The gun-fights of a cowboy movie gave one illustration, but so did the Vietnam war.

The student banners of the 1960s blazed forth the Reichian message, 'Make Love, Not War', as if one were the alternative to the other. 'To touch the truth', ran the headline on the front page of the listings magazine, *Time Out*, 'is to touch your genitals.' In its inside pages, it offered a guide to Reichian events in London, presumably incomplete.

Grotowski's 13-Rows theatre at Opole might be described as a better Orgone Box. His methods were intended to break down social self-consciousness and to release sources of spiritual and physical energy. He encouraged an openness within his company, demanding the trust of a confessional. To break down actors' armouring, he introduced a training regime, described in his book, *Towards a Poor Theatre* (1969). Whatever charges might be levelled against his company, that of self-indulgence was the least appropriate, for his actors trained like athletes and were absorbed in their high-seriousness, half-way between a humanist religion and a science of self-discovery. But he was often accused of self-indulgence, when his results shocked the faint-of-heart and played upon sensitive nerves. *The Constant Prince* strayed close to blasphemy and since clothes were a symbol of armouring, some nakedness was to be expected from a Grotowski event, but not striptease, which he despised. Among his followers, it was sometimes hard to tell the difference.

Such workshops, arts laboratories and centres for theatre research sprang up all over Europe and North America during the 1960s, their names proclaiming their objectivity and scientific aspirations. The arts labs attracted professionals and amateurs alike. If you went along to one, you might want to rehearse for a show but instead be asked to take part in psycho-drama, an improvisational theatre in which you were expected to reveal all. The techniques derived from many sources, Grotowski of course, but also from psycho-analysis and oriental meditation.

One familiar sound of a Sixties summer was of a theatre group, sitting in a circle in a public park, humming softly to themselves. What did they think they were doing? They could have been imitating the chant of Buddhist monks clearing their minds for Nirvana. Some went so far as to shave their heads and wear saffron robes. They might have been training their voices or taking part in a therapy session. Before the 1960s, voices were trained at drama schools to cultivate the Sound Beautiful, in diction classes to round the vowel sounds and to attack the consonants, in singing class to mellow the tone and to regularise the pitch. During the 1960s the idea of establishing a neo-Platonic ideal as to what a voice should sound like, and imitating it, would have been dismissed as old-fashioned, bad from almost every point of view, philosophically (by pretending that absolute standards exist), politically (by seeking to eliminate accents) and as a way of creating a beautiful sound.

The new aim was to encourage actors to seek their natural voices, which meant, in singing, finding that humming pitch which caused least strain. It did not matter whether they were singing in or out of tune, because nobody played a note on the piano to ask them to imitate. Instead they were asked to trace the sources of strain in their voices, which suggested that they were trying to sound unduly *macho* or frail. By such means, armouring could be detected. Having discovered natural pitch, actors concentrated on the timbres of their voices, the roughness, smoothness or inner disharmonies. The key was relaxation. Voice-training sessions were often preceded by physical exercises whose purpose was not muscle-building but to make the body supple and free of tensions. In this state, the voice lost its signs of strain, but found its physical characteristics, from the resonating chamber of the chest to the fritillary flutterings of the larynx.

Having found their natural voices, actors were asked to listen to the voices of others. In a group hum, you could not only hear the sounds of the collective but sense their physical presences as well. If the group was a friendly one, which they often were, for peace and love were aims, the result was an enhancement of the community spirit. The group members subtly adjusted their voices to respond to the calls around them. It could be a moving experience. You felt not only that you were getting to know your neighbour better on some subliminal level, but also that you were creating the basis for a new world order, from the roots up, from the posture of the spine to the worship of the sun. Communism, or at any rate the communal spirit, came naturally. Who needed money, when we were all the same at heart? There were text-books on the subject.

The man who invited Grotowski's *The Constant Prince* to Paris and thus set this spiritual chain-reaction into motion was Jean-Louis Barrault. Like Olivier, Barrault was established as a classical actor before the war. Both had run commercial companies (with their wives) in the 1950s and became directors of national theatres, in Barrault's case the Théâtre de France, better known by its old name, the Odéon. Among his other achievements, he brought new life to French classical acting, its broad gestures, its liquid diction. He was a pioneer of 'total theatre' where the audience was surrounded by the action of a play, instead of gazing at it from afar. He had worked in black box studios during the 1930s, where he had met Artaud, whose ideas found expression through Barrault's work, in his use of masks, mime, chanting and ritual. Like Artaud, he was attracted to oriental theatre. It was the Artaud-like quality in Grotowski's work which persuaded him to invite *The Constant Prince* to the Théâtre des Nations, of which he was the director.

In this context, *The Constant Prince* was at an advantage, for it was not necessary to understand Polish to know what was happening while the Prince was being tortured. Other companies came from so many parts of the world that to comprehend the verbal language of any one was an unexpected pleasure. It was hard enough to understand the story synopses provided in French. The proliferation of international festivals over the next fifteen years led to a special kind of touring production, which relied on colour, spectacle and athleticism at the expense of words. The theoretical stress on cultural universality became a self-fulfilling prophecy. Those performances which could best transcend the language barriers were those most often chosen.

Among Third World countries, an invitation backed by hard currency to visit a festival in Paris, Edinburgh or Toronto was an honour and so travelling productions were more highly prized than those that stayed at home. This meant that sophisticated art forms were sometimes neglected in their home countries in favour of Westernised *kitsch*, 'airport art', while audiences were given the misleading impression that Third World cultures were more accessible than they were.

Nor was it coincidental that the Théâtre des Nations, staged bienni-ally, had its home for many years in Paris. Its main sponsoring body, but not financially, was the International Theatre Institute (ITI), a UNESCO category 'A' NGO (non-governmental organisation) founded in 1947, which had its offices in the main UNESCO building in Paris. Its main source of income for staging the Théâtre des Nations came from the

French government, whose Minister of Culture during the 1960s was the novelist, André Malraux. Malraux's concern for the arts was evident, but he might have had more difficulty in raising the money for the Théâtre des Nations, if it had not suited the aims of General de Gaulle.

De Gaulle was elected as President of France in 1958, under a new constitution devised to end the instabilities of the Fourth Republic. He received much support from the colonial settlers in such outposts of the French Empire as Algeria. They assumed that he would defend French interests. De Gaulle granted independence to the colonies instead, including, against much French settler opposition, Algeria; but he tried to strengthen cultural and trading links with the newly independent countries. He believed profoundly in France's civilising mission. At times, the Théâtre des Nations was like a grand family reunion, under the auspices of UNESCO certainly, but with a large number of companies from small countries in part connected by heritage to Paris. It was a vivid way of illustrating the global extent of French influence.

De Gaulle wanted to demonstrate the independence of France from US domination. In 1963, he rejected an offer of US Polaris missiles, seeking to develop a missile system of his own. Unlike Harold Wilson, he condemned in 1965 the US presence in Vietnam and criticised US behaviour in Latin America. In June 1966, he carried out his threat to take France out of NATO. The US Secretary of State, Dean Rusk, made light of this withdrawal, but it was the first major split in the Western Alliance.

De Gaulle's alternative strategy was not isolation, but to build up Europe as a credible third force by strengthening the links with West Germany and by vetoing the entry into the EEC of Britain, an ally too closely tied to the United States. He paid state visits to the muttering and rebellious Soviet colonies in Eastern Europe, presenting himself as a more credible honest broker between East and West than Wilson could ever have been. As a result, he was in a position to make a bid for the support of Third World countries who feared China, distrusted the Soviet Union and hated the United States. The staging of the Théâtre des Nations can be regarded as an act of cultural diplomacy, at worst as electioneering but, at best, as an appeal to a wider humanity.

Unfortunately for his grand plan, West Germany was much less willing to weaken its links with NATO and the United States, nor was it in a position to do so. It relied upon American, British and French forces to keep the Soviet army at bay, which had stationed large forces in East Germany. There was a time in the early 1960s when de Gaulle with his old friend, the West German Chancellor, Konrad Adenauer, speculated that a larger Europe (without Britain) might be strong enough to hold its own with the super-powers; but Adenauer resigned in 1963, at the age of 87, and his successor, Ludwig Erhardt, took a more pragmatic line.

De Gaulle's France was left in the awkward position of being half-in and half-out of the Western Alliance, a fact of which his left-wing opponents took advantage. As the war in Vietnam grew increasingly bitter, his independent stance brought him no credit, for he could do nothing about it. A wave of student and trade-union protests spread across Europe and North America during 1967, which derided him not as a leader who tried and failed, but as an irrelevant fantasist.

While the war in Vietnam was the main target for students, it was not the only one. Among young Europeans, who were not liable to be drafted, it was primarily a symbol of everything else that was wrong with Western civilisation, its racism, its sexism and its consumerism. The war was how a capitalist society behaved in action. If rebels like Tariq Ali in Britain, Rudi Dutschke in Germany and Daniel Cohn-Bendit in France could not point to more convincing examples from the communist world, this did not prove that they were wrong, but it did make it more difficult to show why they were right. Their arguments had to be expressed in somewhat abstract terms, borrowed partly from Sartre, partly from Mao's Little Red Book and partly from anecdotes in praise of the Cultural Revolution in China, which few had experienced.

The *événements de mai* actually began in March 1968 with the arrest of six students who were staging an anti-American demonstration. It provoked a series of strikes and sit-ins which spread across the country, until the Rector of the University of Sorbonne in Paris tried to ban all students from the campus. Thirty thousand students rioted in the streets of Paris, faced by water cannons and tear gas from the police. Their demands were many, but they concentrated upon the release of the arrested students and an end to state censorship. On 21 May the trade unions, communist-led, called a general strike and France was paralysed for a week.

De Gaulle was on a state visit to Romania, but hurried back to Paris to declare a state of emergency. He dissolved the National Assembly and summoned the Chiefs of Staff to suppress all subversion. 'The voice we have just heard', said François Mitterrand, the Socialist leader, 'is the voice of dictatorship.' De Gaulle called a general election on 30 June 1968, in which he won a landslide victory against a background of demonstrations and riots. 'Elections are treason', proclaimed the student banners. De Gaulle was surprised by his majority. How could events which had created so much fuss have so little substance?

For many years afterwards, left-wingers in France, Germany and Britain wondered why they missed their opportunity in May 1968. Some accused the bourgeois intellectuals with their shallow loyalties, while others blamed the Soviet Union for choosing that moment to dispatch their tanks to the borders of Czechoslovakia. Who would vote for the French Communist Party whose Big Brother in Moscow was threatening the Prague Spring? In London, Tariq Ali gave this explanation: 'One of the central myths of bourgeois ideologues in the West was to equate the socialist project with the crimes of Stalinism. Since there was no other model of existing socialism, it was also difficult to demonstrate in practice what we were fighting *for* in those days. Everyone knew what we were against, but positive models could not be found in any advanced country.'[5] The post-mortem on Stalinism had lasted in the Soviet Union for more than twelve years already. Was Brezhnev's regime much better? The students lacked those hopeful examples of socialist countries which had inspired their parents, Ben-Gurion's Israel, Gandhi's India, and argued in the style of Plato that an Ideal Socialism existed of which all earthly versions were very imperfect copies.

Another bourgeois objection was that the students were always discovering utopias around the world which on inspection turned out to be police states. The Prague Spring, admired by Tariq Ali, was closer in spirit to social democracy than any system which he recommended; but the example further afield, and therefore more attractive, came from China. Mao Tse-Tung had announced his 'great proletarian cultural revolution' in August 1966 and its aim was to re-kindle the spirit which had swept him to power in 1949. Mao was aware that China was still a backward country and he blamed a whole class of intellectuals of 'revisionism' and 'bourgeois reactionary thinking'. They included school and university teachers, artists of all kinds and those who worked with their heads rather than hands. The Red Guards of student revolutionaries paraded their former professors through the squares of Peking wearing dunces' caps and herded them up to work on the farms. Throughout China, independence of mind was thought to be treason. Learning was elitist. Mao's words from 1927 were much quoted, in the West as well as the East: 'A revolution is not a dinner party, or writing an essay, or painting a picture, or doing embroidery . . . a revolution is an insurrection, an act of violence by which one class overthrows another.'

Barrault made the mistake during the *événements de mai* of openly espousing the students' cause by allowing them to use the Odéon for a public debate. He was sacked by Malraux and took his revenge in what was once a wrestling hall in Montmartre. There he staged *Rabelais*, an epic of 'total theatre', in which man was divided into three parts: Gargantua (the sensual appetites), Pantagruel (the thirst for knowledge) and Panurge (the physical instincts). In the second act, he tried to 'sweep us away' into the 'alternative reality' of 'a surrealist dream, in the universe of drugs, which allows all hallucinations, all apparitions'.[6]

He used every showman's trick at his disposal, circus, music-hall, masks, formalised movements à la Kabuki, chants, puppetry, nakedness which was not quite striptease, lots of visual and verbal gags. 'The intention,' as Innes pointed out, 'was liberty with a capital L, but unfortunately . . . the productions reduced this to simple eroticism.'[7] Was it to *Rabelais* that the hopes of total theatre were eventually reduced, Grotowski's scorn of verbal languages, his attempts to revive ancient myths? The answer has to be 'No', for they influenced such directors as Brook, Barba and Andrei Serban in other ways, but *Rabelais* set the style for later Barrault productions, Jérôme Savary's Grand Magic Circus and Ariane Mnouchkine's spectacle, *1789* (1970), which commented as much upon the events of 1968 as it did upon its real subject, the French Revolution.

Barrault's weakness, according to some French critics, was his 'prodigious, almost naive, capacity for recouping what is fashionable'.[8] It was a fault which Olivier did not share, who made his farewell NT performance as John Tagg, a dour Glaswegian Trotskyite in Trevor Griffiths's *The Party* (1973). This was a debate play about why the British left-wing failed to respond adequately to the *événements de mai*. It took place in the London home of a TV director who holds 'a small private meeting' of the Revolutionary Socialist Party (RSP) to seek a 'coherent focus' for the left and to ask whether they should join the French students on the barricades, should they be erected in London.

The RSP was the lightly fictionalised version of the Workers Revolutionary Party (WRP), the Trotskyite movement which was then recruiting members with success in Equity, the actors' union. Tagg was modelled on the WRP's national organiser. Various reasons were given as to why socialism was fragmented and why the Tories were gaining ground in the local elections, but nobody except Tagg did more than confirm the sense of defeat. Britain, the others concluded, was not in a revolutionary phase: this was happening elsewhere, in Cuba, China and Vietnam.

Tagg brought them back to the imperative need to further the class struggle. 'A revolutionary party or faction that fails to establish itself in the working class . . . can lay no claim whatsoever to serious attention.' He dismissed the 'students, blacks, intellectuals, social deviants of one sort or another, women' who had gathered under revolutionary banners. They might reflect the discontents in capitalist societies, but only the working classes were in a position to destroy the system itself. Intellectuals could not do so: their 'main weapon is the word'. 'The intellectual's problem is not vision but commitment. You enjoy biting the hand that feeds you, but you'll never bite it off.'[9] Thus he attacked the velvet prisoners of the West and poured cold water on the idea that what was happening in Paris was anything more than patches of protests tacked together.

Once the common target of the student revolutionaries had gone and the US troops had left Vietnam, its broader aims were almost forgotten. But the *événements de mai* left behind pockets of bitter disillusion, terrorists like the Angry Brigade, the Red Brigade and the Baader-Meinhof gang, who wanted to inflict as much damage on the bourgeois society before they themselves were rounded up. Student socialists became polarised into the soft and hard left, both of which were almost equally alienated by the centre, represented in Britain by the Labour Party.

The soft left, as represented by the utopian communes of the mid-1960s, tended to opt out of party politics altogether. It was too corrupting. It interfered with their true aims of seeking the one-ness of mankind and the union of man with nature. The hard left was better organised, with its newsletters and discussion groups, which it called cells. Sometimes it infiltrated the bourgeois parties to gain influence or to discredit those who were influential. The aim of the French Situationists was 'to disrupt the spectacle'. The spectacle meant the trappings of the bourgeois society, its law, its logic, its education, its art, its literature, everything in short which kept the democratic system intact. What the soft and the hard left had in common, apart from hating capitalism, was their anti-intellectual stance. They took on board the Structuralist idea that the injustices of society were embedded in verbal languages and so, to demonstrate their integrity, they spoke these languages badly. What may have contributed to their defeat was their mind-boggling jargon.

Among the fringe and break-away theatres of Europe, a new kind of socialist theatre emerged, passionate, violent and committed to the collapse of civilisation as we know it. 'I'll be a one-man crime-wave when I get going,' threatened Hepple in Howard Brenton's *Revenge* (1969). British left-wing writers became famous throughout Europe for their hard-line opinions, among them Edward Bond, Howard Brenton, Howard Barker and Nigel Williams, and the strength of their vocabularies. After 1968, the Arts Council thought it wiser to subsidise them and to welcome them by degrees to the velvet prison.

Another side-effect was the way in which so many European directors left the major subsidised theatres of which they had been part. It was like a mass exodus. Hall left the RSC in 1968, although he went to the NT in 1973. Peter Stein stormed out of the Munich Kammerspiele, where he had been tipped as the next Intendant. In Italy, Giorgio Strehler quit the Piccolo Teatro in Milan, the first *teatro stabile* which he established with Paulo Grazzi in 1947, to form a new company, Gruppa Teatro e Arzione. Dario Fo left mainstream theatre to set up with Franco

Rame a theatre collective, Nuova Scena, under the auspices of the Italian Communist Party. In Holland there was the Tomato Revolution, where students pelted the stage of one national company, frightened one actor to death and transformed the state's cultural policy for a generation.

The *événements de mai* had one major political consequence. In April 1969 de Gaulle resigned, having failed to win an absolute majority for his proposal to amend the Constitution. He wanted to take extra powers in the event of further riots, but he had come to realise that a wholly independent France was an impossible dream in a world dominated by the Cold War. He softened his resistance to the British application to join the Common Market. The students had forced him to take sides but unfortunately from their point of view, he chose the wrong one.

9

THE AGE OF AQUARIUS

'Come to the cabaret, old chum'
(From *Cabaret*, 1966)

In 1963 a small audience arrived at the Living Theater's studios in New York to find that the doors were padlocked and the premises seized by the Internal Revenue Service which was trying to recover four years' non-payment of taxes. They were met by the group's founders, Julian Beck and Judith Malina, who took them to an left open side window, through which they could scramble to see a performance of Kenneth Brown's *The Brig*.

The Living Theater was the nearest equivalent in the United States to Grotowski's Theatre Laboratory, a 'poor theatre', whose members shared and shared alike; which came under the influence of Artaud; which plunged its audience into 'total theatre'; which encouraged nakedness as a sign of liberation and spray-painted the auditorium with muscles. It was founded in 1946 with aims that were political as well as aesthetic. 'We insisted,' said Beck, 'on experimentation that was an image for a changing society.'[1] In the 1950s, they presented an adventurous programme at the Cherry Lane and other Off-Broadway theatres, with plays by Cocteau, Stein, Jarry, Brecht and Pirandello, mainly anti-naturalistic; but their production of Jack Gelber's *The Connection* was so convincing a study of drug addiction that critics could not decide whether or not the actors were high as kites.

The Brig was equally naturalistic. It went through, whistle by press-up, the brutalising routine meted out to US marines in a detention camp in Japan, a symbol for the militaristic society that Beck deemed the United States to be. The Living Theater took pacifism as one of its points of departure, others including a rejection of many social habits, such as money, immigration controls and clothes. The farewell-to-the-US performance in 1963 took place under the kind of circumstances in which they found themselves often in their career, locked out of or into studios by those who did not respect their stand against taxes.

The Living Theater then hastily departed for Europe, where they were welcomed and celebrated at the Théâtre des Nations in 1964. They joined other American émigrés, such as the director Charles Marowitz in London and the book-shop impresario Jim Haynes who started the Traverse Theatre in Edinburgh. They left behind one of their members, Joseph Chaikin, who had grown impatient with the other-worldliness of the Beck–Malina approach.

Unlike some members of the commune, Chaikin had gone to college (Drake University, 1950–3) and was a trained actor who had appeared in such commercial hits as *No Time for Sergeants*, where 'we counted laughs . . . and tried to meet the audience on the dumbest common level'.[2] What Chaikin most disliked about such plays was that they presented comic stereotypes, which audiences might take as models for their own behaviour. By such means, the public learnt how to label and codify the levels of authority. 'Such theatre,' he commented, 'sells the audience a moral order of social and internal life based on type and function'.[3]

He joined the Living Theater in 1959 to escape this abuse of the theatrical process which in his view amounted to little more than an indoctrination, but began to doubt whether the Living Theatre for all its good intentions actually worked. There was too much amateurishness and too little attention paid to the new acting skills that Beck had introduced but not developed. Chaikin wanted to improve choral speaking and to develop the physicality of the actors into a primary language, substituting the gesture for the word. He distrusted words. 'I despair of conversation and conventional language,' Chaikin said, 'It doesn't carry meaning any more. It's facile.' Ideally, he wanted each play to have 'its own code in the use of words'.[4] In September 1963 he brought together some actors and writers to form the Open Theater, by which he meant 'open' to new ideas and change.

Two months later, an incident occurred, so terrible and unexpected that it imposed a change of outlook upon them, as it did upon the nation. The assassination of President Kennedy on 22 November 1963 was a greater shock to the United States' image of itself than the murder of Abraham Lincoln in 1865. Lincoln's death was not seen on television nor was there much doubt as to who committed it, a mad actor avenging the lost cause of the South. Kennedy's death was shrouded in mystery which years of official and unofficial investigation did little to dispel. The official version was provided on 27 September 1964 with the publication of the Warren Commission's report, which concluded that Kennedy was killed, like Lincoln, by one assassin. The prime suspect, Lee Harvey Oswald, was arrested at a cinema. The Warren Commission was not sure about his motive, but Oswald was a shady character anyway, the chairman of a pro-Castro 'Fair Play for Cuba'

Committee, who had defected to the Soviet Union in 1959 and returned with his Russian wife to the United States in 1963. It was considered reasonable to assume that some foreign power was behind the murder, perhaps the Soviet Union or Cuba. Oswald was not able to testify before the Commission because, two days after his arrest, still in custody, he was shot by a patriotic nightclub owner, Jack Ruby. This incident was also televised. Ruby stood trial for Oswald's murder, was convicted and sentenced to death. While his appeal was being heard, he died in prison from a chance blood clot in the lung on 3 January 1967.

Meanwhile, fresh evidence was being discounted, suggesting that Kennedy could not have been shot from the angle from which Oswald was supposed to have fired. Was there a second assassin? Conspiracy theories abounded – that Oswald was really a double-agent employed by the CIA, that there was a Mafia contract on Kennedy's life, that white supremacists from the southern states were involved, perhaps the Ku Klux Klan. It was not necessary to believe in any of these theories to conclude that this was a very American murder. The Commission's members, chosen by Kennedy's successor, Lyndon Baines Johnson, added to that impression, among them the white-haired Chief Justice himself, Earl Warren, with the former Head of the CIA, Allen Dulles, at his side. Were they going to ask questions about the rumoured role of the CIA?

If their Report were taken at its face value, there still remained much to disturb the mind, such as the easy availability of guns and the presence of ghetto madmen eager to take the law into their own hands. Ruby's lawyer claimed that millions of Americans thought that his client should have been given a Congressional Medal of Honour. Was he right? Was lynch law so close to the surface in the American psyche? The killing was so like the parade of murder stories on television, the motorcade, the glamorous wife Jackie Kennedy spattered in blood, the lone avenger, the solid cops and the squeal of sirens.

Above all, it was Jack Kennedy who had been murdered, the handsome President who had promised to take the United States towards a New Frontier, who had sworn to rid the country of corruption and racism, who had forced the Soviet Union to back down over the Cuban missile crisis, who had stood by the Berlin Wall and said 'Ich bin ein Berliner'. Some left-wing radicals affected to despise the Kennedy image, privately hoping that they were wrong. His murder demonstrated that they were both wrong and right: he had tried to reform America and died in the attempt. Others were less gloomy. They pointed to the presence in the administration of Kennedy's brother, Robert, who, as Attorney General, was still fighting against the Mafia's infiltration of the trade unions, and to Lyndon Johnson's record on civil rights.

On 2 July 1964, Johnson signed the Civil Rights Act, which was intended to outlaw racism in public life. On television, Johnson called on the American people to 'eliminate the last vestiges of injustice in America'. 'Let us close the springs of racial poison,' he begged. Such laws were not easy to implement. The American Constitution already gave all men and women equality under the law, but that would have come as little comfort to a black man falsely accused of indecent assault in Alabama. Who would interpret these laws, the supporters of Martin Luther King, the civil rights leader, or those of Governor Wallace from Alabama?

In Kennedy's time it was possible to believe that a young and energetic president, who could send men to the moon, could transform the America left by Eisenhower. A mood of criticism had penetrated Broadway and ventured as far as Hollywood. To offset the influence of George Abbott, there were younger writers and directors, often compared with Britain's angry generation. These included Edward Albee, whose one-act play, *The Death of Bessie Smith* (1959) described how the dying blues singer was refused admittance to a white hospital. In 1960, he wrote another one-acter, *The American Dream*, which suggested that it was time for America to wake up. His plays were more roughly constructed at that time than any which Abbott would have tolerated, but, like Osborne, his vivid dialogue masked the poor craftsmanship.

Stanley Kubrick's black film comedy on how the world was destroyed, *Dr Strangelove* (1963), could never have been made in the mid-1950s nor in 1964. It featured an honest president who had to grapple with the generals and scientists in the Pentagon. This was close to George Kennan's assessment of affairs, but there was an optimism in its satire as if it believed that by anticipating the worst, it could stop it from happening. The assassination of Kennedy cast a dark shadow between the 'can-do' social dramas of the early 1960s, where problems were there to be solved, from the Open Theatre's full-blooded assaults on the American way of life.

The Open Theater worked as a team, the writers, actors and designers sitting down together to discuss what they wanted to do before limbering-up, humming, improvising and otherwise behaving like dedicated theatre professionals. Their shows were written by individuals, including Megan Terry's *Viet Rock* (1966) and Jean-Claude van Itallie's *America Hurrah* (1966). They had scripts which could be published, although the real texts, the ones which governed their performances, were conceived more like orchestral scores, not to be read but embodied by the actors.

Van Itallie's *America Hurrah* consisted of three sketches, *Interview*, *TV* and *Motel*, bold, forceful and akin to pop-art. It could be compared with the blown-up, comic-strip images of Roy Lichtenstein. *Interview* was set in a white office where four nervous applicants meet four bland interviewers in white masks. A process of indoctrination began, leaving them unable to face the world outside, where monsters lurk, priests, analysts ('Blah, blah, blah, blah – *penis*, blah, blah, blah, blah – *mother'*) and politicians. In *TV*, employees in a TV station discussed ratings over coffee, while in the background a TV screen ground through the daily routine, a newscast in which 60 peasants in a friendly Vietnamese village were killed by accident and a Second World War movie where deodorant lovers are brought together in the final reel ('I've learnt a lot ... Maybe that's what wars are for.').

'With *America Hurrah*,' commented the critic Robert Brustein, 'the concept of theatrical unity finally becomes meaningful in this country.'[5] The last sketch, *Motel*, choked with loathing. An inflatable doll of a motel-keeper with a brisk and motherly voice drooled on about the décor, the toilet that flushes automatically, the plastic flowers from Japan; before welcoming two grotesque lovers, huge-headed, who smashed up the bed in an elephantine attempt at love-making. They did not stop with the bed. Their multiple and prolonged orgasms beat up the TV set too, crushed uncrushable flowers and their kind hostess. Exit motel.

'The triumph of this occasion,' wrote Brustein, 'is to have found provocative theatrical images for the national malaise we have been suffering in Johnsonland these last three years: the infection of violence, calamity, indifference, gratuitous murder and . . . brutalizing war.'[6] The man who designed the puppets of *Motel* was Robert Wilson, the pioneer director of performance art. *America Hurrah* represented a coming-of-age of Off-Off-Broadway. Chaikin, who directed, was not looking over his shoulder to see whether producers would buy his show. He had settled for the fact that they would not and was proud of it. From then on, actors or writers did not apologise if their production failed to arrive on Broadway. Off-Off-Broadway acquired an identity of its own.

What started out as an economic divide became a cultural one. Broadway may not have been as complacent as Off-Off-Broadway insisted, but it did promote the assumption that Middle America would muddle through somehow. Neil Simon was the most popular Broadway playwright of the 1960s and his comedies were wry rather than over-cheerful, for instance, *Barefoot in the Park* (1963), *The Odd Couple* (1965), and they could be acidic. He wrote books for musicals, *Little Me* (1962) and *Sweet Charity* (1966), and he was the kind of professional writer whom Abbott respected. Each line worked, each motive was clear and a comparison between Garson Kanin's *Born Yesterday* (1949) and *The Odd Couple* reveals the wider range of ideas which Simon brought to his task of writing popular theatre. His plays may have reminded audiences that there *was* a better side to life and to that extent they can be considered soft-centred, but none the less they were thoughtfully observed.

In the mid-1960s, Broadway was suffering from one of its periodic crises of confidence. Many efficient shows which would have enjoyed respectable runs in the past closed after a couple of weeks. Only a smash-hit was good enough. The critic-director, Harold Clurman, blamed the decline on economic factors. In 1965 he pointed out that, due to escalating costs and state taxes, a member of the public would have to pay at least $2.50 for a ticket to a Broadway theatre and possibly as much as $6.90.[7] Audiences were getting older, because only those with few family responsibilities could afford the prices, and the theatre had become as a result less adventurous and more nostalgic.

Even the musicals, according to Clurman, were not what they were: *Fiddler on the Roof* (1964) had two good tunes, *Man of La Mancha* (1965) possibly one. The latest Richard Rodgers musical, *Do I Hear a Waltz?* (1965), with lyrics by Stephen Sondheim, ran for only half a year. Clurman thought that musicals were in a decline. To his, and everybody's surprise, two British musicals did quite well in 1962, *Stop the World – I Want to Get Off* and *Oliver!*. But the Broadway musical tradition was not so much declining as in a state of transition and the changes were not solely driven by economic factors but by aesthetic ones as well.

Throughout the 1950s the younger musical writers had tried to break up the old formula for musicals, in which plots were arbitrarily interrupted by cues for songs. The newcomers want to 'through-compose' their musicals, to tie the songs and dances more closely to the action. The songs should not be 'ternary' in form (verse-chorus-verse) and the acts should not invariably begin and end with choruses. Oscar Hammerstein Jr, whose protégé was Stephen Sondheim, wanted each song to tell its own story.

Their first triumph came in 1957 with *West Side Story*, but this was a hard act to follow. There were some attempts, mostly failures, but the scale and complexity of through-composed musicals made them risky investments. Musicals reverted back to type, *Gypsy* (1959), *The Sound of Music* (1959) and *Camelot* (1960). George Abbott directed *A Funny Thing Happened to Me on the Way to the Forum* (1962), for which Sondheim wrote the lyrics and Harold Prince produced. The memory of *West Side Story* left a sense of frustration among director-choreographers like Jerome Robbins and Bob Fosse that they could not repeat the success. Prince turned from producing to directing for this reason. In 1966 he staged a 'dark' musical, *Cabaret*, based on Christopher Isherwood's *Goodbye to Berlin* (1939), previously made into a stage-play, John van Druten's *I am a Camera*, and turned into a film.

The plot of *Cabaret* sounds like Hollywood with its love affair between a British night-club singer, Sally Bowles, and an American writer, Cliff; but Prince introduced touches of German Expressionism, a leering MC, who explains the background events for those who might have forgotten about Hitler, and some Kurt Weill-like songs. To denounce Nazism in New York in the mid-1960s was no giant step for mankind, but it did reveal that Prince had broader intentions than those normally granted to musicals. He was still a Broadway producer. His first aim was to attract the paying public. He kept the love story to the front, fascism to the back and withheld the reason why Sally and Cliff could not get together in the end. 'Audiences had enough to handle, two doomed romances, Nazis, Sally's abortion, without inflicting Isherwood's homosexuality on them as well.'[8]

This, as Prince realised, was what was wrong with Broadway music-als. The pill was so coated with sugar that it damaged the teeth. In his film *The Producers*, Mel Brooks parodied *Cabaret* as the bad-taste smash-hit *Springtime for Hitler*. But *Cabaret* was ambitious in ways other than thematic. It was not a 'through-composed' musical, which suggests that the linear development of the plot was all-important, so much as a 'depth-composed' one. The sets and music were used more to convey an atmosphere than to tell a story. It was the first of the 'concept' musicals, which Prince later developed with Stephen Sondheim, whose six musicals with Prince are good examples, and with Andrew Lloyd-Webber.

Some critics unkindly remarked that a concept was a 1960s word for an idea, but with the thought extracted. When thinking became too diffi-cult, you conceptualised. 'Concept' musicals did release choreographers and designers from the tyranny of the book. Prince never liked to start a production without a detailed idea as to what the show would look like and he encouraged composers to write music which commented ironically on the action. It could be regarded as Broadway's reply to total theatre. But the sets were costly, the tunes less easy to sing and such factors may have contributed to the fragile economics that Clurman noted. The double-edged merit of Abbott's productions was that their costs so carefully matched what audiences could be expected to pay.

Clurman also remarked on the bad effect that Broadway success seemed to be having on Albee. He liked *The Death of Bessie Smith*, *The American Dream* and 'the superbly virile and pliant dialogue' of *Who's Afraid of Virginia Woolf?*, Albee's first Broadway hit. But he complained of *Tiny Alice* (1965) that Albee had 'lapsed into abstraction. Its locale is generalized . . . its action unreal.'[9] He disliked its 'stilted literacy', blamed the influence of the French Absurdists and remarked that it provided Broadway with a skilful imitation of a profound play with 'Here is High Art' written all over it, but which avoided saying anything else.

Clurman, like Brustein, looked to Off-Off-Broadway for the new American theatre to be born. It could not be Off-Broadway (the experimental theatres of the 1950s), because they had become unionised and with the rising costs, had evolved into try-out theatres for Broadway. Off-Off-Broadway was different, a poor people's theatre, whose actors worked in hamburger bars and might even be blacks. Under the leadership of Chaikin, Ellen Stewart at the Café la Mama and Richard Schechner at the Performing Garage, it was fighting a determined battle against Broadway and the rest of the United States. The movement had spread across the country to Chicago, Minneapolis and the West Coast. Californians claimed to have invented it. 'We are trying in our humble way,' said Ronnie Davis of the San Francisco Mime Troupe, 'to destroy the United States.'[10] Who could imagine Barbara Garson's *MacBird* (1967) on Broadway, a *Macbeth* satire with John F. Kennedy as Duncan and Lady Bird Johnson as Lady Macbeth? It was in such bad taste.

Financially, Off-Off-Broadway survived on box-office income and gifts from well-wishers. At the Open Theater, actors paid fees to maintain the theatre before they were allowed to join the workshop sessions. Clurman thought that they should be subsidised on the European model, but it was hard to think of any government which would have supported something like *MacBird*. Off-Off-Broadway was fired by a missionary zeal. It drew its strength from two main grievances, racism and the war in Vietnam, which merged at a certain level and joined a host of other causes, from the hounding of Mexican immigrants to gay liberation. Rock music turned political, as did Country and Western, under the influence of Bob Dylan. Night clubs became subversive with the dry songs of Tom Lehrer and the improvised scatology of Lennie Bruce, who got sent to jail sometimes for being funny in possession of drugs.

Few Americans under 30 were unaffected, even those who in reaction turned ultra-patriotic. In March 1965 Johnson sent the first combat troops into Vietnam to support the South Vietnamese army, their 5,000 US advisers and the US airforce bombing of Hanoi. It was intended to be a small-scale operation. When the last US combat troops left in 1972, more than 45,000 US soldiers had died in Vietnam and 2 million Vietnamese. Scarcely a week passed without news of some fresh atrocity. Students, dreading their draft notices, would open their papers to see a photo of the South Vietnamese General ('Buddha will understand') Loan shooting a terrified suspect in the head or read of the massacre at Mylai where Lieutenant Calley was accused of killing at least 109 'oriental human beings'. A 23-year-old soldier wrote 'the bones were flying in the air, chip by chip'.[11]

Calley was charged with these murders in 1969 and the word 'oriental' in his indictment revealed how the war had come to be seen in racial terms. The villagers were not described as Viet-Cong sympathisers or suspected of 'harbouring terrorists'. Civil rights leaders treated the war as an extension of their struggles in the United States. Race riots, which the Civil Rights Act had done little to prevent, spread across the country and mobilised opposition to the Vietnam war as well. It was said to be a white war, waged to secure white supremacy in a world where nine-tenths of the population were coloureds or blacks.

What could President Johnson do, stuck in the White House? He had tried to woo and bomb the Viet-Cong to the conference table. They had refused. He had fought the Civil Rights Act through Congress and been forced to send in the National Guard to quell race riots in New York, Cleveland, Chicago and Detroit. Tormented by failure, and threatened by a split in his party, he announced in March 1968 that he would not stand for re-election. On 4 April 1968 Martin Luther King was gunned down at a rally in Memphis, Tennessee. There were race riots in dozens of cities around the United States. On 5 June 1968 Robert Kennedy, who had decided to run for the White House, was shot and fatally wounded outside his hotel in Los Angeles, after winning the Democratic primary election in California.

In his essay, 'From protest to resistance' (1968) Eric Bentley discussed the value of the theatre in such a situation. His claims for it were modest – to bear witness, to keep up the spirits of the rebels and, quoting Julian Beck, to shake the rigidities of the audience. He put in a plea for literary, as opposed to non-literary, political theatre; or rather, since he was answering a letter from the Off-Off-Broadway director, Richard Schechner, in the *New York Free Press*, argued that this kind of discrimination was unnecessary. They were all fighting on the same side.[12]

But were they? Bentley was born in England in 1916. He was of a different generation from the student protesters, a well-established critic, director and playwright, who wrote books and translated plays by Brecht, and protested against Joe McCarthy in the 1950s. His instincts were those of an old-fashioned liberal-socialist and his methods were those of verbal persuasion. His language was an acquired skill, which Bentley employed better than almost anyone else writing about theatre. But could he speak for those who were in the front line of the battles in Vietnam or Detroit? Would they have trusted him? What means of communication could they use? It was as hard for him to speak the jargon of Flower Power, of rock musicians, of drug culture, of the Black Panthers or Christian Revivalists, as it was the other way round.

All sign systems divide, as well as connect. They separate those who can use them from those who cannot. One problem which America faced with all the others in its summer of discontent, 1968, was the lack of a common language to bridge the gap between the generations, between black and white, between conservatives, liberals, Maoists and Trotskyites. Words were mistrusted by the young, twisted by the old. The government still referred to the 'peace offensive' in Vietnam, targets were called 'pre-selected areas of impact' to make them sound less warlike. Truth was not the first casualty of the Cold War, but language. At a time when sign systems everywhere were under scholastic scrutiny for signs of indoctrination, when in the East bureaucracies were developing ideologically sound communication techniques not dissimilar to Havel's Ptydepe, and some European radicals were claiming that the only valid forms of self-expression were revolutionary graffiti, it was hard to find a language that was outside the struggle.

Bentley could not understand why the Living Theater burnt dollar bills on stage, when they were asking for money off it. 'When you're solicited, you wonder if they're just collecting kindling . . . The *avant-garde*,' he concluded, 'never had any sense!'[13] But the Living Theater's theatrical gesture did not prevent them from having to buy brown rice with the tokens they detested. They needed to have money to survive and to burn.

This mutual incomprehension was not always hostile. It could be gentle, forbearing, eager to please. It was the dawn of the Age of Aquarius. In November 1967, Grotowski visited New York to conduct a course at New York University's School of Arts. 'In this country,' he said pedantically, 'I have observed a certain external friendliness, which is part of your daily mask. People are very friendly, but it is terribly difficult for them to make authentic contact: basically, they are very lonely. If we fraternize too easily, without etiquette or ceremony, natural contact is impossible.'[14] The influence of Grotowski on Off-Off-Broadway can be illustrated by the contrast between van Itallie's *America Hurrah* and *The Serpent* (1968). *The Serpent* was not a polemic, but a re-telling of the Biblical story of Genesis to envelop the day-to-day crises with a vision of the separation of the sexes, the origin of evil, the slaying of Kennedy by Cain.

'There are no costumes,' wrote Clurman, 'the actors are barefoot in simple work-clothes. Percussive and flutelike sound is employed. There is the music of plant and animal life in their generative stages, to which the actors add their own little bleats, neighs, moos. At one point the serpent is seen in a swaying tree (formed by the actors' bodies), aglow with glistening red apples, an enchanting image.'[15]

This yearning for a lost innocence, pre-conscious, pre-verbal and almost pre-natal, was in sharp contrast to the violence which, as the Black Panther leader Stokeley Carmichael said, was 'as American as blueberry pie.' As a fashion, it spread to Broadway in Galt MacDermot's *Hair*, described as an 'American Tribal Love-Rock Musical'. It was conceived by two hippy actors, Gerome Ragni and James Rado, spear-bearers with Joseph Papp's Public Theater in New York. They teamed up with Galt MacDermot, who composed music for Papp's *Hamlet* in which they were playing, and *Hair* opened at a discotheque called Cheetah.

There it was spotted by a young producer, Michael Butler, who brought in Tom O'Horgan to re-stage for the Biltmore Theater on Broadway, where it opened on 29 April 1968, and ran until the Vietnam war was over. O'Horgan strengthened the slight plot about a student who joined a hippy commune to evade the draft and made the most of MacDermot's pleasant music, soft and soaring rock. He also borrowed another Off-Off-Broadway technique by asking the cast to stand naked under dim lighting at the end of act one, a Broadway breakthrough, anticipating *Oh! Calcutta* (1968) and Tom Eyen's *The Dirtiest Show in Town* (1970).

Hair sentimentalised, of course, the protest movement. While members of the Living Theater were not chosen for their good looks, on Broadway they were. The students were attractive kids who were having a ball, dressing up in fancy clothes if they dressed at all, falling in love, getting high, before facing up to their duties as American citizens. Being liberated was fun and something which you could only do in a free society.

Four months after *Hair* opened on Broadway, the Democratic Convention was held in Chicago, to nominate a candidate for the forthcoming presidential election in November. Three senators were the main contenders, two in favour of withdrawal from Vietnam (Eugene McCarthy and George McGovern) and one (Hubert Humphrey) who was not. A vast gathering of protesters collected in Grant Park to march on the convention hall; but the mayor of Chicago, Richard Daley, gave orders for the police to move in and break up the demonstration with truncheons and teargas. The following day a Senator complained about the mayor's 'gestapo tactics' and Daley's response was televised but not reported. It was thought to be unprintable. Humphrey won the nomination, but lost the race for the White House to the Republican Richard Nixon, in earlier days a staunch supporter of Joe McCarthy. This result, in which the Alabama Governor George Wallace also ran and won 10 million votes, indicated that most Americans still supported the Vietnam war, but it was becoming unpopular. Nixon took note.

The scenes from Chicago demonstrated the narrow dividing line between law-and-order and oppression. They took place within a week of the Soviet tanks rolling into Prague and were accompanied by Berlin riots where Rudi Dutschke was shot, by the *événements de mai* in Paris and the demonstrations in London outside the US Embassy in Grosvenor Square. There may have been more chaotic years than 1968, but none so easily watched on television or when the world could be seen as a fragile globe, spinning in space, from an Apollo 8 spacecraft circling the moon.

The man who followed Albee as America's playwright most likely to succeed was Sam Shepard, a Californian, born in 1943, whose one-act plays for La Mama won Obie (Off-Broadway) Awards from the *Village Voice* in 1966. In 1970 he went to London on a four-year visit, where he wrote *The Tooth of Crime* (1972). On his return to the States, he wrote some haunting full-length plays, *Curse of the Starving Class* (1976), *Buried Child* (1978), *Fool for Love* (1979), *True West* (1980) and *A Lie of the Mind* (1985). Shepard abandoned any attempt at formal story-telling, but he used fragments of US folklore (the rattlesnake), consumerism (the stocked or empty fridge), desolate landscapes, rock music and a roadside bar to provide an alternative American Dream.

His plays proceed by a kind of associative logic, akin to jazz: very American, curiously austere. He offered the culture of the scrap-heap, the combing of a rubbish dump to see what crops up, which probably won't be much of use anyway. An object startles with its odour of lost optimism. It gets thrown back. Love is a memory that sometimes gets recalled. What was it exactly? A rub of the scrotum.

There are kinfolk somewhere, best avoided.

10

THE FLOATING ISLAND

'I heard the news today, oh boy!'
(From *Sgt Pepper's Lonely Hearts Club Band*, 1967)

In October 1966 the Royal Shakespeare Company staged a collage-documentary-debate about the Vietnam war, *US*, whose title was thought to be equally apt in small or capital letters. It was directed by Peter Brook at a time when he was trying to combine the shock tactics of Artaud with the coolness of Brecht. Part One described what was happening over there, the self-immolation of a Buddhist monk, a US news conference, a seek-and-destroy mission and a bombing raid in which as much hell was let loose as could be easily raised within the Aldwych Theatre.

The second half was a debate about protest. An Englishman wanted to follow the example of the US Quaker Norman Morrison who burnt himself to death on the steps of the Pentagon, and a left-wing protester (Glenda Jackson) tried to convince him of the folly of the gesture. When she failed to do so, she denounced the British complacency. She called for napalm in Hampstead to bring home to the people the truth of what was happening in Vietnam.

'As Miss Jackson, pallid and square-shouldered, delivers her final harangue against cosy English isolationism,' wrote Michael Billington, 'the combination of her words and her presence leaves an unforgetable imprint on the mind.'[1] He felt that '*US* distorts the truth by its suggestion that Hanoi is constantly offering an olive-branch, repeatedly flung back in its face by Washington . . . [and by ignoring] the Vietcong atrocities'.[2] Others thought that it was far too well balanced. Tariq Ali in *Town* complained that it did not convey 'anything coherent',[3] while D.A.N. Jones in the *New Statesman* likened it to a play 'written in 1940 by a kindly Rumanian, hoping England . . . will negotiate with the Nazis'.[4]

The play ended with a powerful Brook image. A small box was brought on stage, from which was released a small cloud of white butterflies, which fluttered around the theatre. One seemed to be caught, a match was struck and its wings shrivelled in the flame.

The target may have been British complacency, but it was hard to know what good could have been done if we had been less so. No amount of napalm in Hampstead could have brought British troops back from Vietnam, because none had been sent. The United States tried to persuade the Labour government to dispatch a token force; but Harold Wilson and his Foreign Secretary, Michael Stewart, had only given them moral support, pleading poverty, although they did maintain bases east of Suez.

Before the election in April 1966 it was rumoured that if the Labour Party was returned to power with a larger majority, it would take a stronger stand. Tariq Ali, passionately opposed to the American intervention in Vietnam, has described how Labour politicians listened sympathetically, made excuses and promised to do better next time. *US*, staged within six months of the Labour victory, may have been a way of prompting their resolve.

'The RSC,' wrote Brook, 'is using public money to do a play about Americans at war in Vietnam. This fact is so explosive.'[5] The play needed subsidy because it was large-scale and used methods which might not work, but Brook would have been naive to suppose that any government anywhere would give grants to a theatre which stood the slightest chance of arousing public opinion against its foreign policy. It was less silly to believe that there was an anti-Vietnam mood within the Labour Party that *US* might encourage or that the government might want to see an anti-Vietnam play at the second national theatre as a way of demonstrating to the world that Britain was a free society, where the public had elected a Labour government. *US* stopped short of demanding the withdrawal of US troops or of denouncing the global containment of communism which justified the US peace offensive.

Brook wanted 'a theatre of confrontation', one which brought 'current events' back on to the stage, which touched the issues which 'most powerfully concern actors and audiences at the actual moment when they meet'.[6] He used the techniques pioneered in the Theatre of Cruelty season and developed powerfully in his production of Weiss's *The Marat/Sade*, of which Brook wrote: 'Everything about this play is designed to crack the spectator on the jaw, then douse him with ice-cold water, then force him intelligently to assess what has happened to him, then give him a kick in the balls, then bring him to his senses again.'[7]

This was strong stuff for a theatre more accustomed to the cocktail glass held in the trembling hand, but not as strong as it might have been, for nobody could decide precisely where Weiss's message or sympathies lay, with the inmates of the asylum at Charenton, with the asylum's director of liberal views or with the Marquis de Sade, who was staging the spectacle? In classical theatre, the intention was to hold back on stage violence to allow the theme to emerge clearly at the crisis, but in *The Marat/Sade*, sensationalism overwhelmed what may have been its message. *US* was in a similar mould. The images stayed in the mind – the burnt butterfly, the puppet corpse of a marine with rockets for eyes which dangled over the proscenium – but what was the message? That war was a terrible thing? Yes, of course . . . and then?

If the Suez affair had shown that the days of imperialism were over, Vietnam demonstrated that Britain was without much influence in the world at all. Kennedy's Secretary of State, Dean Rusk, said in 1962 that Britain had 'lost an empire and has yet to discover a role', considered to be the sort of simplification to be expected from an American. But events kept confirming his point. Neither Macmillan nor Wilson could to do much to persuade the South African government to end apartheid. South Africa left the Commonwealth in 1961, but the ties could not be severed for economic and military reasons, as well as kinship. South Africa was part of the perimeter ring of Western defences. In 1965, Ian Smith's white government in Rhodesia declared unilaterally its independence from Britain. Wilson tried economic sanctions to bring down the regime in a matter of 'weeks rather than months'. It didn't. Meanwhile, General de Gaulle was blocking British efforts to join the EEC.

For those of us who lived in Britain, it felt as if we were on a floating island, tethered to the United States, tugging at our moorings but afraid to drift. Nor were domestic politics more encouraging. Wilson had come to office promising to end restrictive practices on both sides of industry, but it was hard for him to do so when the trade unions, the chief source of funding for the Labour Party, were among the offenders. The economy stayed sluggish, unable to achieve the 3 per cent annual growth rate which the new Department of Economic Affairs had promised and which was supposed to pay for better social services. The only thing to rise reliably was inflation.

When such measures as a wages and prices freeze had failed to cope with inflation, Wilson was forced in 1967 to de-value the pound. He went on television to explain that this did not mean *necessarily* that the pound in the pocket was worth less than before, only that it was not worth so much in international exchanges, a distinction so subtle that it became a joke. The contrast between the government's rhetoric and its practice was comic as well as alarming. To that extent, *US* was a play of its time, not because it was confrontational but because it wasn't but pretended to be. Even this modified example of free speech was out of line with what was happening elsewhere in the media.

In February 1966 the BBC cancelled the screening of a film on nuclear warfare, Peter Watkins's *The War Game*. The Director of Television, Kenneth Adam, insisted that BBC had taken this decision 'independently', but it was the month before the election. The BBC might have been accused of stirring up trouble within the Labour Party, which was divided on the subject of the British independent nuclear deterrent, but it was not screened after the election either. Programmes taken off by the BBC before an election had a habit of being never seen again. The satire programme, *That Was The Week That Was*, was removed before the 1964 election and did not return. It was not only programmes that were at risk, but the independent spirit that the BBC had shown under its Director-General, Hugh Carleton-Green.

The appointment of Carleton-Green in 1960 had changed the tone of the BBC. Instead of being a deferential organisation where the News matched the cut-glass accents in which they were read, it became one which took the liberty of asking Ministers the sort of questions which might be expected from an adult electorate, sometimes in regional voices. The BBC's Board of Governors supported him. Its Chairman was Lord Normanbrook, who as a former head of the Civil Service knew where the public interest should be distinguished from that of the government. When he died in 1967, Wilson appointed someone more sensitive to the needs of politicians. He chose the wartime Radio Doctor to take his place, Lord Hill, a Conservative peer.

Carleton-Green saw this as an attempt to tame the BBC and resigned in 1968. There could be no return to the days when an announcer in a dinner jacket asked Sir Anthony Eden whether he had a message for the nation, but in other ways the government tried to exert pressure, which met with resistance inside the BBC. The more George Wigg MP, as Postmaster-General, asked BBC producers to provide transcripts before transmission, the more prolonged became their excuses. The BBC had a constitutional duty to be 'impartial', an impossible task which was interpreted to mean that both sides of an argument should be presented.

There could, of course, be more than two sides, but the binary assumption fitted in with classical logic, whereby through the clash of opposites the truth might emerge. The BBC may have relaxed its rule on 'above average' accents, but in other ways it obeyed Aristotle. If an opposition spokesman was interviewed on a programme, someone from the government was entitled to reply. If one refused to appear or both parties held similar opinions, as was the case with the Vietnam war, the BBC had three options. It could drop the item, stage a mock battle in which the opponents quarrelled with each other for being in agreement or provide an 'empty chair'. This was reserved for occasions when a subject seemed to be worth airing, but where only one side was present. The presenter pointed to the empty chair and stated that so-and-so had been asked to state his case but had declined.

In political terms it was like pleading the Fifth Amendment and BBC rarely used it.

The country was impotent, the government was devious and the future was bleak. Graduates from Oxbridge, who might have sought careers in the civil service, chose satire instead. The revue, *Beyond the Fringe* (1960) set the fashion and one of its members, Peter Cook, also owned the satirical magazine *Private Eye*. The mood of irreverence spread beyond Oxbridge revues and the BBC, where it did not begin. There was fun to be had from turning a top-down society bottom-up. The sex scandals of Macmillan's last months were particularly amusing, except for those concerned.

It was the kind of humour in which the playwright, Joe Orton, specialised. 'Like all great satirists,' wrote his biographer, John Lahr, 'Orton was a realist';[8] but he was neither and such praise did him an injustice. *Loot* (1966) and *What the Butler Saw* (1968) were not satires on the police or psychiatrists and if they were intended to be so, they failed. They were shaped like the Vernon Sylvaine farces of the 1950s, all doors and mistaken identities. Orton excelled in mocking middle-class gentility, taking polite phrases and turning them inside out to make them sound saucy. He had a wild and black imagination, and took a worm's eye view of human nature, but he contained his excesses within prim diction, trimmed neatly like a suburban hedge. 'The Friends of Bingo have sent a wreath,' said the widower, McLeavy, in *Loot*, relishing his dead wife's funeral arrangements, 'The blooms are breathtaking.' He shared this skill not with Oscar Wilde, with whom he was sometimes compared, but with Frankie Howerd, the comic who became an unexpected hit at Peter Cook's Establishment Club. The tradition of class-inflected smut was also a feature of intimate revues, to be found in the *double entendres* of Max Adrian and the Hermiones, Gingold and Badderley.

The difference lay in the extremes to which this was taken, the boldness of the bawdry. 'They'll carry you to your grave,' Dr Prentice in *What the Butler Saw* warned his wife, a closet nymphomaniac, 'in a Y-shaped coffin!' The sexual habits of the middle classes amused other dramatists of the 1960s, including Giles Cooper and Frank Marcus, but the joke wore thin as Britain became less puritanical. The target may have lain elsewhere, not so much in what was happening behind the lace-curtains as in the refusal to admit that anything was happening.

Sex was a way of deriding the pomposity of British society, its class-structure, which was now easier to mock because it had come to mean so little. When Britain ruled the world, the edifice of authority had to be supported, because much depended upon it. Now that it ruled so little, there was no need to sustain the pretence. Those who had been confronted at school by atlases with vast areas of imperial pink that they might be asked to defend heaved a sigh of relief. With the loss of territory went the myths of Empire, Pax Britannica and the obligation to keep up appearances. Above all there was the comfort of knowing that on the other side of the world a major war was taking place in which Britain for once was not involved.

Young Americans flocked to London as a haven from their draft notices. In April 1966, *Time* magazine described it as 'the city of the decade', 'Swinging London', where you could be young, free and uninhibited. The Beatles set the trend in pop music, Carnaby Street the fashion, in the form of the mini-skirt. If Stephen Potter's *One-Upmanship* caught the mood of the 1950s, the *Carry On* films did so for the 1960s, seaside postcard comedy, cheerful, raunchy and vulgar in a way which meant nothing to those who had not been trained to be polite.

On the Edinburgh Festival fringe in 1966, a play by an unknown dramatist put this freedom into a different perspective: Tom Stoppard's *Rosencrantz and Guildenstern are Dead*. It was bought by Olivier's NT and staged at the Old Vic in 1967. At the time, it was likened to *Waiting for Godot*, in that Hamlet's two friends sit around the court, chatting, playing dice and waiting for things to happen. Unlike *Godot*, the audience knew roughly about what happened in *Hamlet*, while Rosencrantz and Guildenstern do not. They are pawns in a game played by others, a metaphor for swinging Britain. In the Soviet Union the hero of *Hamlet* was Fortinbras, in Germany it was Hamlet (too thoughtful for action), in Poland it was Claudius, but in Britain it was T.S. Eliot's 'attendant lord' or Stoppard's Rosencrantz and Guildenstern.

Similarly, in Stoppard's *Jumpers* (1972), George, a professor of moral philosophy, theorised amiably about moral values when the barbarians were at the gate. In *Travesties* (1974), Henry Carr, a consular official in Zurich in 1917, remembered his stage triumph in *The Importance of Being Earnest* and fretted for his lost trousers, while around him, Joyce writes *Ulysses*, Tzara cuts up a Shakespeare sonnet and Lenin plots a revolution. Stoppard's Britain was an Edwardian air-bubble of misplaced confidence.

Stoppard loved Britain. He regarded it as a great privilege to hold a British passport. He played cricket almost as well as Harold Pinter. But he was born in Czechoslovakia in 1937, escaped in the following year to Singapore and came to Britain in 1946. His education was British, but he never forgot the anarchy from which his family had fled. He was a pioneer in Britain of Czech Absurdist drama, adapting the plays of Kahout and Havel; but it was another Czech writer, Milan Kundera, who coined a phrase to describe Britain in the 1960s, 'the unbearable lightness of being'. In a world where an individual felt responsible for what happens to mankind, all actions, even trivial ones, were weighed down with the burden of duty. This could be described as the unbearable heaviness of being. If that duty is removed and a person is led to believe that no action on his/her part will make any difference, this provides a sense of freedom which is also unbearable. Anything can be done, but nothing matters.

Almost anything could be done in Swinging Britain if you knew when and where to do it. You could stage a Happening by wheeling a naked girl across a balcony during a Writers' Symposium. You could join a Grotowski-style commune or an agit-prop company touring the factories. You might even be subsidised. You could sit in a cellar, sipping orange juice laced with LSD, and wonder where the flowers went. Strip-clubs mushroomed around central London, of most use to those out-of-town visitors who did not know where the best parties were. The poet Philip Larkin may have mourned that 'sex began in 1963' ('rather too late for me'), but it was not too late for one of the rare post-war impresarios to become a multi-millionaire, Paul Raymond, whose club theatre in Soho was billed as 'the world's centre for erotic entertainment.'

There was also a virulent strain of Sixties depression, which could be found in its theatre. It was not attached to any cause, like Vietnam, but to a general malaise. It could be illustrated by the contrast between the optimism of Arnold Wesker's socialist parables of the 1950s and the gloom of *Their Very Own* and *Golden City* (1965), where he contemplated the collapse of his dreams. Wesker, like Joan Littlewood, had a reason to feel gloomy. Both had seen their plans for workers' fun palaces put to one side, while the national theatres were brought into being. After the success of her documentary musical about the First World War, *Oh, What a Lovely War!* (1963), brought her goal no nearer, Littlewood left the country in disgust, not returning to direct until 1972.

For others, the anxiety might be described as Existential, which could mean either alienation or the frustration at not knowing quite what one wanted to be in a society where in theory one could be almost anything. It could be blamed on the loss of class roots as the meritocrats moved upwards. This worried such dramatists as David Storey and David Mercer. Both came from Yorkshire and looked back on their childhoods with a mixture of nostalgia and resentment. They despised the limits of the working-class districts from which they had come, felt treacherous about doing so, but longed for its security as well, the confidence of knowing your place in society and keeping to it. And how under those circumstances could they talk to their parents?

Families were a problem at a time when the talk was of sexual liberation. In 1964 the psychiatrist R.D. Laing published an authoritative book on the subject, *Sanity, Madness and the Family*. He argued that what was often interpreted as madness could be a healthy response to intolerable outside pressures. His case histories often laid the blame on the nuclear family, but society at large was responsible as well. In a world where mass destruction could be contemplated as a form of defence, who was mad, the man who said 'Yes' or the man who said 'No'?

Laing's influence could be detected in Mercer's plays, whose heroes of the 1960s were those who retreated into madness or eccentricity, such as Peter in *Ride-a-Cock-Horse* (1965), Morgan in *A Suitable Case for Treatment* (1966) or the Reverend Flint in *Flint* (1970). One of Storey's Laingian heroes was the provincial teacher in *The Restoration of Arnold Middleton* (1966), driven to isolation by his life at home and to madness by the offers of help. Mercer and Storey did not blame just the family, but the tug-of-war between the home and the outside world. 'If everyone could hold in his mind through one single day,' said Brook, 'both the horror of Vietnam and the normal life he is leading, the tension between the two would be intolerable.'9

At times, the depression grew very black. Harold Pinter's *The Homecoming* (1965) was an example. It was Pinter's third full-length play to be seen in London, the others being *The Birthday Party* (1958) which ran for a week and *The Caretaker* (1960), which was a hit. His style came into vogue, described by Bamber Gascoigne as 'distilled naturalism'.10 The language followed the speech-patterns of everyday life in the districts of London where Pinter was brought up, but it was charged with a street menace, the threats which, according to Pinter, often followed Jews as they hurried past gangs of thugs in Hackney alleyways. 'Are you all right then?' 'Yes, I'm all right.' 'Well, that's all right then!'

He underlined innocent-sounding phrases with long pauses or switched directions startlingly. 'I'll take that glass.' 'If you take that glass . . . I'll take you.'11 He studied Beckett and *A Slight Ache* (1959) is like *Molloy*; but what he chiefly borrowed from him was his irony and mordant wit.

The title of *The Homecoming* was almost Polish in its levels of irony. On the surface it refers to the return of an American college professor, Teddy, to the North London house where he was brought up. He brought his wife, Ruth, with him, but left their children behind. His mother had died and the household was now all male, occupied by his father, his three brothers and his uncle. Ruth filled the place of the lost woman of the house. Teddy not only came home, but brought 'home' with him.

Teddy's male relatives started to treat Ruth as their joint property. She became their mother, common girl friend and nice little earner, for they proposed to set her up as a call-girl in Soho and she did not complain. She rather liked the idea. She too had come home to the sexual roots of her nature. Teddy, too polite to object, returned to the quiet campus in the United States. It may not have been his real home, but it was less barbaric. One moral of *The Homecoming* might be that the more you treated a girl as a male sex object, the better she liked it. This was a bleak idea in itself, made harsher by the thought that the family was shown to be a battleground of male fantasies, controlled by a dominant female. Teddy's 'uncle' – but are they related? – collapsed from a heart attack. Nobody pays attention.

Pinter was likened to Edward Albee, but his pessimism ran deeper. Like Albee, dialogue was his strength, but he rarely indulged in one-line gags. As he became fashionable, the street-corner menace became, in his phrase, 'the weasel under the cocktail cabinet'. His settings moved upwards through the ranks of the bourgeoisie, until by *No Man's Land* (1975) and *Betrayal* (1978), he settled for somewhere near Hampstead. His opinions moved further left at the same time.

Before the dust had settled from *The Homecoming*, linked with *The Marat/Sade* and David Rudkin's *Afore Night Come* in Hall's 'dirty plays' row with Emile Littler, an even blacker play opened at the Royal Court. Edward Bond's *Saved* (1965) presented an image of working-class desolation in South London, a social desert contaminated by capitalism. The characters were barely literate, barely articulate, unable to love or feel affection. Hooligans in one scene stone a baby to death in its pram, which its unmarried mother had left unattended, but this savagery did not provide the play's moment of deepest despair. This was reserved for the final scene, where the five main characters exist, side by side, in a dump of inertia. One flicks through a copy of the *Radio Times*, another mends a broken chair. The dead baby has been forgotten.

Saved was not licensed by the Lord Chamberlain's Examiner of Plays and the Royal Court was turned into a club theatre for the production. Even then it was not safe from prosecution, for plain-clothes policemen lurked around the bar to see if anyone was being served with an unlicensed drink. It was clear that, sooner or later a prosecution would be brought against the play which had so shocked its London audiences. It became a test case for the 'permissive society'. Olivier appeared as a witness for the defence at the court hearings and wrote in *Plays and Players* that '*Saved* is not for children but . . . the grown-ups of this country should have the courage to look at it; and if we do not find precisely the mirror held up to nature . . . at least we can experience the sacramental catharsis of a very chastening look at the sort of ground we have prepared for the next lot.'[12]

Olivier placed *Saved* within the Western tragic tradition. Its purpose was not simply to shock but to purge. Such horror stories could be found in any local newspaper, where they were half-read and half-forgotten, lingering at the back of the mind. Bond made us think about them freshly and enquire about the causes. The aim was social virtue. When *Saved* was released to the general public, the case for stage censorship collapsed. The Lord Chamberlain's Examiner of Plays was finally declared redundant in 1968. Olivier's argument might not have applied so easily to the savagery in other Bond plays, the cannibalism of *Early Morning* (1968) or the eye-gouging machine in his *Lear* (1972).

The cruelty in Bond's plays, rooted in the pessimism of the mid-1960s, could be justified, if needed, from several points of view. It reminded us that class-divided or, more broadly, unjust societies were always on the brink of civil war. His plays may have been grim, but they were well-written and sometimes poetic; and there were classics which contained more atrocities, *Titus Andronicus*, for example. Didn't they belong to what could be regarded as a genre of modern Revenge Tragedy?

Since the turn of the century, left-wing critics had asserted that good plays, forward-looking ones, attacked the bourgeois societies of which they were part. The alternative was to be complacent, boulevard or (if German) 'confectionery'. Better plays hit harder which, in Bond's case, meant often more violently. His aim was to develop a working-class culture, which started by defining the enemy, bourgeois capitalism. How could anyone who supported the war in Vietnam object to Bond's plays?

Nor could anyone complain that the violence was gratuitous, although it might seem far-fetched. Bond did not write horror movies. His violence was part of his attack on society, one way in which it differed from Greek tragedy. One sought to disrupt, the other to pacify. The aim of catharsis was to get rid of vengeful emotions and to end cycles of revenge killings, whereas Bond's plays were more of an incitement to violence. They offered an excuse for terrorism. The argument was that the ruling classes provoked violence, to which the working classes eventually would have to respond in kind. It was only after a classless society had been achieved that the wheel of blood would spin to rest.

The trouble with Britain, according to the hard left, was that it had not had its revolution, unlike the countries in Eastern Europe. Even at the time this sounded rather like somebody with a headache envying those dying of cancer; but the disillusion with Wilson's government was such that moderate socialism seemed the worst betrayal. Apart from the equivocation over Vietnam and nuclear weapons, Wilson seemed to be perpetuating the class system by introducing life peerages for those who had served with distinction on one of his quangos. The fact that the House of Lords still existed, and showed no signs of going away, indicated how unshakeably top-down British society really was. Peter Barnes's *The Ruling Class* (1968) painted an eery picture of the Upper Chamber with cobwebbed corpses whom only the prospect of a debate on hanging could revive.

It may seem to be a paradox that a country so little inclined towards radical change nurtured a brand of theatre which could think about nothing else. Plays from the medium- to hard-left (in egg-boiling terms from about fifteen minutes to three hours) spread to the menus of continental theatres. Between the first club production of *Saved* at the Royal Court in November 1965, and its first run for the British public at large in February 1969, there were no fewer than thirty productions on the continent, mainly in German-speaking theatres. Britain's lack of influence abroad and its plump body-politic at home gave its theatre the chance to kick over the traces in a manner which it had never previously enjoyed. London swung, because Britain dangled.

Subsidy was another factor. The contrast between the old commercial managements and the new state-aided ones could be seen vividly in 1966 when Coward's *A Suite in Three Keys* played in the West End, while *The Homecoming* was at the Aldwych, with *US* on the way, and *Saved* was available for club members at the Royal Court. In 1968, the Arts Council decided to provide financial support for alternative theatre companies, which were often small, agit-prop and temporary. Why did it help companies whose aim was to destroy or at best disrupt British society? Was it pursuing a Potter-like policy of proffering a helping hand to those whom it wanted to push in the gutter?

The Arts Council's Drama Panel shared the view that new plays were often subversive and they did want to be accused of indirect censorship by withholding grants for political reasons. Questions then arose as to what its values were and where subsidies should stop. When Hall took over the Shakespeare Memorial Company, it had a reserve in the bank, a small trading profit and no grants. When he left in 1968, it had gained a London theatre, its company had increased in size and its audiences had risen from 348,539 to more than a million. It received grants of £226,500, but it had a deficit of £161,126 and no reserves at all. With a success like that, who could afford failure? If the Arts Council wanted to take on board radical new companies, there was likely to be, as one Treasury official warned, 'a bottomless pit of demand'.

Brook had no quarrel with the RSC and he liked Hall, but he feared the parochialism of national theatres. 'Official culture,' he once said, 'is mostly ridiculous.'[13] In the modern world people knew what was happening in Tibet or Vietnam. They could see it on television. But, as *US* proved, they had not developed an international culture to handle these global facts. In 1970, Brook moved to Paris to establish the International Centre for Theatre Research (CIRT). He did not know where the research might lead, but he had in mind something elemental, truthful to all nations and all people, which could confront modern confusions with a mythology so innocent of ulterior motives that it might even be mistaken for a new religion. The French government lent him a disused tapestry gallery for the purpose.

11

TOWARDS MUSIC

'In desiring to become, you begin to live'
(René Daumal, quoted in *The Conference of Birds*, 1977)

In West Germany, the first performance of Edward Bond's *Saved* took place in April 1967, in a studio theatre attached to the Munich Kammerspiele. It was hailed as the Production of the Year by the theatre magazine, *Theater Heute*[1] and made the name of its director, Peter Stein, who was barely 30. It helped to establish a genre, the Volkstück, whose parallel in Britain was kitchen-sink drama, and it startled the citizens of Munich.

Stein's *Saved* was staged in an open room under plain white lighting in the style of Brecht, with no attempt at naturalism but with authentic objects, a rowing boat, a juke box. The scene where the baby was stoned to death was presented with terrifying realism. What also took the audience aback was the fact that the play had been translated by Martin Sperr into a Munich dialect. While the distinction between High and Low German had become less marked, it was customary for dialect plays to be warm-hearted and faintly funny, as if the working classes were not expected to take part in the deeper issues of life.

Saved changed that. Instead of nudging the working classes towards the periphery of events, it placed them at the centre. The consequences of capitalism were not to be found just in places like Vietnam, but in the hooliganism of the streets, the urban decay and the dereliction of the mind. The common man was not an innocent bystander, but a maimed animal limping in the shadows of concrete skyscrapers. The difference between British kitchen-sink drama of the 1950s and the Volkstücke of such writers as Franz Xaver Kroetz (*Dairy Farm (Stallerhot)*, 1972) lay in the bleakness of the vision. Wesker was never so pessimistic.

Despite its many early productions, the wider shock-waves from *Saved* spread slowly. All German-speaking countries prided themselves on their regional and municipal theatres, the most lavishly endowed in Europe. There were 132 municipal companies in West Germany,

120

of which most received more subsidy than the RSC and the NT put together. In 1973/4, the Deutsche Oper in West Berlin received DM 32 million (about £6 million), which was about the amount given by the Arts Council to all the theatres in Britain.[2] Their audiences were loyal, their political support unwavering and their actors were rarely attracted away to the private theatres or television. There was a high-seriousness to match, a disdain for the 'confectionery' theatre elsewhere.

By the late 1960s many of these theatres felt old-fashioned. This was partly due to the late acceptance of Brecht, although his influence, when it came, came in a rush; but even Brecht's plays were showing signs of age with their proletarian diction which nobody spoke in real life. The repertoires were dominated by the familiar dramatists, Shakespeare, Molière, Schiller, Goethe and Shaw, with only Friedrich Dürrenmatt and Anouilh, apart from Brecht, popular among the moderns.[3] The respect in which these theatre were held discouraged small initiatives. Each production had to be a statement for mankind.

The German state theatres had large companies, long periods for rehearsal and big financial resources; and in these not unimportant respects, the working conditions for actors and directors were the best in Europe. Some, however, were run autocratically and after the successes of *Saved* and an equally trenchant production of Brecht's *In the Jungle of the Cities*, Stein, who had seemed destined to become a resident director at the Munich Kammerspiele, came into conflict with its Intendant.

In 1968 he staged Peter Weiss's *Vietnam Discourse*, loosely modelled after Brook's *US* but it pulled fewer punches. The Americans were condemned for invading Vietnam and the German public was accused of condoning crimes committed in the name of freedom. The narrator was a popular cabaret singer, Wolfgang Neuss, who got so carried away by the force of the arguments that he tried to take up a collection for the Viet-Cong. The Intendant promptly sacked him. Stein and his co-director, Wolfgang Schwiedrzik, resigned in sympathy.[4] Stein swore that he would never work in a German state theatre again. He hated the system, the huge companies, the stale repertoires, the authoritarian structures, the wealth, the affectations of culture and the complacent audiences.

With some colleagues who included the director Klaus Peymann, Stein wrote a manifesto for a new kind of theatre collective, which would work through discussion on a limited number of projects, each requiring the full commitment of the company. There would be no more reverential productions of classics. Each performance should be considered as part of a sustained process of enquiry. Stein brought together a small group of like-minded professionals who were prepared to leave the security of their state theatres to undertake what amounted to an open-ended socialist de-construction of bourgeois habits of mind.

They worked together on three plays by Bond and Goethe's *Torquato Tasso*, which they took out on tour as guest productions. They were not always welcomed. In Zurich their reception was frosty, but their reputation grew among critics and radicals. In 1971 they received an offer which they could hardly refuse. The Senate in West Berlin proposed that Stein's company should be provided with a home attached to the Schaubühne am Halleschen Ufer, a grant equivalent to half a million pounds and a building, the Mendelssohn-Bau on the Lehninplatz, which they could convert to their requirements. In return, they had to present a minimum of four productions a year and 250 performances.

Such largess to a 33-year-old director with a reputation for making trouble would have been unthinkable in Britain or in most other German cities, but the authorities were seeking a left-wing replacement for Erwin Piscator, who died in 1966. It was part of their propaganda but Stein, whose sympathies lay to the East, did not see why that was any reason to refuse the offer. If the West Berliners wanted to waste their money, he said, they should do so on a theatre rather than another Starfighter.[5]

Stein's manifesto, published by *Theater Heute* in December 1969, provided a model for the many groups which broke away from the repertory theatres around Europe in the early 1970s. Few were as lucky as Stein's company and many did not survive, but they had other characteristics in common. They were democratic collectives in which some were more equal than others. They liked trenchant working class plays by Bond, Kroetz and later Nigel Williams, but they attempted Brechtian epics as well and radical re-interpretations of the classics. They travelled and were ready to set up shop almost anywhere, in tents, in factories and empty cinemas. Mnouchkine's Théâtre du Soleil found a disused armaments warehouse, the Cartoucherie. A focal point was an old farmhouse near Amsterdam, the Mickery, which the smaller groups visited.

The International Centre for Theatre Research (CIRT) in Paris might be regarded as one of them, but Brook was not a young rebel and his aims were different from Stein's. He remained an associate RSC director and as a parting gift, he directed *A Midsummer Night's Dream* (1970) to which he brought all the stage magic at his command, acrobatics in a white gymnasium, whirling plates and floating feathers. Then he moved with his wife, Natasha Parry, and his family to Paris, which became his home city. 'It wasn't a sudden decision,' he recalled,[6] nor a demonstrative one, but of all the directors who left state theatres after 1968, his departure was the most significant. What was more extraordinary was that he did not publish a manifesto but simply said that he was searching for a theatre which would appeal across nations and cultures in a manner 'akin to music'.

Brook had been at the centre of British theatre for twenty years. He was only five years older than Hall, but they might have belonged to different generations. He began his career as an *enfant terrible* during the war, staging iconoclastic shows in the London's little theatres while he was still an undergraduate at Oxford. Sir Barry Jackson, the founder-director of the Birmingham Rep, asked him to direct *Love's Labour's Lost* at the Shakespeare Memorial Theatre in 1946 when he was only 21. He was responsible for two of the best Stratford productions in the 1950s, *Measure for Measure* (1950) and *Titus Andronicus* (1956); but Binkie Beaumont used him as a pair of lungs to breathe some life into such frivolities as André Roussin's *The Little Hut*. Brook was a West End director before Hall left university. During the 1960s, Hall gave him the support at the RSC to try out his ideas at LAMDA and to bring the results to the Aldwych. Brook, rather than anyone else, earned the RSC its world-wide reputation as an innovatory company.

His family came from Russia, although he was born in London. He spoke several languages and was open to influences. 'I have never believed in a single truth,' he wrote, 'I believe that all schools, all theories can be useful in some place at some time. But I have discovered that one can only live by a passionate, and absolute, identification with a point of view. . . . For a point of view to be of any use at all, one must commit oneself totally to it, one must defend it to the very death. Yet at the same time, there is an inner voice that murmurs: "Don't take it too seriously. Hold on tightly, let go lightly."'[7]

On his European tours with British companies he had been impressed by the way in which non-English audiences responded to Shakespeare. They may have read the plays, but did they know them so well that they could follow every line? Was the acting so expressive or was there a beauty with the sounds of words which transcended their meaning? In 1968 Barrault asked him to conduct acting workshops at the Théâtre des Nations. Brook discovered that he could communicate with actors from various cultures, despite the fact that they could not rely on a common language.

In some respects it was easier. If you simply listened to words, you did not notice the tone of voice or the body language. If words were a problem, you watched details of other people's non-verbal behaviour and formed an impression of their natures which might be more reliable than what they actually said.

This was when the CIRT project took shape in his mind, but the seeds were sown before then, from his friendships with Grotowski and the French director Micheline Rozan, from his impatience with classical repertoire and from his wish to escape from the confines of

123

narrow nationalism. Like Stein, Brook was lucky in finding sponsors, the Ford and Gulbenkian Foundations, and the Shiraz Festival which commissioned the first production.

When he announced his plans in 1970, some colleagues believed that he was seeking a super-ecleticism where all the world's stage techniques could be tipped into a common pool from which the right one could be drawn when required. This was exactly what he did not want. He did not like the idea of a simple exchange of expertise, with a British actor showing the others how to speak Shakespeare and a Japanese one teaching Kabuki. Instead he hoped that the actors would shed 'their ethnic mannerisms',[8] so that national differences would be revealed at a deeper level.

There remained the large question as to what this group of actors would actually do. What plays would they perform, and how? Brook began by inviting them to study the structure of sound. He found an ancient Greek text, 'eleleueleleyu . . .', and asked them to approach it 'like an archaeologist, stumbling across an unknown object in the sand'.[9] By 'tasting the letters on the tongue', the actors sought the sounds and rhythms without knowing what they might mean. A 'meaning' did emerge, an instinct for an appropriate stress, which varied from actor to actor without being individualistic, for it was a response to a text.

One visitor to the closed workshop sessions, the poet Ted Hughes, was fascinated by this experiment with sound, which corresponded to his own search for the right-sounding syllable in a poem. Hughes noticed the link with the ceremonial languages of religions. An example might be the use of the Latin liturgy in a Catholic church, but Hughes sought deeper, pre-Christian roots. He found them in the 2,000-year-old Persian language, Avesta, only used for ritual purposes. The intellectual meanings of the words were guarded secrets, but Avesta communicated through sound, the delivery and when it was used. 'In Avesta, there is never any distance . . . between sound and content.[10]

From these fragments, Hughes devised an ancient-and-modern, religious-and-secular, public-and-incomprehensible play, Orghast, CIRT's first world offering in 1971. It was staged in the ruined temple of Persepolis, near Shiraz, high up on a hillside whose beauty 'beggars belief'[11] and the two parts began at sunset and at dawn. The spectators sat cross-legged on mats. A ruined temple provided exits and entrances, from which the actress Irene Worth emerged to deliver oracular utterances. 'Balls of fire were hurled down from the tomb's plunging hillside entrance.'[12]

The Shiraz Festival was under the personal patronage of the Empress of Persia, wife to the Shah, and it was one of the Shah's aims, as a pro-West leader of a Muslim country on the borders of the Soviet Union, to raise Iran's profile in the Western press. It was one of the exotic places to which such familiar visitors to international festivals as the Living Theater, the director Robert Wilson and the composer Karlheinz Stockhausen would come. The Marxist critic Jonathan Hammond dismissed it as 'decadent bourgeois Western art, interlaced with a few home-grown products and traditional Persian and Indian culture, ironically juxtaposed against a pre-capitalist society ... with no visible modern culture of its own'.[13] When the Shah was driven into exile in January 1979, and Iran became a fundamentalist Muslim state, the party was over.

Brook himself came to feel that *Orghast* was too rarified, 'Holy' rather than 'Rough' theatre, to use the distinctions of his book, *The Empty Space* (1968). He wanted to discover whether his company could make contact with 'an optimum audience ... vivid in its response and having a total openness to form, because it had not been conditioned in any way by Western forms.'[14] He took thirty CIRT members around the Sahara to find a public uncontaminated by Western contact. A film crew and a journalist, John Heilpern, went with them. The Saharan villages were not the only ones totally open to form. The CIRT actors had no idea what to expect either. They had a few improvisatory concepts and placed their trust in music, rhythmic speech and a simple set, a rug in a market square. For the villagers of In-Salah, it must have been a strange sight to see such simplicity surrounded by cameras and a battery of lights. Under normal circumstances, they had no electricity. As Brook proudly remarked, 'nothing remotely resembling this had ever happened before in the market.'[15]

A clue as to why this odd adventure took place can be found in the title of Brook's book, *The Empty Space*. When most people think about the theatre, it is far from empty. It is filled with clowns and murders. Brook saw it as a void in which anything could happen. He did not want to find that space filled with the trappings of Western society. In the quest for emptiness, he had something in common with Roland Barthes, who argued in *Writing Degree Zero* (*Le Degré zéro de l'écriture*) (1953) that any writer was liable to get trapped in the hidden assumptions of the language in which he chose to write. Writing 'degree zero' meant cutting away the unnecessary attachments to a word to use it solely with the meaning that the author intended. It was, like the empty space, a philosophical abstraction. In In-Salah, the villagers had their assumptions as well and so they were not 'totally open to form'. Brook was trapped in his assumptions by supposing that they were.

The Saharan journey might have had a religious resonance, a renunciation of the world to discover the true meaning of life, except that none of the CIRT actors were going into the desert alone to commune with God, but were surrounded by cameras. Brook 'scandalised an anthropologist by suggesting that we all have an Africa within us'.[16]

125

'This was based on my conviction that we are each only parts of a complete man: that the fully developed human being would contain what today is labelled African, Persian or English.'[17] To search for other pieces of 'the jigsaw' to complete the 'inner Atlas', CIRT went elsewhere in Africa and the results were seen at the Adelaide Festival in 1980, a trilogy of *The Conference of Birds*, based on a twelfth-century Sufi poem, *The Ik*, from Colin Turnbull's study of a mountain tribe on the verge of starvation, and *Ubu roi*, the parody of empire building.

Whatever the motives for the wandering, it had the effect of transforming a random collection of actors into a team which functioned as one, with a simple but sophisticated style, bold and precise in gesture, a corporate rhythm and the knack of story-telling. They returned to Paris after three years of travel, where Brook started to look for a performance space. Micheline Rozan found it for him, an abandoned music hall near the Gare du Nord, 'wrecked, charred, streaked with rain, pockmarked, yet noble, human, glowing-red and breathtaking'.[18] This became his empty space in Paris and he made no attempt to fill it with machinery. He left the Bouffes du Nord more or less as he found it. Some simple seating was installed and the place was made safe. But the Bouffes du Nord was never empty. Its century's experience was carved on its walls. It had merely been stripped of modernity. That may have been what Brook was seeking, not an empty space but one uncluttered with the twentieth century.

Stein's company at the Schaubühne started out in the opposite direction, with a manifesto, a political philosophy and a resolve to raise the consciousness of the working classes, but they too were drawn to the distant past. At first, they began rehearsals by discussing *The Communist Manifesto* before limbering up and humming. Klaus Peymann found all that democracy rather hard to take and left to improve Shakespeare at the Bochum Schauspielhaus. They staged documentary plays for working-class audiences, but they chafed at the simplicities of an approach in danger of drifting towards agit-prop. They took on a task not less left-wing but more demanding of their talents – to de-mythologise bourgeois drama, starting with *Peer Gynt* (1971), Labiche's *The Piggy Bank* (1973) and Gorki's *Summer Folk* (1974), followed by a modern play, Peter Handke's *They are Dying Out* (1974), whose title reveals what he thought of the middle classes.

Stein wanted to trace the history of the bourgeoisie, but when his company started to unpick the tangle of needs and prejudices which might help to define the European middle-class outlook, they began to find that the Marxist interpretation of history was not wrong, but limiting. They found themselves in the position of not knowing where to stop. They did not want to stop. The process was too interesting. It was always opening new areas of enquiry.

Like Brook, Stein was fascinated by open spaces. In 1976 he staged a promenade production, *Shakespeare's Memory*, in the Spandau film studios, as part of the process for his *As You Like It*, staged at Spandau in 1977. The word 'memory' was ambiguous. It could mean our memories of Shakespeare or Shakespeare's memory of a medieval world transformed by the Renaissance. Stein was trying to pin-point the historical moment when the pastoral order gave way to the new urbanism and capitalism might be said to have begun. What fascinated him about *As You Like It* was the contrast between life at court and the Forest of Arden. He changed the order of the early scenes to make the comparison more marked. At first, the audience stood in a great hall, as if in a manor-house, surrounded by raised platforms. The room was coldly lit and there was a sense of aggression, erupting into the wrestling match. The audience then filed through a narrow tunnel, dripping with rock water, into a pastoral world, with a beech tree, a pool and a farm, where they were allowed to sit and take their ease.

Stein converted *As You Like It* into a play for our times, tinged with ecological green, turning Shakespeare into an unconscious prophet of modern city decay. A dramatist who worked with the Schaubühne, Botho Strauss, went further by writing a modern version of *A Midsummer Night's Dream*, called *The Park* (1984), where Shakespeare's woodland has been desecrated into an urban slum. Stein's *As You Like It* had the merit of invigorating a comedy which had begun to seem merely cute, but, as Anikst might have pointed out, he narrowed the range of meanings.

Like many Elizabethan writers, Shakespeare contrasted two extremes which he whittled back towards a moderate centre. He did not endorse one way of life over the other. The other objection to Stein's *As You Like It* was that the split in sensibility, if it happened at all, did not begin with the Elizabethans, but earlier still. What inspired the Renaissance, what did the very word mean but the re-birth of classical learning? If Stein meant to solve the riddle of Western habits of mind, he had to go back to their origins in the Greek city-states, his next hurdle.

In 1980, he staged Aeschylus' *The Oresteia* in a production which attempted to re-construct Greek theatrical practice, but responded imaginatively to the text. The audience sat in an amphitheatre, confronted by a bare stage on which stood a single statue of a Greek warrior, an image which stressed the character of the civilisation to which Europe was so indebted. The smell of battle was never far away – or the force of Agamemnon's hurtling chariot. There was no naturalistic fighting, but the contrast between the formal movements of the masked chorus and the unseen slaughter which they described provided its own tension. In a 400-page programme, Stein and his *dramaturg*, Marleen Stossel, described Athenian culture and how Socratic logic, binary

127

in form, progressed through conflicting opposites. It was a mental discipline imposed upon those who were suffering the chaos of war. It was militaristic in its very nature.

From that point of view, the Cold War itself could be seen as a wide-screen projection of Athenian logic. One side declared its position, which was immediately countered by the opposite side, until either the problem was solved or, as sometimes happened, both sides became entrenched in bigotry until there was really no alternative but open war. It was what the popular sociologist, Edward de Bono, inventor of 'lateral thinking', called 'rock' logic in his book *I Am Right, You Are Wrong* (1990). He argued that 'water' logic (based on perceptions not syllogisms) should guide humanity as it moved into yet another millennium.

Plato might have countered syllogistically that to avoid such stalemates, it was necessary to believe an Ideal World. There had to be some standards against which the propositions of the conflicting sides could be measured. *The Oresteia*, far from being a symbol of the militaristic society, demonstrated how a peaceful society should react to the upheavals of war. To end blood feuds, Athena instituted the jury system. To pacify unruly passions and the torments of guilt, Orestes sought purification, catharsis. The ancient Furies were tamed into the Eumenides, the kind ones, who only punished those who by common consent deserved to be.

While Stein was examining ancient Greek texts to discover the origins of the Cold War, Brook was engaged in a similar quest but further afield. Brook was influenced by the teachings of George Ivanovich Gurdjieff, the Russian occultist, who died in 1949. Brook made a film about Gurdjieff, *Meetings with Remarkable Men* (1977) and there are likenesses between CIRT and Gurdjieff's Institute for the Harmonious Development of Mankind, established at Fountainebleau in 1922, surviving for fourteen years. Both stressed physical and mental discipline, the universality of human needs, and both the study of the world's religions.

After his African trilogy, Brook began research into his next major project, a stage version of the ancient Sanskrit epic, *The Mahabharata*. There could be no question of a direct adaptation. It was eight times as long as *The Odyssey* and *The Iliad* combined and contained sections of much theological complexity. It was more of an act of homage than a realisation of the text. 'We are not attempting a reconstruction of Dravidian and Aryan India of three thousand years ago. We are not presuming to present the symbolism of Hindu philosophy. In the music, in the costumes, in the movements, we have tried to suggest the flavour of India without pretending to be what we are not.'[19] What they did attempt was to tell the story in three parts, about the struggle between two tribes, the Pandavas and the Khauravas, who belong to the same demi-godlike family, but are torn apart by, among other resentments, a dice game. Jean-Luc Carrière provided the script.

Brook did try to offer the Hindu concept of *dharma* as an alternative to Christian Good and Evil. 'What is *dharma*? That is a question no one can answer, except to say that in a certain sense it is the essential motor. Since it is the essential motor, everything that is in accord with it magnifies the effect of *dharma*. Whatever does not agree with it, whatever opposes or is ignorant of it, isn't "evil" in a Christian sense, but negative. *The Mahabharata* cuts to shreds all the old, traditional Western concepts, . . . founded on an inessential, degenerate Christianity in which good and evil have assumed very primitive forms.'[20]

The Mahabharata was first performed on three evenings at the Avignon Festival in 1985, not in a theatre but in a quarry outside the town, the Carrière Callet, whose cliffs provided a majestic setting. At the end of the week, the three parts were played consecutively on one evening, starting at sunset and ending at dawn, like *Orghast*. It was a little like a short pilgrimage to get there, a boat along the river, a walk up a rocky hillside not unlike India, the scent of the flowers, the sound of ox-horn trumpets and the first sight of a huge natural amphitheatre with its battery of lights. But the most striking feature of *The Mahabharata* was the way in which the actors told the story, simply, athletically and with team precision.

Their appearances were impressive, Ryscard Cieslak's blind and ravaged King Dhritarashtra, Maurice Benichou's Krishna, Bruce Myer's haunted Karna and the unnaturally tall, gaunt figure of Sotigui Kouate's Bishma. Their props were simple, sticks for spears, one large wheel for a chariot (and Fate), strips of dyed silk and Indian cloth; but they were used with an unforced symbolism to convey scenes of warfare, coronations, journeys into the wilderness, arrivals at court and spiritual revelations.

The flexibility of Brook's production enabled *The Mahabharata* to travel around the world and to adapt itself to many different spaces, including the Bouffes du Nord and a Glasgow tram-shed. On film it was less convincing. One effect at Avignon was hard to repeat. In the distant hills, a small fire was started, which leapt down the cliffs in seconds to end by a pool of water. The four elements were part of his staging, fire, water, the red earth and the scented air. They all performed well in Avignon.

In India, the story of *The Mahabharata* is told in many forms, as the Bible is in Europe, in films, comic strips and music. One episode, where King Dhritarashtra begs the god Krishna to restore his sight, only to plead for blindness again when he sees the destruction on earth, has been expanded into a full evening of *Bharat Natyam* dancing. Brook's version lacked the background understanding of the Hindu gods, which may have been why there seemed to be so little difference between Christian and Hindu versions of good and evil. The Khauravas were wicked and the Pandavas were good but innocent. The meaning of *dharma* was lost.

The Mahabharata also demonstrated how much Brook's methods as a director had changed since his days at the RSC. He had become more creative but less experimental. In the 1960s a Brook production usually implied daring effects and dazzling *coups de théâtre*. Now he gave the impression of wanting to avoid anything which might distract from the telling of a story. Although many images in *The Mahabharata* startled with their power and grace, they emerged unselfconsciously, as if woven into the fabric by accident. It could be called a post-Modern production, although he had to work for a lifetime to be as post-Modern as that.

CIRT was one of the few groups where multi-culturalism developed beyond the point of tokenism. Many companies had black or Asian actors within their casts; but CIRT's multi-culturalism was such a way of life that a uniformity of colour or accent would have seemed odd. Brook was so inventive in his choice of playing spaces that it was hard to look a quarry in the face again without wondering to what use it could be put.

Stein's Schaubühne was no less influential. The haunting birch forest in his *Summer Folk* was reproduced in productions around Europe, from Bergen to Belgrade. His main impact was felt in the repertoires of the German state theatres and of those modelled on their example. Standard Shakespeares in the standard Schlegel-Tieck translation fell out of fashion, replaced by more faithful texts in searching productions. A comparison between the programmes of the late 1960s and of the early 1980s reveals how quickly the plays of younger German dramatists were now being snatched up, not only for the studios but the main stages: Kroetz, Handke, Mueller, Thomas Bernhard and Botho Strauss.

In 1985 Peymann replaced Achim Benning as the Intendant of the Burgtheater in Vienna. It was controversial. Peymann was a left-wing radical from West Germany, associated with Handke and Bernhard, noted for his assured, but startling, treatment of Shakespeare's plays. Benning was a leading Austrian actor. Slogans sprayed on walls – 'Prussians, go home!' – were referring to Peymann. Almost at once the Burgtheater changed character. The sentimentality went and so did the too-easy familiarity that such stars as Klaus-Maria Brandauer and Fritz Mulier enjoyed with their public. In their place came cool actors from the Bochum Schauspielhaus, like Gert Voss. Plays attacking the Austrian record of fascism appeared on the main stage, such as Bernhard's *Heldenplatz* which was chosen to celebrate the Burgtheater's centenary. One of its targets was the Austrian president, Kurt Waldheim. It caused an uproar.

Stein's Schaubühne fulfilled an Archer–Barker demand for a national theatre. It was not solely a place where classics were performed but where they were also researched. It was different from Tynan's recipe, 'the best of everything', or Hall's, 'a shop-window for the best of British Theatre'. Stein's *Oresteia* and Brook's *Mahabharata* were both concerned with the origins of war, as if they had separately decided to concentrate on the one issue which concerned them most. The first performances of *The Mahabharata* came at an apt moment. Every generation everywhere will interpret the fight between the Khauravas and the Pandavas in its own way, but in Avignon it was like a plea to end the Cold War. For the first time in forty years this seemed just possible.

The last months of Chernenko's life were depressing for those who hoped for change. The old guard in Moscow were clamping down on dissidents. Even Lyubimov was sacked from the Taganka. After Chernenko's death, a new General Secretary of the Communist Party was appointed in March 1985, a younger man, cosmopolitan and more friendly in his ways, Mikhail Gorbachev. In Moscow, there was a perceptible feeling of relief. Few dared to hope that the barriers which had divided the world for so long would be dismantled in the near future, but Anikst was one of those who confidently predicted that it would happen in his son's lifetime.

It was this new feeling of optimism which so perfumed the night air as we walked up the rocky paths to the Carrière Callet.

12

THE NATIONAL THEATRE
IS YOURS

'Where the fuck are we?'
(From *The Romans in Britain*, 1980)

With its customary timing, the NT moved from the Old Vic to its new building on the South Bank eleven months after its last deadline on 23 April 1975, a symbolic date, Shakespeare's birthday, and about six years after Stein had declared that big state theatres were a thing of the past. By March 1976 the complex was not complete, but Hall sidled his company into the one auditorium which was nearly ready, the Lyttelton. The others opened during the course of the next few months, the Olivier and the Cottesloe, although some stage equipment still did not work.

Hall decided to move in prematurely because he was convinced that otherwise the place would never be finished. Other directors might have welcomed an extra year at the Old Vic to strengthen the company which could be enlarged later; but Hall came to the NT, as he had done to the Shakespeare Memorial Theatre, with a grand plan in his mind. He faced up to his task with the zeal of someone who once taught business management to army officers. He had three theatres to fill, he sketched out his programme and employed a large company, only to discover that the enemy was advancing in a pincer movement and nothing was what it seemed.

Hall could not be blamed for the building delays, nor could the NT's Board, the South Bank Board, which commissioned the place, for the contractors who failed to deliver or the men on site. Excuses, as well as insults, were flying in all directions. One culprit was the government which should have removed the ceiling price on the costs before November 1974, because inflation had made it of academic interest. Wilson's Labour Party had been returned to power in March 1974 and they could blame the previous Tory government under Edward Heath. Heath could blame the sudden rise in oil prices in 1973, which had triggered off a spiral of inflation in which incomes chased prices, and vice-versa, and caused havoc, of which one sign was the mess on the South Bank.

To de-construct still further the house that Jack was having such difficulty in constructing, this example of instability in world commodity prices could be blamed on past colonialism or recent de-colonialism, according to the two prevailing Cold War opinions. The same authorities were agreed that Britain could have handled the situation better if it had either had a command economy, as in the East, or a free market system, as in the United States. Its own supply of oil might have helped, but Britain had not started to tap the oil-fields in the North Sea. It had to put up with the demands of the oil-producers.

Some countries fared worse and others better. In Britain, the annual rate of inflation was 26 per cent, but in Israel it had reached 180 per cent. The failure to cope with what was not so unpredictable a crisis was a sign of how rigid the political systems had become, how stale the mental habits behind them. Both Wilson and Heath tried to enlist the support of the unions in the battle against inflation and when that failed, introduced a prices and incomes policy. Many union leaders were sympathetic, but they were paid to improve the living standards of their members. If they seemed too inclined to accept wage restraint, there were those in their ranks who would attack such deals as con-tricks of capitalism.

There was no inflation in the Soviet Union. Wages were fixed, prices were fixed and the rouble, to which all Eastern European currencies were tied, was as steady as a rock. One attraction of socialism was that it protected people from the uncertainties of the market. Inflation was the particular problem of societies like Britain which tried to combine some elements of a command economy with a degree of democratic freedom. While the Soviet Union may have avoided the curse of inflation, it had other difficulties, summed up by the title given to Brezhnev's time, the Years of Stagnation. Nothing was happening. The old Stalinist factories were falling apart, the shop assistants still totted up bills on abacuses and the most familiar sign in the back streets was that of the little repair shops. If you wanted to buy something special, such as an orange, you went to the black market, which was subject to inflation. If you required a special service, you needed *blat*, the bribery which became so widespread that it amounted to a secondary system of exchange.

After 1973, as the memory of the Vietnam war receded, the claims of the left came under critical scrutiny. David Hare's *Fanshen* (1974), produced by Joint Stock, a Stein-like collective, offered an account, based on William Hinton's book of the same name, of how one Chinese village transformed itself through socialism. It was a success touring the small theatres but by 1975, when more was known about the Cultural Revolution, its utopianism sounded, to say the least, dated. Hare and Howard Brenton turned their attack towards Western corruption (*Brassneck*, 1973) and cynicism (Hare's *Plenty*,

1978). The argument of many left-wing writers of the time was that the economies of socialist countries may not have grown as they might under capitalism but more care was taken of real people. The curse of the West was consumerism: the full shelves in the shops were a matter of reproach. It caused environmental damage. As unemployment became a threat in Britain, they pointed to the Soviet Union where nobody was unemployed, by law.

Anyone who had thoughtfully travelled in Eastern Europe knew that such claims were ridiculous. There was more corruption in the Soviet Union than in Britain, the social services were if anything worse, factories were more polluting and the British unemployed were better off than the *baboushkas* who chipped the ice from the steps of Moscow's Lenin Library. The conviction that socialism must be better somewhere was hard to shake, but it left a trail of unreality across Western drama.

The divisions in the labour movement grew between those who were still convinced that full-blooded socialism was the only answer to Britain's problems and those who believed that this cure was worse than the illness. Heath sought an agreement with the National Union of Miners in 1973/4, failed, went to the country on a 'Who governs Britain?' slogan and lost to Wilson. Wilson's successor, James Callaghan, tried to sit out the 'Winter of Discontent' in 1979, called an election and lost to Heath's successor, Mrs Thatcher. Britain was becoming ungovernable.

In August 1976, Hall faced a strike of stage technicians, NATTKE members, who figured that now was the time, before the new theatre was open, to sort out their futures. It was settled by a compromise in which the basic pay was in line with the West End, but they had the chance of making a lot more on overtime. Such deals were a consequence of becoming an 'industrial/commercial complex',[1] in the NT's words, and not a theatre in the normal sense, where people might be prepared to work for less.

This did not go down well with other theatre managers, who complained in October 1974 that the demands of the new NT might absorb the country's stock of skilled technicians.[2] Nor was this danger confined to backstage staff. Hall wanted to assemble the best acting talents in the country for his company. He hoped that the NT would become a shop window for British theatre, a laudible aim, but this was no comfort for managements who might find that their best professionals were being lured to the South Bank. It cheered few of them to know their taxes paid for the subsidies to undermine their work.

The gap between the amount of money given to the NT and the best subsidised regional theatre (apart from the RSC) widened in Hall's first years. In 1973–4, the last Olivier year, the NT received £450,534 as opposed to £121,200 given to the Birmingham Rep, a ratio of under 4 to 1. In 1975–6 (*before* the move to the South Bank in 1975–6) Hall's

NT received £1,931,500 while the Nottingham Playhouse got £177,303, a ratio of nearly 11 to 1. The big leap in the NT's subsidy can be explained by the preparations for the new theatre, but it helped Hall to out-bid his rivals.

In his *Memoirs*, Hall bitterly complained about the hostility of the press[3] and the jealousies of the profession, Olivier's old guard among them;[4] but he had embarked upon a course which was bound to bring him into collision with half the theatres in the country. It came at a time when every theatre was suffering from inflation but particularly those new theatres which had been brought into being in the late 1960s as monuments to civic pride. The cost of window cleaning at the Birmingham Rep could have paid for one production. Overheads like these were unavoidable. The only place where economies could be made was on the stage.

The most tightly run ships best rode out the storm. In Scarborough, the Stephen Joseph theatre prospered – on a 'new plays' policy, more-over. Since these were often provided by Alan Ayckbourn, Director of Productions since 1970, the best British writer of well-made comedies, and often produced 'in-the-round', keeping the set costs low, this was less surprising.

Hall's NT was able to buy what others were reluctant to sell. In this respect, his position was distantly similar to the Prince Littler Consolidated Trust in the 1940s, except that the war was now with inflation and Hall did not use his own money. Conscious of the jealousy that his privileged position aroused, Hall went out of his way to assert that all theatres should be given more subsidy and that the negligible amounts given in Britain were a scandal when compared with those given to German theatres or to those in the East whose citizens were poor but valued Culture.

There was another strand of opinion which was having doubts about Hall. They might be called mature radicals, knowledgeable and above-the-battle. They included critics and arts editors who had supported Hall and the NT movement in the past. They agreed that Hall had been a dashing leader of the RSC, and shown his mettle in his support for Brook, but that he could be somewhat glib.

'The theatre,' Hall said in a TV interview with Tynan, 'is society's debate with itself – at flashpoint.' The last two words were over the top. Hall talked about 'high-definition' acting, a Tottenham Court Road phrase which he applied to almost anything he liked. But there could be 'good' in something struggling to define itself, not sharp or precise, but provocatively cloudy. Hall's image of the NT as a shop-window for British talents could be a substitute for having an artistic vision of his own. His use of the word *talents* was suspect too, as if some were innately gifted while others were not and that the best companies assembled them together. When asked what he would like to direct at the NT, Hall answered with deep sincerity, 'The Oresteia,' and added, toughening up, 'or a season of German Expressionism in association with the National Film Theatre'.[5]

His better side as the NT's Director was shown by the way in which he brought writers and directors from the regions and gave them their heads. Bill Bryden came down south from the Edinburgh Lyceum to explore the flexibility of the Cottesloe's stage. His team's promenade performances, Lark Rise (1978), and The Mysteries (1979), were a delight. Richard Eyre (from Nottingham), Michael Rudman (from the Traverse and Hampstead) and Peter Gill (from Riverside Studios) joined the company, as did Alan Ayckbourn, although he retained his links with Scarborough. He brought in the Oxbridge radicals, Hare and Brenton, who had risen through the ranks of Portable Theatre, Joint Stock, the Royal Court and the Nottingham Playhouse to the NT with commendable speed for those who wanted to 'disrupt the spectacle'.

British theatre was well-stocked with those who had good track records, not only in terms of its own history but internationally too. This was often attributed to the Swinging Sixties but the Feeble Fifties made their contribution as well, with Pinter, Scofield, Ayckbourn, Finney and Hall himself, while the Thrombotic Thirties and the Tintinabulating Twenties provided Gielgud, Richardson and Peggy Ashcroft. If for no other reason, Hall's NT should be celebrated for providing such a rich feast.

By 1980, Hall had become the most powerful British impresario since the heyday of Beaumont. His most notable protégé was the young director whom he had picked out to succeed him at the RSC, Trevor Nunn. After an uncertain start, Nunn's RSC gained in confidence and offered Shakespearian spectaculars in Stratford and London, his musical of The Comedy of Errors (1976) among them; but the best examination of the texts came in the studios, notably Buzz Goodbody's Hamlet (1975) and Nunn's Macbeth (1976). In its rich self-assurance, the RSC was the only contender to the NT which, since they were both now 'centres of excellence' and funded accordingly, was itself a tribute to the power of subsidy.

From the Arts Council's point of view, despite mutterings from its Drama Panel, it was convenient to have someone like Hall who could be entrusted with the kind of value judgements inherent in the giving of grants. Hall was a member of the Council itself from 1969–72. The amounts of money given to the NT and the RSC were not within the province of the Drama Panel, but negotiated at higher levels. It was not its business to discuss whether the NT was worth nearly sixteen times the amount given to the Sheffield Crucible, as was the case in 1981–2.

The government was happy that at last the NT could be deemed a success, a 'centre of excellence' in the broadest meaning of the phrase, that is, not confining itself solely to excellence. One of the Arts Council's original purposes had been to spread artistic excellence around the country, 'raise and spread', the old motto. In those far-off days, it was hoped that the regional reps might mount a challenge to Beaumont's West End; but, as Hall pointed out, there was only a limited supply of real talent in the country. It was better to assemble the talents in two centres of excellence and send them out on tour or, in the RSC's case, for festival seasons at Newcastle. In that way, the NT and the RSC could properly be described as 'national', although, as Hall reluctantly mentioned, such touring policies were expensive. But there need be no loss of regional access to 'high-definition' productions, if enough money were given to the nationals.

Hall's support from the Great and the Good remained firm. In 1974, MPs in the Commons described his opponents, who must have included Olivier, Tynan and Jonathan Miller, as 'gnats', 'rats', 'jackals' and 'gadflies'.[6] Five years later, questions had to be asked in the Lords about the NT's attempt to block the sales of the officially unofficial history of the National Theatre.[7] Plurality in parliament in this instance was not a privilege to be extended to those who held an alternative point of view.

Apart from the impact that the nationals were having upon the rest of the theatre system, there was the more difficult question of aesthetic standards. Hall wanted a nucleus of high-definition productions, surrounded by those which he might have described as a bit fuzzier. He balanced the broadly centrist plays in the NT's repertoire with the broadly leftist, but Michael Blakemore was one of those who thought that his choices were too uncritical. Blakemore was unhappy that Hall wanted to direct William Douglas-Home's *The Kingfisher* in the Lonsdale vein, tears-through-the-smiles, although this project was thwarted by the commercial management which owned the rights. If the NT was going to stage everything from boulevard romances to trenchant hard-left stuff, it would not be setting the standards but merely reflecting them. The press might jump to the conclusion that *The Kingfisher* was being put on to secure a privately profitable West End transfer.

Blakemore left the NT shortly after it had moved to the South Bank, the last member from Olivier's regime to do so. For several years. Hall faced little opposition within company or outside it, apart from the usually friendly rivalry with the RSC. He contributed his own high-definition productions, among them Beckett's *Happy Days* with Peggy Ashcroft and Pinter's *No Man's Land*, to which Gielgud and Richardson brought the long experience of their acting lives. Hall's Shakespeares were un-Kott-like and mainly uncut. Nobody, he said, ever cut notes from

Mozart's music. Mozart was Salieri's victim in Peter Shaffer's *Amadeus* (1979), his greatest success at the NT, which went to Broadway, into the West End and was made into a film. Mozart was an uncouth lad, but he had a gift for music which must have been inspired by God, for his manuscript, apart from its wonderful music, was clean and neat, unlike the crossings-out of lesser composers. Salieri, an envious, older musical hack, resented Mozart's natural talent and plotted his downfall. Whether he murdered him or not is left unresolved.

It might have been a parable for his times, as Hall saw them. Talent was an innate gift and inspiration was divine. It had to be protected from those envious people who wanted to destroy it. The New York critic John Simon was probably among them. He had taken Shaffer to task for his repeated use of the love–hate of an older man for a talented boy, a cap which fitted *Amadeus* as much as it did *Equus* (Dysart and Strang) and *The Royal Hunt of the Sun* (Pizzaro and Atahualpa). He disliked the way in which Shaffer seemed to disguise homo-eroticism. 'The play pullulates with dishonesty' he wrote of *Equus*.[8] Others felt similarly about *Amadeus*, although the reviews were in general enthusiastic.

The poet James Fenton, then the critic for *The Sunday Times*, objected to the clichés about artistry. Because Mozart was divinely gifted, he sat down at a piano and thumped out a marvellous tune. It was art with the problems removed. It precluded hard choices and difficult decisions. It emphasised facility in a way which would have won the approval of Vasari, the Mannerist critic of the Renaissance. Shaffer changed the text for Broadway, but there was a symbolism both in the success of *Amadeus* and in its image of Art, as conveyed by Hall's NT.

Facility does not always mean glibness. Ayckbourn wrote his plays quickly, but he was always thinking about them and asking why his local audiences, who meant more to him than the West End, laughed at this line rather than that. His private workshop was Scarborough where he settled after twelve years as an actor, BBC producer and writer, having had two West End hits already. Here he polished his skills. No British comedy can match the intricacy of *The Norman Conquests* (1974), three plays set in one house over one weekend with the same three couples, but set in different rooms. What happens off-stage in one is on-stage in another. Laughter accumulated from play to play. The more you knew, the funnier it seemed and few complained that it was the same plot.

This was craftsmanship in the Beaumont and Abbott tradition and *The Norman Conquests* triumphed in reps around the world, but they could not have been written without Scarborough. The place itself was his secret asset in the competition with other good writers of well-made comedies from his generation, Michael Frayn, Simon Gray and Alan Bennett, who made their names in the 1970s. Frayn's *Noises Off* (1982), a farce about a disastrous run of a really terrible old farce, played almost everywhere in the 1980s, even at Havel's old theatre, the Balustrade. Gray's *Quartermain's Terms* (1981) was comparable with the best of Rattigan. Ayckbourn wrote plays where his grasp of story-telling matched his wit. This allowed him to take some startling risks, among them asking the audience to decide what the endings should be.

His bigger gambles lay in leading his Scarborough public where they did not want to go but, for one reason or another, Ayckbourn thought that they should. At the end of the first acts of well-made comedies, writers usually want to send out punters laughing to the bars, but in *Joking Apart*, he did the reverse. The story is of an attractive couple, Anthea and Richard, with three children and a circle of friends who feel inadequate in their company. In the absence of their hosts, their friends talk about them and their remarks are as poisonous as acid rain. Their malice brought the first act to a telling but sombre conclusion.

In the last act Anthea's daughter, Debby, asked her mother why all their friends are 'lost-looking'. Anthea replied that as a family they have been 'very lucky' and 'it really is up to us who have, to help the others a little bit'. This provoked a laugh at Scarborough, where it was first produced in 1977, for their help has wrought havoc all round. In retrospect, *Joking Apart* can be seen as the first stage attack on what came to be known, under Mrs Thatcher, as 'the dependency culture'. Ayckbourn was rarely a didactic writer, but in *Way Upstream* (1983), he warned against the anarchy into which he felt Britain was sliding. This was more effective in its Scarborough simplicity than in the pond with real waves at the NT to which it transferred, but it was not one of his successes. In comparison with other attacks on what was wrong with Britain, his level-headedness looked like concession.

In 1980, Michael Bogdanov had directed Brenton's *The Romans in Britain* which became a *cause célèbre*. Brenton drew an analogy between the Roman invasion of Britain and the English occupation, as he saw it, of Northern Ireland. In one scene, a centurion tried to rape a naked male Celt and enlarged the anus with his sword to make the passage easier. It provoked a court case on the grounds of obscenity, which the NT won, but it distracted from the point that Brenton was trying to make. Was he trying to say that England was buggering Ireland? High-definition productions are much improved when high-definition thought goes into them.

This was one problem with Hall's NT. The range of productions might seem to be admirable, but it sacrificed content to style. Hall's *Oresteia* was superficial when compared with Stein's at the Schaubühne, though more convincing than the RSC's eleven-hour epic, *The Greeks*, an amalgam of plays adapted by John Barton to tell the story of the Trojan Wars. Left-wing plays jostled with revivals of musicals and boulevard comedies. So broad a tolerance had a reductive effect, but the pre-eminence of the nationals meant that Hall had little choice but to try to please everybody.

Hall's NT was brought into being by a government policy confident that the state should be able to fund all acceptable shades of opinion. It was not an attempt at thought control, but at thought restraint. If an artistic hierarchy could be created, where the underlings struggled to get into the two top companies, the system could be steered from top to bottom in the British manner. When in 1987 he started to tidy his desk for the Last Goodbye (to the NT), he helped to appoint his successor, Richard Eyre. It was the year when Alastair Milne resigned angrily from the BBC and the consensus which had held Britain together over twenty years, Butskellism Mark 2, broke up. The notion of the state handing out patronage to the arts was no longer accepted so readily and Hall himself was in some trouble. A change had taken place in British politics which despised the old nostrums and treated the former virtues of 'tolerance' and 'compromise' as little better than dirty words.

When Margaret Thatcher came to power in January 1979, she looked and sounded much like an Ayckbourn character, a nice lady, with an over-impeccable accent, upwardly mobile from Grantham, busy and bright, spreading havoc among those less fortunate than herself. Her image became more calculated in office. She took voice lessons from an NT actor to sound less shrill in the House of Commons. Her hair was crisp and *bouffant*. Her phrases were rounded to be more quotable by a dramatist, Ronald Millar.

Hugo Young has described her childhood as the daughter of a thrifty shopkeeper in his biography, *One of Us*, whose title is both apt and ironic. Margaret Thatcher never saw herself as belonging to the establishment, certainly not of that sprawling octopus with its tentacles in the universities, the arts, the media and the *quangos*, which had ruled Britain since the 1960s. She rebelled, and surrounded herself with like-minded rebels, and the implication of her phrase, 'one of us', was that so-and-so was 'not one of them'. She appealed to an old brand of Toryism (though not to 'shire' Toryism) which placed an emphasis on patriotism, self-help, good housekeeping, low taxes and less government. As a woman, she was not a member of any male London clubs and her assertiveness, according to Young, stemmed partly from her determination not to be patronised by those who were.

In her view, the words 'consensus' and 'compromise' were tainted, because they suggested that the arguments had not been considered sufficiently carefully to reach an agreement. This particularly applied to management–union deals where both sides put up their bargaining figures, splitting the difference. Such settlements took no account of what the public was prepared to pay. When the bargaining bodies had monopolistic powers, the results bore no relationship to market forces and if governments financed such deals out of taxation or by printing money, the effects were inflationary and everyone suffered. This, according to Mrs Thatcher, was a major cause of Britain's decline.

She wanted to reverse the process, to keep management–union deals away from government, to de-nationalise industry and to restrict the supply of money. Monetarism, a term associated with the US economist Milton Friedman was more than economic theory and only slightly less than a moral philosophy. It rested on the belief that money was the language of transactions, representing the exchange of goods or services between one person (or a group of people) and another. If a government printed money to buy its way out of trouble, it ran the risk of not only of de-valuing the currency but of de-basing all the transactions which went with it. Inflation was not just an economic problem but in a wide sense a social one. If people could not rely on the currency, how could they plan for the future or manage their affairs in the present?

Many economists found this analysis simplistic, not only in such a précis. A standard description of inflation was of too much money chasing too few goods, which suggested two solutions, either the restriction of money or the increase of productivity. If money became so restricted that it sent profitable firms into bankruptcy, there could be inflation from lack of goods, as well as from unemployment. Something more delicate was required, a balance between goods and money, but governments could do little about productivity, not being productive themselves. They were confined to the one-sided solution of restricting money supply.

Friedman's theory could be applied to sign systems which were not currencies. Mrs Thatcher once remarked that 'the prime tool of government was plain English'. If a government controls the flow of information, and the framework in which it is presented, how can anyone trust what is being asserted? Monetarism had a direct message for the arts. How could any government decide how much art people wanted to see to allocate grants accordingly? How could it fix the levels of subsidy for various kinds of art? It was impossible, but governments had bequeathed such a system. One odd feature of Thatcherism was not that the arts suffered from a lack of subsidy but that her economic liberalism did not extend to freeing the arts altogether from state intervention.

When she came to power, she promised arts lobbies that she would not make 'candle-end economies', which was taken to mean that she would not cut off their subsidies. During her years in office, grants to the Arts Council kept pace with inflation and sometimes rose above it, although they did not make up for the losses from the rate-capped local authorities or the abolished Metropolitan Councils. One way to earn more money might have been to have made films for the video industry or for TV. Broadcasting was facing a technology-led revolution. It was now possible with optical-fibre cabling (rather than satellites) to have an almost unlimited number of channels, but when the Home Office cautiously allowed a few more, it accompanied each liberalising measure with more layers of censorship. They were introduced to defend the 'Consumer Protection Requirements', so-called to remind the public that they were being censored for their own good.

Thatcherism was compounded of paradoxes. In his biography Young pointed out how the meaning of monetarism shifted during her years. Her aim may have been to reduce the powers of central government, but in many respects she increased them. There were fewer *quangos* but those that remained were stocked with her supporters. After her election victory, she quoted St Francis of Assisi, 'Where there is discord, may we bring harmony . . .', but no Prime Minister seemed to welcome more the prospect of confrontation. To cure inflation, she risked mass unemployment and brought in laws to curb the power of the unions, accepting the prospect of riots in the streets. The test of strength against those whom she dubbed the 'enemy within' came in 1984, when the National Union of Miners staged a national strike against pit closures. She chose her ground carefully and, unlike Heath's, her government won.

The broad-left treated her simply as a class enemy. *Ditch the Bitch* screamed the title of one play from the Theatre Workshop, Stratford. But her class was not that of the old establishment or of the new yuppies, but of those middle classes who tried to do their best under circumstances which in the 1970s always seemed to be against them. Under Thatcher, British velvet prisoners were most at risk, as the last months of Hall's NT regime illustrate.

In July 1986 *The Sunday Times* ran articles accusing Hall and Nunn of making fortunes at the expense of the taxpayer. Several examples were given, but the one which set the trend was that of *Amadeus*. The rights to *Amadeus* were acquired by the US commercial producers, the Shubert Organization, one and a half years before its world première at the NT. The production costs were carried by the NT, but the bulk of the profits went to the Shuberts. Any commercial management would have wanted to secure a good cut of the royalties in return for this favour. According to *The Sunday Times*, the NT received 10 per cent of Shaffer's royalties, some $320,000, whereas Hall as its NT and Broadway director received £2 million. Hall said that it was only £720,000, but in any case the British taxpayer received a raw deal and Hall a profitable one.

Questions then arose as to why it was not known at the time and took so long to be publicised. In 1977, the Arts Council and the NT's Board were warned that such deals were likely unless steps were taken to prevent them.[9] In 1983 a letter in the *Evening Standard* described the *Amadeus* arrangement,[10] but only in 1986 did it become a scandal. One answer might be that there was no longer a shell of the Great and the Good to protect Hall. Even the Arts Council seemed reluctant to support him in public. Another could be that in 1985 the NT staged Brenton and Hare's *Pravda*, whose central figure, a power-mad press tycoon, was thought to be modelled on Rupert Murdoch, who owned *The Sunday Times*. Were the articles his revenge?

This incident did little good to the cause of the arts lobby. The Arts Council's influence dwindled. Subsidised theatres were told to seek business sponsorship and more from the box-office, but the original aim of giving grants to the arts had been to counter the effects of commercialism. Mrs Thatcher's ideological ancestors were said to be Adam Smith and the Manchester liberals, but whereas Smith and Gladstone championed free speech, she left the impression of wanting all views to conform to her own. This led to cabinet resignations and in November 1990 to a party *coup* in which she was replaced by John Major whose manner was as conciliatory as hers could be provocative, although their views might be similar.

Mrs Thatcher sometimes tried not to give the impression that she was a leader in internal exile. Her supporters continued to claim that she had fought against the British weakness for compromise, which preserved privilege at the expense of national purpose, and that in her three terms of office she had rallied the Western will to fight back against communism. World communism in any case was suffering the fate which Marxists once predicted for capitalism. It was collapsing from its internal contradictions.

13

BROADWAY BABIES

'Good times and bum times,
I've seen them all and, my dear,
I'm still here.'

(From *Follies*, 1971)

While Peter Brook sought a universal theatrical language 'which touches people as music does',[1] it could have been argued that he was trying to re-invent the wheel, for the most popular genre world-wide *was* the musical, as it had been for decades. It may not have been a kind of theatre to which he was attracted, with its lavish sets, rampant technology, cheap tunes and trite plots, but in most major cities outside communist countries, where there were big enough stages, Western musicals were the chief attraction.

In the Soviet Union, about a third of the 625 main subsidised theatres were operetta houses. The critics ignored them, the seat prices were high because the subsidising authorities thought them less worthy of grants and there were fewer block bookings from the trade unions; but the operetta houses were usually packed. In 1984, a new musical was in rehearsal in the Siberian city of Novosibirsk. It was written by a local composer, Anatol Dierov, and called *It's That Cat Again*, a title which echoed the Western musical *Cats*, which many had heard of but nobody had seen.

It had the makings of something dreadful with its story of a randy tomcat on the tiles and a chorus of pussies in boots, wearing fish-net tights and stetson hats. The artistic director, Eleanor Takova, was asked how this squared with the policy of 'raising the consciousness of the people' and she replied that it taught the public about the value of social relationships.[2]

It's That Cat Again was part of a repertoire which included Offenbach's *Orpheus in the Underworld* and Romberg's *The Student Prince*. The operetta house was the most charming theatre in Novosibirsk, less bombastic than the huge opera built by Stalin in 1942 as a kind of

144

Kremlin beyond the Urals and less didactic than the local rep, the Red Torch. It was a turn-of-the-century building set in a park whose birches in winter tinkled with icicles. To drive up to its pillored entrance in a sleigh laden with furs, to mingle with couples dressed up in preserved evening dresses and dinner jackets, and to watch a musical play about maidens, princes or tomcats was to catch sight of Soviet society in what might be deemed its un-reconstructed form.

Such operettas may have been harmless trips down Memory Lane, but they reflected a yearning for the days before the Revolution which could be felt throughout Eastern and Central Europe. In Poland, a longing for the past almost amounted to a national disease, while in Hungary, there was a brisk trade in Austro-Hungarian memorabilia. In the large but musty ballroom of the Balkan Hotel in Sofia, Bulgaria, a string trio in velveteen jackets played selections from Strauss, while courting couples dipped their tea-bags in luke-warm water.

The attitude of the communist authorities to such displays of bourgeois backsliding was mixed. Perhaps they could do nothing about them, but probably they were divided between preserving the standards of a lost culture to prove that they could be civilised too and getting rid of them altogether to show that a socialist society was different. This conflict in ideological priorities can be traced back to the early years of the Revolution. Havel's play, *Restoration*, described how it affected an architectural department which never knew whether to tear down old buildings or to preserve them as if in a museum.

The authorities did wish to stress that the old ways were class-oppressive and when a reactionary operetta was revived, it was often accompanied by lengthy programme notes which explained in what historical context it should be interpreted. Whether they were read or not is another matter. There were plays which used operettas to present the spectacle of old-world societies dancing to disaster, such as Slawomir Mrozek's *Tango* (1964) and Witold Gombrowitz's *Princess Ivona* (1938) and *Operetta* (1966).

Mrozek and Gombrowitz were Polish Absurdists living in exile in France, which did not endear them to the authorities, but *Operetta* in particular combined music and spectacle with a sound ideology. It should have been a perfect retort to the operetta houses, unless it was directed to leave the impression that the relics of an oppressive social order were not responsible for the disasters which befell them. Those who remembered the Second World War understood that the upper classes encouraged the Nazis to thrive. Those who did not might enquire who precisely were the barbarians who had destroyed these charming people.

The stylistic attempts to modernise operettas by grafting rock, jazz and blues on to a Viennese frame, as in *It's That Cat Again*, were usually doomed to failure. This was partly due to a lack of first-hand contact with the Western genres, which had to be imitated from smuggled cassettes, but the main stumbling-block was the absence of anything which in the West could be called a youth culture. This seemed odd, because the communist countries spent much time and money on promoting youth activities. Most towns had children's theatres and puppet companies for the very young, while in the local palaces of culture, teenagers were trained in ballet and ballroom dancing, in singing, musicianship and acting. There were more infant phenomena in the Soviet Union than any society could conveniently accommodate and even disco-dancing was taught by trained tutors, counting the beats.

The same methodical approach was taken towards youth culture as was adopted on political matters by the Komsomol, which many teenagers joined as the first step towards advancement in the communist party. In the 1940s, Mikhail Gorbachev was a Komsomol leader, organising holiday camps and rallies. Promoting culture was one of its activities, but it did not encourage independence of thought or fashion. The autocratic nature of Soviet society, oppressively top-down, was reflected in the way in which its students were kept under control. Even to receive a phone-call from a contact in the West was a privilege granted only to those students who had passed their exams. In the Years of Stagnation, the most potent symbol of geriatric rule was the wizened relics on the podium for the May Day parades in Moscow, the veterans of the Second World War, bent with age and medals. When Brezhnev died in 1982, aged 72, and was succeeded by the former head of the KGB, Yuri Andropov, who died after fifteen months in office, and was succeeded by Konstantin Chernenko, aged 73, who died in March 1985, it seemed as if one qualification to lead the communist world was to have been measured by the undertaker.

This was not an accident of history but a flaw in the system, for there was no settled procedure for transferring power from one generation to the next. If Marxist-Leninist principles were observed, it did not matter who carried them out, although the presence of old revolutionaries at the helm could be of symbolic value. Almost throughout the communist world, the leaders ruled until they dropped. Mao Tse-Tung was supposed to be in charge of China until he died in 1976 aged 82. At the lower ends of the Soviet bureaucracy, the quickest way to get promoted was to be the favourite son of a hero about to die.

Even theatre companies were top-heavy with elderly or middle-aged stars on life-long contracts. It was not unusual to find a 50-year-old actor playing Romeo. Among the operetta companies, the principals could be well on into their second childhoods and risking cardiac arrest. When the Czech critic and Shakespearian translator Milan Lukes took over Prague's National Theatre in 1985, his first aim was to lower the average age of the company by about 20 years. He chose youthful plays, like *Love's Labour's Lost*, cast them from promising graduates from drama schools and dressed them in what were by Czech standards daring costumes, slinky Monroe dresses and leather jeans; but there was something old-fashioned about this youthfulness which contrasted with the young tourists from the West who flocked into Wenceslas Square. It was not just a matter of style, although the permanent waves of the girls were somewhat tell-tale, but of mental attitude. It was as if they did not know what was expected of them, whether to be coquettish like Monroe or sullen like James Dean.

The attraction of the West for the post-war generation in the East was how its young people were allowed to behave, sometimes badly, sometimes with style, sometimes both badly and stylishly, as was the case with its rock stars. In 1959, Kruschev on a visit to Hollywood objected to the indecently exposed thighs in *Can Can*, which may have inspired the wardrobe mistress of *It's That Cat Again* to allow more room for the legs. In the 1960s, the Beatles were banned as prime examples of Western decadence, but by the early 1980s, their songs were played on amplified balalaikas by the bands in Intourist hotels. In 1984, the forbidden records included anything which might be described as Heavy Metal or Punk Rock, but a hot form of illegal barter were the smuggled cassettes of *Frankie Goes to Hollywood*.

Western youth culture was hard to control, for each restraint increased the attraction. It was also difficult to explain why such groups as the Rolling Stones should be banned, when *Street Fightin' Man* talked the language of revolution. In at least two ways rock music upset the unspoken laws of communist censorship, by encouraging cosmopolitanism and by providing an example of capitalist freedom. The fact that Mick Jagger was denouncing the police was less important than that he was allowed to do so. In discos across Europe and North America similar sounds could be heard, similar lyrics could almost be heard sometimes (praising peace, denouncing the military) and amplification systems were turned a notch or so higher each year apparently to compensate for the deafness of the authorities. Youth seemed not to be knocking at the door, as in Ibsen, but creating subterranean shock-waves as cellars called out to cellars from Novosibirsk to Detroit. In Britain, Liverpool was temporarily the epicentre.

Most Soviet towns had their Western-style pop groups, whose gigs rarely took place in the palaces of culture. They had their folk singers too, like Bob Dylan, of whom the most famous was the actor Vladimir Vysotsky, although he was never a Dylan imitator. Vysotsky was a star at the Taganka, where he played Hamlet as the perplexed student in 1970, but his concerts drew such crowds that the authorities banned them within a hundred miles of Moscow. The public made pilgrimages to remote towns to hear Vysotsky sing. On his death in 1980, the streets leading to the Taganka were sealed off by the police to prevent a riot of flowers. Lyubimov staged a memorial tribute to Vysotsky, also banned by the authorities, and yet few of his lyrics seemed subversive, except by recording events.

There were official attempts to counter this unpredictable but effective form of propaganda, which was undoing so many positive influences from the Komsomol and the palaces of culture. In 1981, the Lenin Komsomol, the leading young people's theatre in Moscow, staged a rock musical, *Juno and Avos*, whose music was not unlike Galt MacDermot's in *Hair* and whose staging was similar to a David Essex musical, *Mutiny*, in London. A raunchier harder-rock musical was produced in Budapest, *The Ballad of Clement the Mason*, whose leather-clad male chorus might have been described as fascistic in the days before Jagger and the Rolling Stones.

In the West, however, Jagger's fans were starting to look middle-aged. In 1977, a revival of *Hair* ran for only a month on Broadway and the last touring companies had packed away their beads and joss sticks. One of the things of which nobody wished to be reminded was the Vietnam war. After the anything-goes *joie de vivre* of the 1960s, the mood in the United States was cautious to the point of being reactionary. Rock musicals had turned away from the Zen Buddhism of *Hair* to Christianity (*Godspell* and, from Britain, *Jesus Christ Superstar*, 1971), but the most striking feature of what had become a glut of musicals on Broadway was the number of revivals among them, and *pastiche* revivals, and re-constructions of what might have been hits in their time if somebody had bothered to write them.

This was more than a trip down Memory Lane but rather a sixties by-pass. The fashion spread to London where Broadway producers liked to try out musicals because the costs were less and support from the taxpayer might be arranged. The revivals included *Pal Joey*, *Oklahoma!*, *Guys and Dolls* and *Kiss Me Kate* from the 1940s and 1950s, *No, No, Nanette*, *Anything Goes* and the pastiche *Dames at Sea* from the 1920s and 1930s, and *Pirates of Penzance* from the 1870s. They were surrounded by new musicals celebrating past eras, such as *Follies* (1971), *Grease* (1972), *A Little Night Music* (1973), *Chicago* (1975), *On The Twentieth Century* (1978) and *Sugar Babies* (1979). When new old musicals became too expensive to produce, new old compilations took over, *Ain't Misbehavin'* (1978) from the songs of Fats Waller, and *One Mo' Time* (1986). Stephen Sondheim entered this Hall of Fame by compiling himself in *Side by Side by Sondheim* (1977).

Of the six musicals on which Sondheim and the director Harold Prince closely collaborated, three were set in the past, one morosely in the present and two poised half-way between past and present. None was cheerful, upbeat musicals in the Broadway tradition, but warily witty, *angst*-ridden and clever. Sondheim liked to mimic the drive of a show-stopping hit, and often stopped the show, but the rampant energy was put in its place by his watchful lyrics:

'Hey, Mr Producer, I'm talking to you, sir,
I don't need a lot, only what I've got,
Plus a tube of grease-paint and a follow-spot!'[3]

Love was a many-splendoured problem. Among 'the little things you do together', if you unwisely got married, were destroying the children, annoying the neighbours and getting a divorce.[4]

Five of the Sondheim–Prince collaborations were 'concept' musicals, the exception being *A Little Night Music* which was in the operetta tradition. *Sweeney Todd* (1979) had a plot, developed by Chris Bond from the Victorian melodrama, but its concept was to evoke a Victorian factory cityscape where the grimy windows shut out light. 'Separating people from the sun' became Prince's metaphor for 'the incursions of the Industrial Revolution on the poetry within people'.[5] Interpreted like this, Sweeney the Demon Barber was both a victim and an avenging angel, a concept not so far removed from RoboCop and the samaritans of the subway.

The others had fragmentary stories, but not much in the way of linear developments. They conjured up times, places and moral dilemmas (usually left unresolved); and had an 'arc', rather than a plot crisis, where the theme emerged to be developed in depth. Concept musicals encouraged designers to use the resources of modern theatres, lasers for *Jesus Christ Superstar*, a wrap-around railway track for *Starlight Express* (1985), holograms (*Time*, 1987), and complicated sound and lighting effects. When Prince went into later rehearsals, he was wired up with communication systems like Frankenstein's Monster. Composers and lyricists were given more space for parody and to extend the orchestrations so that they commented ironically on the action. The occasional Wagnerian *leit-motif* could be detected. The songs were extended into individual stories and often sung by characters who had little connection with whatever plot wasn't quite there.

Sondheim was an expert at parody as a composer and lyricist. Like Prince, he received a training in the Broadway disciplines. His childhood mentor was Oscar Hammerstein Jr, whom he knew from the days of *Oklahoma!*. After Hammerstein's death, Sondheim wrote lyrics for Richard Rodgers (*Do I Hear a Waltz?*, 1965), Hammerstein's partner. He studied musical composition with the composer Milton Babbit, and Prince first employed him as two-talents-in-one for *A Funny Thing Happened on the Way to the Forum* (1962). 'I'm a pasticheur,' Sondheim modestly remarked, 'I can imitate virtually any style of music after hearing it briefly.'[6] He was never, unlike Bernstein, attracted to grand opera nor, unlike Prince, to Brecht. His forte was the musical.

To describe his tributes to the Broadway masters in *Company* (1970) and *Follies* (1971) as *pastiche* would under-estimate their inventiveness. He could ham his originals so outrageously that it amounted to caricature, but he also borrowed their styles to develop them with intricacy and sophistication. In *Company*, he chose one of Irving Berlin's favourite tricks, patter verses counterpointing a slow soaring melody. Berlin wrote such a song for *Call Me Madam* ('You're Just in Love'). Sondheim's 'Getting Married' had a *kitsch* wedding hymn as its melody, while the patter verses expressed the panic at the thought of wedlock.

Follies was set in an old vaudeville house, scheduled for demolition, where the Weismann Follies used to be staged in the years between the wars. Dmitri Weismann (modelled on Ziegfeld) invited his middle-aged stars back to the scene of their former glories. The slight plot described how they'd gotten on all these years, but it provided a framework for Sondheim's parodies of the song styles of Broadway's musical theatres – of Sigmund Romberg ('One More Kiss'), of George Gershwin ('Losing My Mind') and of Cole Porter ('I'm Still Here'). One song recalled Frank Loesser's 'Standing on the Corner' (watching all the girls go by) from *The Most Happy Fella* (1956). In comparison, Sondheim's 'Waiting for the Girls Upstairs' was sadder in tone and more complicated in texture, an octet where the two principal couples, Mr and Mrs Stone (affluent, jaded) and Mr and Mrs Plummer (less affluent, frustrated), were joined by the ghosts of their younger selves, when they were just Phyllis, Ben, Sally and Buddy, hopeful and making up their minds. The lyrics described the taut nerves of two young men about to go on the town with their girls from the chorus, senses attuned to the sights and sounds backstage.

> 'Clicking heels on steel and cement,
> Picking up the giggles floating down through the vent.'

The music contrasted their old high hopes with their new low mid-life crises. 'Weren't we chuckleheads then?' mused Ben.[7]

The song was a tribute to a world well lost, not to Follies the Show, but the follies of innocence. The parody was so much richer than the original that it may seem unnecessary to have recalled Loesser in the first place. There was a dramatic point. Loesser's song evoked Eisenhower's America, catchy, optimistic and cheerfully sexist, whereas Nixon's America was cynical and worldly wise, still suffering from the sickness of the Vietnam war. The parody of a Cole Porter list song, 'I'm Still Here', gave a quick summary of the tough times that one girl, Carlotta, battled through to survive:

> 'Been called a pinko, commie tool.
> Got through it stinko by my pool.
> I should have gone to an acting school,
> That seems clear.
> Still someone said, "She's sincere."
> So I'm still here.'[8]

In *Merrily We Roll Along* (1981), the Sondheim-Prince musical which did not quite work and brought their association to a big gap (if not an end), this mulling over the past is expressed by backtracking the lives of Kennedy hopefuls who sell out to the system, putting wealth before principles.

Sondheim was a virtuoso in love with his craft. He devised crossword puzzles for the *New York Magazine* and his compact lyrics required actor-singers with good diction and a strong sense of irony, like Elaine Stritch and Len Cariou in New York or Julia Mackenzie in London. His songs were more tuneful than they were sometimes credited with, but this did not make them easier to sing. This may have been a reason why none of his musicals with Prince was a smash hit: the longest first run belonged to *Company* with 706 Broadway performances. The loss of story-telling was another factor. Despite his gift for lyrics, Sondheim rarely wrote good dialogue, which he left to the scriptwriters.

Company was based on eleven one-act plays by George Furth about the problems of maintaining marriages or other meaningful relationships in modern Manhattan. Sondheim and Prince chose three stories, to which Furth added a further two, and they devised a frame (as in *Follies*) of a party to celebrate the birthday of a bachelor, Robert, who stayed unpartnered at 35. There was no reason why he should not get married. He wanted to do so to feel the anguish of 'Being Alive', but he couldn't make up his mind, to the irritation of his girl friends, who sing 'I could understand a person, if he actually was dead!'[9] He wasn't, merely paralysed by an emotional *rigor mortis*.

Furth's dialogue, gag-ridden in the Neil Simon manner, was much upstaged by Sondheim's lyrics, cynical to the point of self-destructiveness. World-weariness so prevailed that you had to abandon hope with the hat-check girl. Nor was the sophistication quite what it seemed. There was an air of unreality to it, as if Sondheim had got into the habit of worrying about minor matters while leaving the major ones intact. If *Sweeney Todd* was a weak attack on Victorian capitalism, *Pacific Overtures* (1976) skirted around the question still in everyone's mind. Why had the US got so involved in the politics of Eastern (and South-Eastern) Asia?

The concept of *Pacific Overtures* was the 120-year-old history of Japanese–American relations, no less, told in a style which set-wise imitated Kabuki and music-wise sounded Oriental without being so. A remote Third World culture had been brought up to date by its contacts with the US, but what was lost from its heritage? It was a tale of colonial expansion, the irony being that modern Japan was expanding in the other direction, into the United States. Couldn't the two cultures have always lived in peace, side by side, independently?

Once that particular stone had been lifted, it was hard to ignore the bugs underneath, for the success of Japan's post-war economy, like those of South Korea and Taiwan, was largely due to US efforts to secure allies on the Pacific front line against communism. Such policies went badly astray in the Philippines and, of course, in Vietnam. It was not the right time to go into these issues on Broadway. In the mid-1970s, US optimism reached its post-war, perhaps its all-time, low. The decade began with the realisation that the Vietnam war was a great mistake. After peace was declared, President Nixon was embroiled in the scandal of Watergate and forced to resign under threat of impeachment.

His successor, Gerald Ford, was beaten in the presidential elections of November 1976 by the Democrat Jimmy Carter, whose claims partly rested on the fact that he came from Georgia, not from any East or West coast political establishment. He was Mr Clean, but his trouble-free record was held to reflect his lack of experience. The Republicans made the most of this, casting doubt on the SALT Treaty, which he signed with Brezhnev in 1979 to limit the number of long-range nuclear missiles.

In 1979, the Republicans had an ideal opportunity to destroy Carter's image as a peacemaker. In November, the supporters of the new leader in Iran, Ayatollah Khomeini, who led the revolt against the Shah of Persia, stormed the US embassy in Teheran, taking nearly a hundred members of its staff as hostages. It was a symptom of the fundamentalist Muslim rebellion against the West. In April 1980, there was an attempt to snatch the hostages in a commando-raid which went badly wrong. Carter took the blame and spent time during an election year in negotiating their release. He failed, or was outmanoeuvred, and lost the election as well.

Within ten years, the most powerful nation on earth had been outwitted and even beaten on the battlefield by two Third World countries whose combined national products failed to match the resources of one major US company, General Motors. The US could have retaliated with massive strength, but was deterred by the prospect of drawing the Soviet Union into the fray. There was a sense of national humiliation, made worse by the conviction that the US was basically in the right. It had tried to defend freedom and its reward was to become an international laughing-stock.

If reasons were required to account for Sondheim's pessimism, it was hardly necessary to look beyond this unhappy mood, which also explained the nostalgia. The appeal of Ronald Reagan, actor-turned-president in 1980, was much more apparent in the US than it was elsewhere, a familiar face on the small screen, sticking to the old simplicities, promising a frontier solution. It was not Reagan but Margaret Thatcher who turned the spirit around with a triumph of leadership. The military regime in Argentina invaded the Falkland Islands in the South Atlantic, pursuing a long dispute with Britain about their sovereignty. In neither military nor economic terms were the Falkands of significance, but there was a point of principle at stake. Amid troubles at home which would have daunted most Prime Ministers, Thatcher assembled a Task Force which steamed in to re-capture the islands, 8,000 miles away, in May 1982, in defiance of geographical logic.

As a military feat it was striking enough, but as a symbol of how the West should stand up against dictatorships, it captured the US imagination. When Reagan invaded the little island of Grenada in the Caribbean in October 1983, it looked like an act of copy-cat statesmanship. Thatcher and Reagan gained political support within their own countries as a result of these events and won the following elections, in 1983 and 1984 respectively. In Cold War terms, the campaigns were side-issues, but they carried the message that, despite Vietnam, at least two of the Western allies were prepared to stand firm at whatever cost.

The gloom eventually lifted from Broadway. After *Merrily We Roll Along*, Prince and Sondheim went their separate ways. Prince was alarmed by the rising costs of Broadway musicals. In 1971, *Follies* had cost $700,000 to produce, whereas the amount which had to be raised in 1981 for Tom Eyen's *Dreamgirls* was $3.6 million.[10] For economic reasons alone, he must have been tempted to look across the Atlantic to Britain where Andrew Lloyd-Webber and Tim Rice had been so successful with *Jesus Christ Superstar*. In 1976, he was given the chance to direct their latest musical, *Evita*, in London.

Evita was in some respects the ideal Prince show, which gave him the chance to present the rise and fall of Eva Perón against a background of recent Latin-American history. It must have been galling for Sondheim to listen to Rice's lyrics and repetitions of Lloyd-Webber's theme tune and to observe how the very lack of sophistication seemed to work to the show's advantage. It ran for eight years in the West End, four on Broadway and bred touring companies like rabbits. The authors' youth was part of the embarrassment. They could afford to side with Che Guevara and wag fingers in admonishment against the Americans. That was the advantage of being born British when the Empire had been erased from folk memory. *Evita* could never have been written by Sondheim whose skills at parody never plumbed such depths of the *faux naïf*.

Sondheim veered in the other direction and embraced Art in a big way. *Sunday in the Park with George* (1984) brought to life a painting by the Impressionist Georges Seurat, whose *pointillisme* provided the inspiration for Sondheim's little phrases floating around a *belle époque* park. *Into the Woods*, a concept-musical devised with the writer director, James Lapine, was a *mélange* of fairy tales, commenting in a sort of psychological way on the questing myths of childhood. 'Eventually,' wrote Craig Zadan in *Sondheim and Co.*, 'the show is about community responsibility', while Stephen Banfield pointed out that it 'draws us towords the widest world issues, environmental and political',[11] which was the problem. A glut of relevancy choked the digestion of one good concept. It might have been written on an Arts Council grant.

In London, *Sunday in the Park with George* was given a posh production at the NT in 1990. The rise of the nationals offered the best training ground in Europe for those who wanted to stage large musicals. Nunn took time off from the RSC to direct three of them, *Cats, Starlight Express* and *Chess*, but a fourth, *Les Misérables*, which he co-directed, was a collaboration between the RSC and the British impresario Cameron Mackintosh. There were failures as well with *Seberg* (NT), *Carrie* and *The Clockwork Orange* (RSC). British regional companies gate-crashed the party, notably the Haymarket, Leicester, which revived *Me and My Gal*.

British musicals for the most part gave up the pretence of being anything other than mass entertainment. They lacked Sondheim's sophistication or Prince's early inventiveness. They displayed technical skills in staging and much *panache*, but their measure for success was the box-office. Their global appeal rested on unsubtleties, broad washes of sentiment (Lloyd-Webber's *The Phantom of the Opera*, directed by Prince, 1986), stage spectacle and tunes which could be whistled, far too often.

Nostalgia was not what it was – nor what it seemed elsewhere. In Poland, some drama students connected with Warsaw's Theatre School and the Teatr Ateneum heard about the compilation musical *Ain't Misbehavin'*, and made the normal mistake of misinterpreting Western trends. They knew that it had something to do with Fats Waller's songs: the title suggested revolt. One of them, Andrzej Strzełecki, and an actor-dancer, Janusz Jożewicz, who was 'nuts' about old Hollywood, compiled a version, *Bad Behaviour*, submitted as an entry to a student drama competition at Łodz in 1985.

Their rivals were competent but lack-lustred, smooth Chekhovs and rough Arthur Millers. The year 1985 was not a vintage one for Polish theatre, which had been purged in the war between the government and Solidarity, the first independent trade union in the Eastern block. Leading actors and directors had been removed from their positions of authority and replaced by younger people, whose loyalties were also suspect. In the truce which followed, the authorities tried to woo back the students into the fold by offering them prizes, of which the Łodz competition was one.

In this company, *Bad Behaviour* was outstanding. It was a strange amalgam of Broadway and Polish performance art, mixed up with soft satire about nuclear warfare and other problems of our time. Its message lay in the students' identification with the blacks of the deep South. They, like Fats Waller, were black and blue, they lived as third-class citizens in a white man's world, they had little choice but to accept their lot and they too found consolation in song and dance.

The jury debated. Could the *samizdat* piece be awarded the prize? Might it be interpreted as a pro-American gesture? There was much thoughtful discussion, until finally they all came to the conclusion that it would be unjust to award the prize to any other company. There was a certain daring to the decision, which enlivened the later conversations at the bar as the jury sought to recover from their arduous labours, and penetrated the press on the following morning, and went on to the notice boards of the Polish drama schools, whose students were astonished to read that a good production of Chekhov's *The Seagull* had been passed over in favour of something called *Bad Behaviour*!

Thus easily was Western nostalgia mistaken for rebellion, at a time when the outward signs of 1960s permissiveness adorned the rock musicals of such theatres as the Lenin Komsomol (the Lenkom) whose ideological messages were Marxist-correct. Thus too in the West, did popular musicals borrow a certain idiom from the East which deplored capitalism and wrung its hands over imperialism. Finally thus did the two sides of the Cold War betray their unease at the rigid roles in which history had cast them.

14

THE UNRAVELLING

'Thought is free.'

(From *The Tempest*)

On the day of Chernenko's death, 11 March 1985, the coils of an immense epic began to unwind across the stage of the Maly Theatre in Leningrad. The theatre may have been small as its name implied, the company young and unknown, but nothing was allowed to stand in the way of their ambition. Their aim was to tell the story of what one village in North Russia, Pekashino, had endured through fifty years of war, famine and corruption, and to tell it objectively, pulling no punches, but in such a way that the soul of all Russia could be felt to rise above each trial and indignity.

Brothers and Sisters was a trilogy, adapted by the Maly's artistic director, Lev Dodin, from a novel by Fyodr Abramov in the nineteenth-century Russian tradition, precisely observed, moral but not moralistic, spiritual. Sometimes the plays were performed on three separate evenings and sometimes in one span, lasting nearly eight hours. It packed the theatre in Leningrad, not so small as to be a black box studio nor large enough to accommodate easily the five hundred people who crammed between its walls each night. Few who saw one episode could resist the temptation to see the others. Hopeful crowds gathered at midday to pick up returned tickets and waited until the show began before drifting away.

In 1986, *Brothers and Sisters* paid a visit to Moscow in a season which included another Dodin-Abramov hybrid, *The Home*, and Aleksander Galin's *Stars in the Morning Sky*, a new play about the prostitutes who were forced to leave Moscow during the Olympic Games in 1984. All three were examples of a new wave in Soviet theatre, sometimes called 'tape-recorder' drama, whose parallels in the West would be the Volkstücke and 'kitchen-sink drama'. In the interests of realism, they broke various taboos – against bad language, non-heroic workers and nakedness, which was seen for the first time on a Soviet stage in Galin's play. The fact that such plays were allowed at all was a sign of the times, but *Brothers and Sisters* went further by confronting its audiences with such a record of state mismanagement that it made *The Man Alive* seem like the comedy that Mozhayev insisted that it was.

Brothers and Sisters came to be known as the first *glasnost* play, proof that the Soviet Union was coming to grips with its problems. It might have been better described the last ditch of the Years of Stagnation, the border between one age and the next. It illustrated the climate of opinion which brought Mikhail Gorbachev to power, not the one which he induced. As the Soviet critic Mikhail Shvydkoi pointed out, Abramov's novel had not been banned. It was a best-seller, in as much as sales figures counted where the state controlled them. There was 'nothing particularly daring or controversial' in the play's text.[1]

Brothers and Sisters had been nearly ten years in rehearsal.[2] It began as graduation exercises at the Leningrad Institute of Theatre, where Dodin taught. His students spent vacations on the collective farm in Abramov's village when the author was alive, labouring with the villagers and recording their memories. When Dodin was given his own theatre, he brought some of them together into his company, where they continued to work in the manner to which they had become accustomed. *Brothers and Sisters* was not an ideological play. It did not challenge the decision to collectivise the land. It concentrated on the years after the war, in which all but two of the adult men in Pekashino lost their lives, leaving the farm to be run by women and children.

As a novel, *Brothers and Sisters* came within the boundaries of post-Stalinist censorship. It was not inflammatory nor did it stray beyond the telling of events into an attack on Marxist-Leninism. As a play, it was powerful and contentious. There were scenes where the ragged peasants watched films where girls waved to the world from tractors never seen in Pekashino or listened to the happy statistics from *Pravda*. They were surrounded by lies. Their farm was in a shambles. Since the state took what they could produce, they were forced to steal milk or kill a cow accidentally on purpose to find meat for a village party.

In one scene, the war-time head of the collective farm, Anfisa, met her soldier-husband again, whom she had thought dead. The actress, Shestakova, held her look of blank astonishment for what felt like minutes and the audience began to sob, at first quietly, and then in waves of anguish. It was as if they were all mourning for lost wives and husbands, their ice-bound children, their parents roughly buried in mass graves under bombardment from Nazi guns. Anfisa was like a Mother Courage, determined to keep her family together and losing them, one by one. The analogy did not end there, for as Mother Courage depended upon the war which killed her children, so Anfisa was a servant of the state.

In its determination to remind its public of what they had endured over fifty years, *Brothers and Sisters* was pitiless. It was hard to believe that it had been brought into being in a country where if you wanted to speak to a friend in confidence, you still arranged to meet in a public park. Dodin did have trouble with the Ministry of Culture in Moscow. They started out by objecting to everything, the play's tone, its content, its bad language. They proposed some drastic changes. Dodin stood firm and won the support of the local Leningrad officials who took up the case on his behalf. They wrangled for months and Dodin had to prove by whatever evidence he could muster that his play was factually true. Eventually Moscow gave way.

On occasions, local cultural officers in the Soviet Union sought not to censor artists but to protect them from worse repression elsewhere. Even the Ministry of Culture in Moscow sometimes defended freedom of speech. Its members seemed puzzled that in so tolerant a society as Britain, broadcasting had come to rest with the Home Office, the law-and-order ministry. In the USSR, to find the media in the administrative patch of the KGB would have smacked of Stalinism. The Ministry of Culture's role was to check on the ideological correctness of the arts, but its officials often boasted of how they had bent rules to help this artist or that. *Brothers and Sisters* may have been an example.

It was none the less surprising that permission was granted. In the early 1980s, there had been many attempts to curb outspoken velvet prisoners. In January 1980, Andrei Sakharov had been sent into internal exile in Gorki for denouncing the Soviet invasion of Afghanistan. In 1984, Lyubimov had been ousted as Director of the Taganka, a post he had held for twenty years, and replaced by Anatol Efros, a thoughtful and brave director who found the task of succeeding Lyubimov too much for him. He refused to sit in Lyubimov's office and died within months of his appointment. The decision to allow the staging of *Brothers and Sisters* suggested that someone somewhere high up in the ranks of the Politburo must have wanted it to be seen, but who and why?

In 1984, there was a hidden power struggle in the Politburo. Chernenko was never anything more than a stop-gap leader. He was so ill at the funeral of his predecessor, Andropov, that 'he could not even lift his hand to hold on to the casket as it was carried into Red Square'.[3] The manoeuvrings among those who might succeed him began before he was appointed, for if there had been agreement as to who would become the eventual leader of the Soviet Communist Party, Chernenko would not have been chosen. The youngest member of the Politburo, whose average age was above 70, was Gorbachev, brought from his home in Stavropol to Moscow by Brezhnev in 1978 to sort out the problems of Soviet agriculture.

Mikhail Gorbachev was born on 2 March 1931, in the village of

Privolnoye, some hundred miles from Stavropol in North Caucasus. It was during one of the worst terrors that the world has yet known, exceeding even that of the Holocaust, when Stalin was fulfilling his threat to eliminate the kulak class. Stalin is reported to have said that 10 million kulaks were 'annihilated'.[4] Those independent farmers who refused to be collectivised were sent to the labour camps of the Gulag or to be executed. Gorbachev's parents survived, probably by collaborating, and their son became a member of the Komsomol at 14, the first step towards Communist Party membership and career advancement. He was one of a small group of rural students to be admitted to Moscow State University, the largest centre of Soviet Higher Education.

In September 1950, while George Kennan was travelling in a more or less parallel direction in the USA, Gorbachev boarded the train for the 1,000-mile journey to Moscow which took him through those cities made famous by the battles against the Nazis during the Second World War. He did not like what he saw. 'I traveled through Stalingrad, which had been destroyed, through Voronezh, which had been destroyed, and Rostov, destroyed. Nothing but ruins everywhere. I traveled as a student and saw it all. The whole country was in ruins.'[5]

In Moscow, he studied law but never practised it. Law was a minor trade in a country where trials were foregone conclusions. He returned to Stavropol where he became the party chief in the region. His success in 1977 in organising a better reaping of the harvest, with his reputation for honesty and hard work, returned him to Moscow as a Central Committee secretary in the Ministry of Agriculture. He was elevated to the Politburo by the unexpected death of his superior, Fyodr Kulakov, who at 60 was one Politburo member young enough to be Brezhnev's successor.

Gorbachev's five-year spell as head of Soviet agriculture was not a success. Through no fault of his own, he presided over some of the worst famines experienced in the Soviet Union since the 1930s. After Brezhnev's death, he became second-in-command to Yuri Andropov, who was trying to groom him for the top job, but Gorbachev was not without rivals. Chernenko's choice was Victor Grishin, the Moscow party chief, but a more formidable opponent was Grigory Romanov, a Brezhnev border baron, the powerful head of Leningrad's party machine.

The riddle posed by *Brothers and Sisters* was: whom did its production benefit? Did it remind the public that the problems of agriculture had not lessened under Gorbachev but got worse? But Romanov was responsible for Pekashino. The sly *apparatchik* in *Brothers and Sisters* would have answered to him. Was Grishin trying to discredit them both? Or, as seems to have been the case, had the plans for openness, *glasnost*, been laid before Gorbachev came to power during his friendship with Andropov, who was also from Stavropol? In any case, the emergence of *Brothers and Sisters* during this uncertainty lent it a political weight.

In the West, *glasnost* was taken to mean openness in a democratic sense, a debate between opposing opinions. A better translation might have been 'accountability' with a dash of 'permissiveness'. The Communist Party was not to be challenged, but the public should be kept informed about social problems and officials could be taken to task. The permissiveness lay in the treatment of dissidents, the relaxed controls on travel and in the spirit of frank talk, if not free speech. Sakharov was welcomed back to Moscow, Jews were allowed to emigrate to Israel and attempts were made to lure Lyubimov back to the Taganka.

Gorbachev's other key word, *perestroika*, 're-construction', did involve a measure of democracy, in that some powers were to be de-centralised from Moscow to the regions, where the decision-making process should take place openly, not behind locked doors. *Glasnost* and *perestroika* were good intentions not so far removed from those with which Kruschev and Dubcek began their regimes. The joke in Moscow ran like this: 'What is the difference between Gorbachev and Dubcek? None, but Gorbachev doesn't know it yet!' The question which dogged all three leaders was the extent to which *glasnost* and *perestroika* could go without knocking over the whole pack of cards. Gorbachev's target was not the system, but the hundreds of officials denounced in his first speech as leader to the Soviet Communist Party Congress in 1986, as 'armchair managers, hack workers, idlers and grabbers'.[6]

His first moves in national *perestroika* were to conduct a purge of slackers and to promote his own generation of middle management to the top offices. Such a wholesale re-construction is hard enough to tackle in a large industry. In the USSR, with fifteen supposedly autonomous republics, it was a Herculean task. Many people were fretting for promotion, but no government can change its civil service so quickly without introducing methods for advancement or demotion. To a singular degree, Gorbachev placed trust in persuasion. His charm and good humour were his assets. He was the first Soviet leader to use television successfully, not in speeches, but in informal walkabouts, Western-style.

'Comrades,' said Andrei Gromyko, the long-serving Foreign Minister at the Central Committee meeting from which Gorbachev emerged as the Soviet leader, 'this man has a nice smile, but he has teeth of iron.' He added that Gorbachev 'can grasp very well and very quickly the essence of those developments that are building up outside our country in the international arena'.[7] Among such developments was the knowledge that the Soviet Union could not afford to sustain the arms race at its current level, still less venture into the precision technology of laser-guided weaponry of Reagan's Star Wars. The sluggish economy was causing trouble elsewhere. China had turned to the West for investment, one legacy of President Nixon's visit to Beijing in 1972.

Gorbachev seized the initiative on disarmament. His proposals in Geneva in 1985, Reykjavik in 1986 and Washington in 1987, where he signed an extension to the SALT treaty with President Reagan to cut the number of long-range nuclear missiles, took Western leaders so much by surprise that they wasted time looking for snags. When they discovered that there were none, they concluded that here was a man, in the words of Margaret Thatcher, with whom they could do business. With this goodwill, Gorbachev could raise some burden of army expenditure and withdraw troops from Central Europe. He could even offer the West a prize for which it was prepared to pay, German re-unification.

From the West's point of view, this was all too good to be true. Decades of animosity evaporated like the mists of morning. The theatricality of the events, the change of mood, the forceful encounters, the scenes of foreign ministers toasting one another in champagne on the banks of the Rhine, conveyed the momentous impression that the Cold War was coming to an end. It would have spoilt the feast to recall how many problems were unresolved. Despite disarmament, both sides could destroy the world many times over. The inequalities in wealth had not diminished nor had the prospect of famine receded from two-thirds of the world's population. The ratio in the *per capita* income between Europe and India in 1880 was approximately 2:1. Now it was nearly 70:1.[8]

Nor did the end of the Cold War necessarily mean peace. The rapid breaking-up of the charcoal burner's fire scattered hot ashes around the forest. The various withdrawals from empire, including Afghanistan, encouraged the republics within the Soviet Union to look for full autonomy, especially in the Baltic states, who had never agreed to be unified in the first place. There were revivals of nineteenth-century nationalisms, the cause of old world wars, throughout Eastern and Central Europe. In East Berlin, the graves of Bertolt Brecht and his wife, the actress Helene Weigel, were sprayed with anti-semitic slogans in red aerosol paint.[9]

Brothers and Sisters contained two prophetic warnings for Gorbachev's *perestroika*. One was that the farmers' distrust of the state was such that they would prefer to let their crops rot in the fields rather than send them to towns without proper payment, not in roubles but in barter. The other was that family loyalties were all-important, God-ordained, which, if taken to an extreme, would lead to tribalism. Taken together, they forecast a prospect for the Soviet Union of complete social disintegration.

If *perestroika* and *glasnost* were to succeed, they required a mental preparation. Western-style democracy, though this was not Gorbachev's aim, rested upon certain assumptions, the stress on individual choice, the readiness to listen to opposing views and sources of information thought to be reliable. A sound currency, as Friedman would have pointed out, depended upon a social good faith. The joke in the Soviet Union was 'we'll pretend to work, if the state pretends to pay us'. The loss of faith in Marxist-Leninism, which was the only widely understood ideology, left a vacuum into which ideas uncritically rushed, nationalistic, even racist, often anarchic. Worst was the pessimism that the problems would never be solved, that there was something in the Russian character which respected the knout and the firing squad and that the sole redemptive force lay in Slav spirituality.

To blame the official culture for what was going wrong would have been deemed impertinent in the Soviet Union and a paradox elsewhere, for if there was one aspect of social living, other than rocketry and athletics, in which the Soviet Union excelled, it would have been what was known as its Culture. It was widely acknowledged to have some of the finest theatre companies in the world: the Moscow Art Theatre, under its precise director Oleg Efremov, the boldly Expressionist Taganka, the cheerful Lenkom, the brave Maly, the Bolshoi Ballet and Opera and, of course, the Moscow State Circus. Its fringe theatres, such as the Theatre South-West in a converted boiler room beneath a block of flats in a suburb of Moscow, could boast of acting standards beyond those of the West and of an inspirational director, Belyakovic.

Its acting schools, its technical and design departments, were renowned. What was missing was something less tangible, the spirit of deep enquiry, hard to find in the West as well. It was as if decades of living in the velvet and not-so-velvet prisons had stifled the readiness to speculate. There were some dissident theatres, conducting running battles with the censors, dangerous duels, but after they had proved their various points, then what?

Once 'tape-recorder' realism had removed the gloss from the Soviet worker, there was a reversion to old-style snobbery. In 1986, Mikhail Bulgakov's Absurdist novella, *Heart of the Dog*, written in 1925, was published for the first time in the Soviet Union. Within months, it had been adapted for the Moscow stage in no less than three versions. It was an attack on the Revolution, in which a scientist turned a dog into something which looked like a human being and could quote Engels, but who remained a cur of the streets, vicious, unpredictable and stupid. Its message was that the proletariat would never be fit to govern. After *Stars in the Morning Sky*, stage nakedness became a sign of the avant-garde, but to be really adventurous, directors sought a wardrobe of fetishes – garters, whips and high-heeled boots. They snatched up previously banned Western plays, camping them until they could camp no more. Genet's plays became popular. One production of *The Maids* at the Satiricon Theatre was set in a drag night-club with much miming to old Hollywood songs, a case of piling Pelion upon Ossa. *The Balcony* in particular offered an exemplary mixture of brothel sex and political cynicism.

Mikhail Shvydkoi blamed a decline in audiences on television and so many remarkable events were now to be seen on the small screen that the theatre would have been hard put to match them. In March 1987, Margaret Thatcher visited Moscow and few foreign leaders can have made so powerful an impression. In the early 1980s, she had been the target of most hostile attacks. She had been dubbed the Iron Lady, a title she welcomed. In 1982, the Falklands War was dismissed as imperialism, ridiculous because the islands were so small. The battles of the 1984 miners' strike were screened on Soviet television to illustrate British class oppression, but the presence of Mrs Thatcher was so unlike the images of her that she was mobbed in the streets like a pop star.

She was interviewed on television and her straightforward account of how democracies worked and the advantages of the free market economy came as a revelation to many Soviet citizens who had never before heard the Western case so clearly put. By 1989, Moscow audiences could watch live debates from a newly elected Parliament of the Deputies, fierce exchanges whose conclusions were not foregone. It was exhilarating but also disturbing for those who were not used to such open disagreements, while for the communist old guard it amounted to little less than anarchy.

Where there was good theatre to be found amidst so much facile experimentation, the public did respond. In March 1989, Brook's CIRT company visited Moscow with a radiant production in English of Chekhov's *The Cherry Orchard*, staged with a simplicity far removed from the naturalism of the Moscow Art Theatre or the Expressionism of the Taganka on whose second stage the production took place, on a rug with few props and minimal furniture. Speech levels were conversational, but when Tom Wilkinson's Lopakhin said the words, 'Sometimes, when I can't sleep, I think "Oh Lord, you've given us vast forests, immense fields, wide horizons. We who live here ought to be giants" . . .', there was a stillness in the full auditorium which would have deafened any applause.

This event was part of a festival and symposium to celebrate the fiftieth anniversary of Stanislavski's death. Five hundred actors, directors and critics assembled from all over the world to discuss stage realism and how, according to Stanislavski, it could be achieved. Even while the delegates were attending workshops, watching performances and listening to papers, that image of reality in which Stanislavski so believed receded into the distance, like one of MAT's naturalistic sets, except that there was no end to it, no point where the lines of perspective joined.

From the United States came members of Lee Strasberg's Actors Studio, who talked about affective memory and when the actor playing *Hamlet* should think about his mother, and from Michael Chekhov's Theater Studio, who described the psychological gesture and when we should open up to the sun and close down with the moon. At the Moscow Art Theatre, Efremov offered a production of *Uncle Vanya* so detailed that it was dubbed 'meteorological' because it was possible to guess the exact moment of the day and the state of the weather. Were such re-constructions 'realistic', when such country estates no longer existed in the Soviet Union? Was Stanislavski concerned with museum culture? At the Taganka, Lyubimov was presenting his *Three Sisters*, which began with the sound of army boots. A side wall to the theatre rolled up and a platoon of soldiers marched in. His Russia was a police state.

Where did realism lie? In whose version? Freud's? Jung's? The historical re-construction or the modern comment? It gradually became apparent that Stanislavski was looking at the twentieth century from the other end of our telescope and that what was huge to him was insignificant to us. Rebelling against the high-flown idealism of romantic theatre, Stanislavski sought a new objectivity, akin to a science, through which the world could be examined with an imaginative detachment. It could never be a pure science, because human experiences could never be placed under a microscope, but if we remembered how we ourselves in the past had behaved, we could cultivate our half-intuitive, half-rational understanding of others. Stanislavski never doubted that there was a real world which artists had a duty to study and that the purpose of such an investigation was the betterment of mankind.

Stanislavski was steeped in evolutionary optimism, similar to the fervour which fired the bolsheviks who gathered around Lenin, to the Modernists, the Futurists and *die neue Sachlichkeit*. But how could we at the other end of the century subscribe to it – when we had seen where the advancement of science had taken us, when the plans for utopia had curled brown on our hillsides, and when standards of living in Moscow were lower for the normal person than when Stanislavski first directed *The Cherry Orchard* in 1904? Stanislavski believed that there was a solution to every problem, but we only saw problems in every one of his solutions.

In a room adjoining the conference hall, a meeting of Soviet regional directors took place. They came from as far afield as Omsk and Vladivostock. Their discussions were in turmoil for much of the time. They were not quarrelling about audiences or grants but about what should be done next in their theatres. 'How can we accept the thought,' said one in tears, 'that the glorious Revolution on which we have wasted so much time and blood was wrong? How can we believe that our enemies were right? It is impossible!' 'For seventy one years,' another stated, 'We have been told what to think. Now nobody tells us what is right or wrong. If I'm allowed to stage everything, then I can stage nothing, for I don't know what I'm supposed to be doing.'

'We've lived,' summed up a director from Omsk, 'in a make-believe world. We're *still* living in a make-believe world.' But all had been trained in realism, according to Stanislavski. The shock of the new can be painful for those who have to endure it.

Out in the streets and suburbs of Moscow, life was becoming more difficult each day. Food shortages were one problem. For reasons best known to Abramov, supplies of meat and vegetables were not getting through to the official shops, where prices were controlled. They had to be bought on the black market, where they were not. For the first time in living memory, Moscow became a dangerous city at night. Muggers and thieves were on the prowl. The new private restaurants, where few Russians could afford to eat, had to pay protection money to local gangs. Even the police looked for back-handers in hard currency.

Muscovites had endured bad times before, too often, but in the past they had been able to blame other people, Western agents if they believed the government, bureaucracy if they did not. Now they did not know who to blame, except in some way themselves. They had been led to believe that they were in the process of building a glorious future, from which they might not benefit but their children would. Now their childen were middle-aged. They had been taught that workers under capitalism were in worse straits than themselves. What they saw from the West on TV were riots, strikes and city slums. There had been no talk of Soviet imperialism, but that they were leading the world's oppressed against the military and economic might of the Western powers. Now they could make real comparisons and reach other conclusions.

Gorbachev's speeches stressed the continuity with the past. *Perestroika* opened up the road to 'revolutionary renewal'.[10] It would release 'the creative energy of the working class', stifled by Stagnation.[11] The Communist Party should become democratic to avoid the threat of facing alternative parties in open elections. In trying to maintain a balance between those who wanted to assert the authority of the party and those who wanted to make a dash for Western democracy and the open market, he chose ambivalence, of which his rival, Boris Yeltsin, took advantage. The more troublesome questions were avoided. Was there to be a market economy? How far would the devolution of power to the regions go? Would the Soviet Union itself break up?

Gorbachev still quoted Lenin approvingly, but quarry-loads of commemorative busts lay unshifted at masonries. The consequences of this flight from Marxist-Leninism could be felt around the world. In some countries, it made negotiations easier. The ANC in South Africa could no longer be accused of being a Soviet agency. In others, regimes were left stranded without any international support. Cuba's trade links with the Soviet Union withered away. Despite the lifting of Cold War fears, many life-long socialists felt so embittered by what they regarded as a betrayal that they became, if anything, more fiery; and in no country were the tensions felt more strongly than in East Germany.

The re-unification of Germany came more suddenly than anybody expected. In October 1989, the Berlin Wall was standing, cutting through squares and boulevards, a concrete symbol of all those other divisions which separated East from West. Its first brick was dislodged, as it were, not in Berlin but in Hungary, where border guards decided that it was no longer worthwhile to check the travel documents to Austria. Within days, the trickle of refugees from East Germany had swollen to a flood. By November, the East German authorities decided that it was not in their interests to control the exodus and the quick integration of Germany then became a priority for both sides, East and West.

It was the outcome that most seemed to want. East Germany had been the pride of the Comecon countries, where living standards were higher than those elsewhere and whose factories were more advanced. It had been assumed that with some Western investment the transition from being a moderately successful economy to a thriving one could be overcome. This was not the case. By West German standards, the East German factories were antiquated and produced goods which nobody would buy. The East Germans for the first time faced the prospect of mass unemployment, while the West Germans realised that what was required to save the East German economy was not investment but huge loans. East Germans had cultivated a moral authority towards the West, stemming from the claims of their leaders that they were the first to fight against fascism. In the theatre, they were proud of an excellence which did not come from money. There was a long list of East German socialist writers who had gained acceptance in the West and a shorter one of West German directors, like Stein, who had looked towards the East. The East German theatres now faced the prospect of being reduced to the status of poor relations.

In 1989, East German theatres were for the first time invited to take part in the *Theatertreffen* in Berlin, bringing together picked productions from German-speaking countries in Europe. In 1990, the festival was overshadowed by the news that, due to the costs of unification, two of the eleven state theatres in Berlin would have to close. Which would they be? Would they *both* come from the East? This raised the question of the merits of the two traditions, the earnestness of one or the opulence of the other.

Two productions signalled the difference. One was simple and sentimental, the other glittering but cold. The Schwerin State Theatre offered some songs from the 1950s, *So haltet die Freude recht fest*, together with images of today. Nine middle-aged actors and actresses stood before portraits of their younger selves and sang about how they loved Stalin and how German youth would lead mankind towards utopia. The message was, 'Look at us! Past our primes, our lives wasted in a vain dream!' They looked fit, not unduly wasted, with families no doubt.

In contrast, the Burgtheater from Vienna staged Büchner's *Woyzeck*, directed by the former painter Achim Freyer. Martin Schwab's Woyzeck was wrapped up in bandages like a mummy from an Egyptian tomb. When he shaved his commanding officer, he circled around the hexagonal stage in tiny paces, while a red-scalped Herr Hauptmann barked orders. It was a 'performance art' *Woyzeck*, rhythmically spoken rather than acted, very stylish. Woyzeck's child was a monstrous foetus, storing up future trouble.

Both productions were anti-verbal and in different ways anti-intellectual. They did not use story-telling to connect one event to another. It was as if the old controversies were now matters of form, an *impasse* in which forward movement had ceased long ago, leaving behind a skeletal waltz, with token footsteps, in narrow circles, on a dusty and treacherous ballroom floor.

15

THEME AND EXPOSITION

'Every story should have a middle, an end and a beginning'
(Not Aristotle)

In November 1990, there were demonstrations in the streets of Bucharest every day, for and against the government. Newspapers of most shades of opinion were sold from damp piles on the curbs. In University Square, women in black lit candles in memory of those killed in the revolt against the Ceauşescu regime. It has been estimated that there were ten thousand deaths.[1] The pavements were coated with thick wax.

At the end of a long boulevard stood the unfinished Palace of the People, erected by Nicolae Ceauşescu at much cost to the people. The palace, the square in front of it and the flanking government buildings wiped out a district of Bucharest when it was built, but before anybody could live in it, apart from soldiers and caretakers, it became a tourist attraction, the pediments defaced by piles of uncleared cement, barbed wire coiled at the gates. The actor, Ion Caramitru, who proclaimed the revolution to the world on television in December 1989, wanted to turn it into a Museum of Dictatorships, but was dictatorship dead enough in Romania to earn its concrete case?

Apart from Albania, Romania was the last communist country in Eastern Europe to resist *perestroika*, and the only one to suffer much bloodshed when the regime was overthrown. In July 1989, Ceauşescu played host to a meeting of the Warsaw Pact countries, where the main item on the secret agenda was how to cope with Gorbachev's reforms. The governments in Poland and Hungary were in favour of them, whereas those of Czechoslovakia, East Germany and Romania were against,[2] but these arguments were academic, for without the Soviet army, none could survive.

Within 6 months, they were gone. Poland had a Solidarity-led government by September. In October, the Hungarian Socialist Party, formed from the younger members of the old Communist Party, pledged itself to support a 'constitutional government based on the multi-party

168

system'. In November, a mass strike forced the Czech government to introduce constitutional changes which included non-communist parties and free elections. The old leaders resigned from ill-health or were overthrown – Kadar in Hungary, Honecker in East Germany, Husak in Czechoslovakia.

Only Ceauşescu felt confident enough to resist, as he had opposed Moscow in the past. His sense of security was based upon the strength of his secret police, the Securitate, and the family network which held his government together. His wife, Elena, was first deputy prime minister. One brother was deputy defence minister, in charge of the party's control over the army, while another was chief of the cadres department at the Ministry of Internal Affairs. His son, Nicu, was the first secretary of the Sibiu party region.[3] Of all the Comecon countries, Romania was ruled most like a feudal dictatorship.

The first signs of revolt within his government began in March 1989, with the arrest of Mircea Raceanu, an official in the Foreign Office, charged with espionage. At the same time, the army had to be called in to suppress uprisings in regional towns, but the military response was not as decisive as Ceauşescu would have wished. The popular rebellion spread, until in December 1989 the Ceauşescus fled from Bucharest to be caught and shot days later. The theatres, the universities and the church led the liberation movement, although what finally toppled Ceauşescu may have been a Moscow-inspired *coup d'état*.

An interim government was installed, the National Salvation Front (NSF), which announced that 'all power structures of the Ceauşescu clan have been dissolved'.[4] The NSF promised to hold free elections in April, to abandon 'the leading role' of the Communist Party and to draft a new Constitution observing the rights of ethnic minorities.[5] To the phrasing, their manifesto was in line with other such provisional governments.

But doubts were immediately expressed[6] as to whether the NSF would carry out the promises and whether they had been made in good faith. The new regime had too many members of the old Communist Party in its midst. The NSF party President, Ion Iliescu, could be regarded as one of them. The Securitate's office in Bucharest was ransacked but the secret police still existed. Nor were there any other political parties ready to take power. Parties were quickly formed and gained some support, but the true professionals were still communists, trained by Ceauşescu. The NSF was sufficiently alarmed by the opposition parties to seek to restrict their chances in the elections. In April 1990, the NSF won by a large majority, but opposition members claimed that they were denied access to television and their meetings had been disrupted. Ion Caramitru refused in protest to allow his name to be put forward as a Vice-President, but charges of ballot-rigging were not upheld by a team of international observers.

Immediately after the elections, there were protests against the results and in May, demonstrations in Bucharest were broken up by a mob of pro-government miners who marched through the streets wielding clubs. Law and order was restored by a display of force, but when the crisis was over, the government allowed demonstrations to take place, as happened daily for the next six months. Following the now familiar lines of *perestroika* younger technocrats came into power, who sometimes talked about the open market and the need for *glasnost*, but who stuck to the ways of the command economy. The shelves in the shops stayed bare and the queues for bread grew longer.

In the first flush of liberation, Caramitru announced that a theatre festival would take place to celebrate the return to freedom, but when 'Bucharest '90' was staged in November, it was against a background of mourning, hardship and civil disorder. He invited the Romanian director, Andrei Serban, who lived in exile in the United States, to return to Bucharest to take charge of their National Theatre and Serban's Classical Trilogy, *Medea*, *The Trojan Women* and *Electra*, was the festival's highlight.

It was not exactly a new production, although Serban turned the National Theatre inside out for the occasion and got rid of half its company. He had developed the trilogy over seventeen years with Ellen Stewart's Café La Mama in New York, exploring ideas derived from Brook, Grotowski and Off-Off-Broadway. Extracts had been seen in Edinburgh and the Bouffes du Nord in Paris. Serban was fascinated by the theatre as ritual and had tried out ways of handling the Chorus to shape the emotions of the crowd. The actors of the Chorus spoke rhythmically and chanted in strange languages, and guided the audience from one stage to the next. The texts were taken from Euripides, Seneca and Sophocles (but not from Aeschylus), spoken in their original tongues, and were incomprehensible, like Hughes's *Orghast* at Persepolis. The audience was not expected to respond to the meanings of the words, but to their sounds, which were combined with gongs, drums and flutes into something akin to a religious service.

Nothing like this had been seen in Romania. The old National Theatre had been one of those companies where once-able actors wheezed through Shakespeare and forgot their lines. Elsewhere, since the Ceauşescus rarely went to any theatre other than the National, a certain dissidency was expected. At the Bulandra Theatre, where Caramitru played Hamlet, Claudius and Gertrude were modelled after the Ceauşescus, granting favours graciously while surrounded by guards. Ghosts were forbidden on Romanian stages and old Hamlet was represented by a follow-spot, which had the effect of enlarging the call for 'Revenge'. In the regions, the Craiova Theatre linked *Ubu roi* with *Scenes from Macbeth*, the model for both central characters being Nicolae Ceauşescu, thus deprived of a chance to be heroically wicked.

The Romanian companies might be Expressionist, they might be politically daring, but they were not in Brook's term, 'holy'. The Classical Trilogy began in the streets, where the audience waited with the women in University Square until they were summoned by a gong to a side entrance at the National Theatre. They were then hustled by robed attendants through the corridors to a large room, the NT's second stage, where they watched a violent family row, Medea chained to a wall and cursing Jason for taking a young wife. (The domestic fights of the Ceauşescus were notorious and, since they ruled through nepotism, dangerous to the country.) The Chorus mingled with the spectators as priests, whispering in their ears, as if their lives were under threat, and sanities too, which could only be saved by an appeal to the gods. Medea's children were led out to have their throats cut, a sacrifice demanding a blood revenge.

The audience was herded into a scene dock backstage, where the Trojan Women, led by Hecuba, were rounded up by soldiers for transportation. It was like being among the protesters of 1968, or the crowds in Bucharest in 1989 to whom Ceauşescu appealed. The cause of the Trojan wars, Helen, was wheeled through the mob on a cart, smeared with mud, head-shaven, raped by a bear. Her features, shorn of femininity were like those of Nicu Ceauşescu, terrified by the thought of his trial. The hatred of the culprit turned to pity. When the execution came, it was a barbaric act.

A huge wall to the scene dock was raised. The Trojan Women were taken for deportation. Queen Hecuba and her daughter-in-law, Andromache, tried to hide the last surviving male member of Priam's family, Astyanax, from the soldiers, who snatched him from them before boarding the ship. Astyanax was taken to a high altar, whose side-slopes were steep. The women clambered up to save him, but when they were within grasp, they slid back down the walls, tearing their clothes and their bodies until they piled up in a mound of white and red on the ground.

The final play, *Electra*, was presented on the main stage, on which the audience sat in two tiered rows, where they could look out beyond the performance area and into the auditorium, whose seats were covered with white sheets. At the back of the theatre, surrounded by an ornate picture frame, was the official box of the Ceauşescus. Serban planned a *coup de théâtre*, one of many. This was where Orestes killed his mother, Clytemnestra, whose body, slumped over the parapet, recalled the limp limbs of Elena Ceauşescu, shot with her husband and shown to the crowds.

In the Greek legend, Orestes was tormented by the Furies for the crime of matricide, although the killing was ordered by the god Apollo to avenge the murder of Agamemnon, Orestes' father. One god commanded, other demi-gods opposed and between them, man suffered. Was Romania both justified and haunted in a similar way? Orestes sought absolution and, in Aeschylus' version, he came to Athens to seek the help of Athena, goddess of wisdom, who summoned a jury to try his case.

But Serban, unlike Peter Stein, did not follow Aeschylus but Sophocles and Euripides. The emphasis was upon the purification of Orestes, not his acquittal in a court of law. Serban was aspiring towards catharsis in a world which had forgotten what the word meant, the restoring to wholeness of the divided soul. He altered the choral rhythms and mingled them with gentle notes from handbells and gongs. To a remarkable extent, he transformed the mood of anxiety into one of stillness and hope. The audience changed its body language. From straining forward, they sat up straighter. They looked broad-shouldered. It may not be too much of an exaggeration to say that when they left the theatre after five concentrated hours, they seemed taller by about six inches.

Religious sects have never forgotten the power of catharsis. In Romania, as in other Eastern European countries, *glasnost* allowed a revival of churches and new congregations experienced the power of the Roman Catholic and Greek Orthodox masses. In the Far East, in India, Thailand, Africa and among revivalist meetings in the US, cathartic rituals can be daily observed to rouse, calm and elevate. But modern theatre is secular. Serban achieved a measure of catharsis without the benefit of faith.

Rationalists have always found catharsis disturbing. There can be something treacherous about the way in which the mind can be so easily by-passed by drums and priestly authority. Brecht thought that brightly lit stages and dark auditoriums lulled audiences into a state of passivity or roused them towards empty sacrifices. These trance-like states could be dangerous as well as therapeutic, particularly when, as in the Greek Dionysiac rituals, they were combined with muscle – or mind – relaxing drugs.

The power to arouse such fervour, and to quieten it, was originally entrusted to priests. Greek tragedy represented a transition between Dionysiac rituals and recognisably modern drama where argument and reason were given pride of place. The Greek dramatists after Aeschylus did not ignore ritual, but they introduced stories in which choices were presented before their audiences, who were asked to consider the causes and effects of the play's action. The Greeks raised the spectator from being a passive recipient of priestly crowd control into a participant on whose judgement the outcome of the drama finally rested.

Serban's Classical Trilogy went some way towards reversing this process. The ancient Greek dramatists did not write in incomprehensible languages. Aeschylus' verse was plain and unadorned. The stories of Serban's Trilogy were imaginatively but not logically connected. They were not all part of the same grand plot. Aeschylus' *The Oresteia* described the step-by-step process which led to Orestes' trial. Serban did not provide explanations, even if it had been possible to understand what was being said. Audiences were expected to interpret the plays in the light of what had happened to them in Romania.

His Trilogy showed how dramatic form can loosely bring together many diverse experiences. Memories of several wars could be traced within its span. The Greek parts were written after the Peloponnesian war in the fifth century BC, but to distance the pain, the authors chose plots from Homer's Trojan wars, which took place five centuries before. Serban devised the trilogy during the Vietnam war, but it was seen at its best after the Romanian revolution. This is how art earns its double-edged reputation for being immortal and universal.

The Classical Trilogy was also typical of the 1970s. It was characterised by a distrust of logic which had gone beyond the stage of assaulting reason in the style of the Absurdists. It had assimilated ideas of a Collective Unconscious from Jung, borrowed a little from Grotowski and aspired like Brook towards a universal language 'akin to music'. It could be said to oppose Athenian drama by seeking to control the 'pre-rational' mind through ritual, while its use of unknown tongues for their rhythmic effect was a symptom of a much wider trend.

The modern distrust of words began in the late nineteenth century, as a revolt against the decorum of the Enlightenment, and by the 1970s, the avant-garde had gone beyond rejecting the 'well-made play' in the Aristotelian tradition, but text-based drama in general. It elevated the non-verbal sign systems of the stage, imagery, body language, rhythm and music. Beckett's last plays were more visual and aural experiences than verbal; while Tadeusz Kantor used words in his Theatre of Death primarily to subvert the illusions of the stage, to remind his audiences that what they were seeing were 'dreams', not 'reality'.

Kantor, who died in December 1990, after a dress rehearsal for his last production, titled with deliberate irony *Today is My Birthday*, wanted to show how the mind, or at least *his* mind, could not escape from the past. Ghostly faces of lost souls (including his own youth), skeletons in cupboards, memories, could not be thrown away because they were in a sense dead. They lived in his mind and his mind lived through them.

Kantor could not have pictured on stage what it felt like to have lived through the fires and pogroms of Central Europe if he had stuck to classical story-telling, with its emphasis on binary logic, progress and reaching decisions. The two modes of thought were incompatible. But the social value of classical reasoning hardly needs to be stressed. Binary logic offered a structure for most European legal and political system. There may be no inherent reason why we should try to puzzle through our problems by sorting out the arguments into two piles, For and Against, instead of into three or, as in some African cultures, a circle. It was a useful way of doing things which had become widely accepted. Classical story-telling taught the public to share in the methods whereby their Guardians sifted through evidence and arrived at conclusions; and it was drummed into the mind by every detective story and court-room drama.

Binary logic has limitations. It could be said to encourage opposition for opposition's sake and might not result in a clear decision. There could be facts which do not fit into either pile or the piles could be of such equal size that it was impossible to declare a winner. The Cold War could be regarded as a prime example of the *impasse* to which binary logic reduced mankind.

A similar case could be made for the avant-garde's distrust of words. All verbal languages have limitations and other sign systems can in some respects be better. It may be easier to convey feelings of 'love' through dance, but it is difficult to dance the idea of 'Tuesday'. 'Love' and 'Tuesday' are different kinds of perception. One is concerned with how we feel about ourselves and the other with how we relate to society at large. The European stress on verbal language could indicate the choosing of social good-order over personal well-being. If so, could the inability to express what we feel be related to our main medium of expression, words, and has led us to accept situations (such as the Cold War) against which our instincts rebel?

The avant-garde's rejection of words and story-telling was not necessarily negative. It affirmed a wholeness of being that European classicism was thought to disparage. It looked towards Asian and African cultures to supplement the deficiencies of our too cerebral habits of mind. It detached the theatre from the process of taking social decisions. Twentieth-century drama came full-circle from being obsessed with politics to becoming bored with such frivolity. Serban's trilogy may have uplifted the soul, but it did not offer help with the problems of Romania.

During the 1980s, there were many performance art companies, a term which embraced almost everything from the Wuppertal Dance Theatre to the living statues of Gilbert and George in London. The American director, Robert Wilson, was fascinated by the effects of brain damage upon perception, heightening some faculties, stifling others. He collaborated with an autistic adolescent, Christopher Knowles, on *A Letter to Queen Victoria* (1974) and *Einstein on the Beach* (1976). In 1980, he moved to Germany where his productions, aided by subsidy, became operatic in scale, minimal in content, proceeding with hypnotic slowness.

Perhaps the fourth generation of performance art directors, in a genre where generations changed with a speed rare in their productions, was led by the young Belgian director Jan Fabre, whose *Power of Theatrical Magic* (1985) was a dispatch to the knackers' yard of the clichés of European art, from Madonnas to Siegfrieds, showing how unsuited such images were to the way in which the body functions. Fabre thus demonstrated that European civilisation had become unfit for habitation. In the interval, the cast sat on the stage, smoking and outstaring the audience.

This was more than just the discarding of Modernism which is sometimes called post-Modernism, but an attempt to prune back European culture, like a zealous gardener, to its roots. It came at a time when there was much speculation as to why *perestroika* was not working. The general conclusion was that the free market could not be introduced piecemeal into the command economy. It required something like democracy to sustain it. As capitalist methods for the production and exchange of goods were introduced to the East, it became clear that there was no framework of law to cope with civil disputes. Soviet law was an extension of Marxism. Conflicts of interest were referred back to a bible in which no-one believed. Western law required a debate between opposing views that Marxist dialectic despite its subtlety suppressed. Unlike court-room dramas, Soviet plays tended to suggest that there should be no such conflicts in the state.

To that extent, the source of the emerging anarchy in the USSR was not only political and economic but cultural as well. It was not so much a question of settling particular grievances as of finding the methods whereby disputes could be discussed and decisions peacefully reached. Democracy needed something more than binary logic, but a decorum as well, a respect for the Chair in debate, an acknowledgement that the interests of the State over-rode those of pressure groups. At a certain point in most court-room dramas, of which *The Oresteia* was again the best example, there is an appeal to Natural Justice, a divine order to which governments and states were subject, expressed through such concepts as human rights and individual freedom.

The problems of the Soviet Union could not be solved simply by better management, but by replacing Marxism with habits of mind which needed to be accepted if democracy were to function. To squeeze out one set of assumptions and to insert another is always a difficult process, but it can be painfully prolonged if we have no means to test what might be called the truth of our mythologies. The value of court-room dramas to the West lies not simply in teaching the public how the law works, but also in detecting the limits of the system, such

175

as the false appeals to Natural Justice and the risks of confronting a corrupt judge.

This example provides a classical defence for the theatre. The one thing which we know about the theatre is that it is not real life. It is a game area for the mind. It gives us the chance to test assumptions in our imaginations, which might be disruptive if we placed too much trust in them. The advantage of live theatre, as opposed to TV drama, is that myths are tried out within small groups of people. Actors can tell from the responses of the audience whether the myth carries conviction. They may have difficulty in persuading the public, but in that struggle lies a strength. If there is nothing interesting in the myth, if it neither amuses nor enlightens, we become bored – which is an excellent way of discarding unwanted myths.

Plato distrusted the power of the theatre to undermine the assumptions on which the state depends, which was why he wanted to ban artists from his Republic or compel them to serve the Guardians. Much of this suspicion lingers today. Governments have little to offer other than a mythology. They produce no goods, feed no mouths, cure no sickness. What they must do is to provide the social trust within which these tasks are performed by others. If the role of the Guardians is undermined by those who have no such sense of responsibility, the state totters.

In *The Anti-Theatrical Prejudice* (1981), Jonas Barish has described how governments and churches have tried to suppress the theatre. It is a long history, but the struggle lies not between artists and guardians, but between modes of perception. It is a philosophical question, one which haunts European culture. It can be traced back to the distinction between two Greek words for a word, *mythos* and *logos*. In Plato's time, *mythos* (a divine revelation or an unprovable assumption) fell out of fashion and started to be used in a derogatory way, mere superstition. *Logos* meanwhile was elevated. If something was factually true, and provable by reason and experience, then it was really true.

Nowadays we tend to use the word myth, derived from *mythos*, as, to quote the *Pocket Oxford Dictionary*, an 'old wives' tale', something inherently untrue; but this does not describe the Greek myths adequately, where facts and imaginative theories were entwined. Their facts may have been wrong, their beliefs to our minds incredible, but when they were brought into being, they were not necessarily known to be false. On the contrary, they were forceful attempts to grapple with reality.

We handle the past in a similar way. Our history books and news broadcasts also mix facts with speculation, for reality can not flood into our minds holistically. We have to choose on what aspects of reality to concentrate and behind these choices lie unprovable assumptions or *mythos*. If we string our assumptions together or use our memories of

176

the past to provide parables for the future, we are constructing myths which may in time seem as incredible, or as truthful, as those of the ancient Greeks.

Myths may not be provable, they may be provably false, but this does not stop them from being useful. Freud was helped by the Oedipus legend whether or not a man called Oedipus existed. Myths are aids to perception, embedded in language, but to call them merely useful underrates their significance. Some may be indispensable or revelatory. Evolutionary progress is a myth, for we can have no idea where the universe is going, but it helped us to get rid of Adam and Eve. Another example could be the strange persistence of Absolutes. We may not know what Truth is, but we can guess when somebody is being economical with It. We can have no knowledge of Absolutes, not being Absolute ourselves, but we seem to be incapable of living without Them.

Myths can also be treacherous, persuading us to see things that are not there; and the elevation of *logos* above *mythos* can lend an arrogance to thought, in which what is assumed to be true is asserted to be fact. When governments employ artists, they usually do so to promote the myths which have brought them to power. This may not stem so much from partisanship as from an enlightened self-interest. Artists can provide a sense of nationhood. They can demonstrate legal procedures or, on a seemingly trivial level, groom an image or stage a conference. Even dissident velvet prisoners are useful to demonstrate the openness of a society, but there can be a considerable gap between the freedom granted to such art forms as the theatre, which few people see, and broadcasting, which reaches many.

The question raised by arts subsidy is not how much money should be given to the arts, but how much power should be given to governments. During this century, societies have become increasingly centralised and governments have become major employers, providers of welfare services, possessors of weapons of mass destruction. At each stage in this enlargement, the political need to control the media has become more apparent. In Britain, the television companies promote politicians in a way which casts doubt not so much on their objectivity (for nobody can be objective) but on their vision. They are Westminster-centred, which is where they derive their mandates.

If governments defend their myths to the point of excluding all others, societies become brittle. There are no other ways of looking at the world than those provided by the state. If such a government is overthrown, there is a pause for anarchy before fresh myths come into being, which was what happened to what was the Soviet Union. But there is also a danger in too much pliability. If myths are treated too lightly, if there are no widely held assumptions on which people can rely, there is nothing to hold a society together other than force. At best, the theatre provides a useful half-way house, between suppressing alternative myths and allowing them to run riot and disrupt the system.

The final downfall of communism in Eastern Europe was swift, categoric and preceded by a caricature of a last-ditch stand. In August 1991, Gorbachev was away on holiday in the Crimea when the reactionary wing of his coalition cabinet decided to stage a coup. In timing, it was like that which deposed Kruschev, but there the comparisons end. The old *apparatchiks* who tried to mastermind Gorbachev's downfall had no idea of the strength of feeling against them or how the old authority of the Communist Party had dwindled. Boris Yeltsin, the Russian president, led the resistance and barricades were raised around the Russian parliament. Crowds gathered and when tanks rolled towards the parliament building, the troops refused to fire and in 48 hours, the coup was over.

What prompted this display of incompetence was the threat of a new union treaty which would have given the republics more autonomy while retaining some control in Moscow, but the failed *coup* strengthened the hand of non-communists like Yeltsin and those republics which wanted to break from the USSR altogether. When Gorbachev returned to Moscow, not quite in triumph, for the hero of the hour was Yeltsin, the balance of power had shifted decisively. In less than three weeks, a different union treaty was devised to give the republics full automony and thus the USSR became a Commonwealth of Independent States.

The mess left behind will take a long time to clear. As I write these final sentences, there is an uprising in Romania, another in Georgia, and a fragile peace has just been struck between Serbs and Croats in what is still Yugoslavia. There are other local wars on the horizon and I would feel easier in my mind if I knew whose fingers were on what triggers left by the Cold War. And yet another giant threat for mankind looms ahead.

On 26 August 1991 while Gorbachev was being told that the USSR was finished, an adviser to Mrs Thatcher, Sir Crispin Tickell, warned the British Association for the Advancement of Science that at present rates of population growth, the 5.3 billion people who now inhabit the planet will increase to 8 billion by 2025 AD. If we share out the available resources and all become vegetarian, there may be enough food to sustain 6 billion. He called for an alliance between science and culture to prepare the public for the troubles ahead. The situation was too serious to be left, he said, to politicians and business managers.

He sounded rather like George Kennan at the University of Notre Dame in 1953. It may be tempting to believe that science and culture, being good in themselves, will espouse good causes, but the experience

178

of the past forty years suggests otherwise. In time, the Cold War may seem to have been a distraction from the real problems facing mankind, a schism in the Enlightenment, as remote as the religious feuds which darkened the Middle Ages. As science wasted its energies on armaments, so culture tended to promote the assumptions which it had the power to question.

Science and culture cannot pretend to be 'pure' in the sense of being detached from the societies of which they are part. It is not their job to peddle answers, but to map out the range of possibilities through which we individually sift for solutions. There is no escape from personal choice and private conscience. If this sounds like the conclusion to which I, as a British Liberal, born in 1934, a vintage year for Liberals, could be expected to come, I must plead guilty to the crime of being predictable. My story in this book is a myth, particularly where I have on occasions dwindled into fact. Its value (or otherwise) rests in the mind of the reader, like all myths, everywhere.

NOTES

1 THE CONSCIENCE OF A DIPLOMAT

1 George F. Kennan (1973) *Memoirs*, vol. 2 (London: Hutchinson), p. 74.
2 Mikhail S. Gorbachev (1987) 'Lessons of History', *Perestroika* (London: Fontana/Collins), p. 38.
3 Kennan, op. cit., p. 197.
4 ibid., p. 52.
5 ibid., p. 67.
6 ibid., p. 79.
7 ibid.
8 George F. Kennan in *Foreign Affairs*, April 1951.
9 ibid.
10 Kennan, *Memoirs*, op. cit., p. 227.
11 ibid.
12 *Time* Magazine (1988) *Mikhail S. Gorbachev* (New York: Time, Inc.), p. 62.
13 Miklosz Haraszti (1990) *The Velvet Prison* (London: Penguin), p. 96.
14 Arthur Miller (1987) *Timebends* (London: Methuen), p. 95.
15 Kennan, *Memoirs*, op. cit., p. 87.
16 ibid., p. 185.

2 THE TRIAL OF ARTHUR MILLER

1 Arthur Miller (1987) *Timebends* (London: Methuen), p. 390.
2 ibid.
3 Dennis Welland (1983) *Miller* (London: Methuen), p. 18.
4 Quoted in ibid., p. 39.
5 Arthur Miller, quoted in ibid., p. 81.
6 Miller, op. cit., p. 321.
7 Anthony Summers (1985) *Goddess* (London: Gollancz), p. 196.
8 ibid., p. 175.
9 Interview in *Life*, August 1962.
10 Welland, op. cit., p. 88.
11 ibid., p. 85.
12 Interview with Alan Yentob, *Omnibus*, BBC2, 7 July 1990.
13 Summers, op. cit., p. 175.
14 Christopher Bigsby (ed.) (1990) *Arthur Miller and Company* (London: Methuen), p. 15.

3 BINKIE BEAUMONT'S WEST END

1 Arthur Miller (1987) *Timebends* (London: Methuen), p. 417.
2 ibid., p. 340.
3 BBC Press Release, 23 January 1951.
4 Miller, op. cit., p. 431.
5 ibid., p. 432.
6 ibid., p. 430.
7 Richard Huggett (1989) *Binkie Beaumont* (London: Hodder & Stoughton), p. 357.
8 Irving Wardle (1978) *The Theatres of George Devine* (London: Cape), p. 171.
9 Miller, op. cit., p. 416.
10 Huggett, op. cit., p. 510.
11 Quoted in Anthony Holden (1988) *Olivier* (London: Sphere), p. 385.
12 Kenneth Tynan, review in *The Observer*, 21 August 1955.
13 John Elsom and Nicholas Tomalin (1978) *The History of the National Theatre* (London: Cape), p. 114.
14 ibid., p. 54.

4 THE HEAT IN BRECHT'S COOLNESS

1 George Devine in *Encore*, April 1956.
2 Irving Wardle (1978) *The Theatres of George Devine* (London: Cape), p. 151.
3 ibid., p. 169.
4 ibid., p. 170.
5 Devine, op. cit.
6 ibid.
7 ibid.
8 Wardle, op. cit., p. 170.
9 John Willett (1964) *The Theatre of Bertolt Brecht* (London: Methuen), p. 81.
10 John Willett (tr.) (1964) *Brecht on Theatre* (London: Methuen), p. 3.
11 ibid.
12 Bertolt Brecht, *Mann ist Mann*, first performance 25 September 1926, Darmstadt.
13 Willet, *Brecht on Theatre*, op. cit., p. 180.
14 Ronald Speirs (1987) *Bertolt Brecht* (London: Macmillan), p. 120.
15 Willett, *The Theatre of Bertolt Brecht*, op. cit., p. 200.

5 AT THE BACK OF THE MIND

1 Deirdre Bair (1978) *Samuel Beckett* (London: Cape), p. 382.
2 Samuel Beckett (1955) *Waiting for Godot* (London: Faber), p. 90.
3 Bair, op. cit., p. 381.
4 Annie Cohen-Solal (1987) *Sartre, A Life* (London: Heinemann), p. 53.
5 Quoted by Richard Stack, 'Ionesco's art of derision', *Plays and Players*, June 1960.
6 Cohen-Solal, op. cit., p. 415.

6 OLIVIER PASSES THE BATON

1 Richard Findlater (ed.) (1981) *At the Royal Court*, Appendix 2.
2 Quoted in John Wakeman (ed.) (1975) *World Authors* (London: H.W. Wilson Co.), p. 1317.
3 Frank Granville-Barker, review of *Rhinoceros*, *Plays and Players*, June 1960.
4 Anthony Holden (1988) *Olivier* (London: Sphere), p. 419.
5 ibid., p. 420.
6 ibid.
7 ibid.
8 John Elsom and Nicholas Tomalin (1978) *The History of the National Theatre* (London: Cape), p. 122.
9 Peter Brook, *RSC Annual Report*, 1968.
10 Sally Beauman (1982) *The Royal Shakespeare Company* (Oxford: Oxford University Press), p. 239.
11 *Twenty-fifth Annual Report of the Arts Council of Great Britain* (1969/70), p. 11.
12 Holden, op. cit., p. 461.
13 ibid., p. 4.
14 ibid., p. 5.
15 ibid.
16 Elsom and Tomalin, op. cit., p. 127.
17 Holden, op. cit., p. 3.
18 Alan Brien, review in *Sunday Telegraph*, 26 April 1964.
19 Elsom and Tomalin, op. cit., p. 200.

7 THE VELVET PRISON

1 Felix Barker, *Evening News*, 8 September 1965.
2 Laurence Olivier (1982) *Confessions of an Actor* (London: Weidenfeld & Nicolson), p. 220.
3 Felix Barker (1984) *Laurence Olivier* (London: Spellmount Ltd), p. 66.
4 From a notice pinned in a hotel foyer in Novosibirsk in 1984, presumably with the intention that it should be read by the BBC producer Richard Bannerman and John Elsom, who were staying there.
5 Geoffrey Hosking (1985) *A History of the Soviet Union* (London: Fontana/Collins), p. 411.
6 Olivier, op. cit., p. 221.
7 John Elsom (ed.) (1989) *Is Shakespeare Still Our Contemporary?* (London: Routledge), p. 96.
8 Jan Kott (1967) *Shakespeare Our Contemporary* (London: Methuen), p. 52.
9 Peter Raina (1978) *Political Opposition in Poland* (London: Poets and Painters Press), p. 113.
10 Dorrick Mercer (ed.) (1988) *Chronicle of the 20th Century* (London: Longman), p. 985.
11 Valerie Zolotuchin, *Teatr* [Soviet theatre magazine], no. 6, 1989.

8 THE SECULAR BAPTIST

1 Essay by Ludwik Flaszen in J. Grotowski (1969) *Towards a Poor Theatre* (London: Methuen), p. 97.

2 Christopher Innes (1981) *Holy Theatre* (Cambridge: Cambridge University Press), p. 174.
3 ibid., pp. 171–2.
4 C.G. Jung and K. Kerenyi, *Essays on a Science of Mythology*, quoted in Innes, ibid.
5 Tariq Ali (1987) *Street Fighting Years* (London: Collins), p. 207.
6 *Theatre Quarterly*, vol. 1, no. 3 (1971).
7 Innes, op. cit., p. 127.
8 *Travail Théâtral*, nos. 18–19 (1975), p. 196.
9 Trevor Griffiths (1974) *The Party* (London: Faber), pp. 47–53.

9 THE AGE OF AQUARIUS

1 Martin Banham (ed.) (1988) *Cambridge Guide to World Theatre* (Cambridge: Cambridge University Press), p. 592.
2 Ronald Hayman (1979) *Theatre and Anti-Theatre* (London: Secker & Warburg), p. 232.
3 ibid.
4 Interview with Joseph Chaikin, quoted by John Lahr (1970) *Up Against a Fourth Wall* (New York).
5 Robert Brustein (1970) *The Third Theatre* (London: Cape), p. 51.
6 ibid.
7 Harold Clurman (1974) *The Divine Pastime* (London: Macmillan), p. 191.
8 Foster Hirsch (1989) *Harold Prince* (Cambridge: Cambridge University Press), p. 66.
9 Clurman, op. cit., p. 116.
10 Quoted by Catherine R. Hughes in *Plays and Players*, April 1969.
11 Dorrick Mercer (ed.) (1988) *Chronicle of the 20th Century* (London: Longman), p. 1008.
12 Eric Bentley (1972 [1968]) *Theatre of War* (London: Eyre Methuen), pp. 356–61.
13 ibid., p. 360.
14 Interview with Jerzy Grotowski, *The Drama Review*, vol. 13, no. 1, Fall 1968.
15 Clurman, op. cit., pp. 253–4.

10 THE FLOATING ISLAND

1 Michael Billington in *Plays and Players*, December 1966, p. 12
2 ibid.
3 Tariq Ali in *Town*, November 1966.
4 D.A.N. Jones in *New Statesman*, October 1966.
5 Peter Brook (1967) *The Shifting Point* (London: Methuen), p. 61.
6 ibid.
7 ibid., p. 47.
8 John Lahr (1973) *Orton, the Complete Plays* (London: Methuen), Introduction.
9 Brook, op. cit., p. 62.
10 A.B. Gascoigne (1962) *Twentieth Century Drama* (London: Hutchinson).
11 Harold Pinter (1965) *The Homecoming* (London: Methuen), p. 34.
12 Laurence Olivier in *Plays and Players*, January 1966, p. 28.
13 Brook, op. cit., p. 122.

11 TOWARDS MUSIC

1 *Theater Heute*, December 1967.
2 Michael Patterson (1976) *German Theatre Today* (London: Pitman), p. 5.
3 ibid., pp. 114–17.
4 David Bradby and David Williams (1988) *Directors' Theatre* (London: Macmillan), p. 190.
5 ibid., p. 195.
6 Peter Brook (1967) *The Shifting Point* (London: Methuen), p. 103.
7 ibid., Preface.
8 ibid., p. 106.
9 ibid., p. 108.
10 ibid., p. 110.
11 Peter Roberts in *Plays and Players*, November 1971.
12 ibid.
13 Jonathan Hammond in *Plays and Players*, November 1972.
14 Brook, op. cit., pp. 127–8.
15 ibid., p. 115.
16 ibid., p. 129.
17 ibid.
18 ibid., p. 151.
19 ibid., p. 162.
20 ibid., p. 163.

12 THE NATIONAL THEATRE IS YOURS

1 John Elsom and Nicholas Tomalin (1978) *The History of the National Theatre* (London: Cape), p. 294.
2 ibid., p. 281.
3 Peter Hall (1983) *Memoirs* (London: Hamish Hamilton), pp. 258–9 and elsewhere. Hall was mistaken in asserting either that I had shown the manuscript of *The History of the National Theatre* to other journalists in Fleet Street or that I was the source of two articles by Max Hastings in the *Evening Standard* (22 and 23 September 1976).
4 ibid., p. 221.
5 From John Elsom's interview with Peter Hall, 30 May 1975.
6 Elsom and Tomalin, op. cit., p. 276
7 This book was Elsom and Tomalin, *The History of the National Theatre*, ibid.
8 John Simon in *The Hudson Review* vol. XXVIII, no. 1.
9 Elsom and Tomalin, op. cit., p. 333.
10 I wrote this letter on 11 February 1983, and it was published a few days later.

13 BROADWAY BABIES

1 Peter Brook (1967) *The Shifting Point* (London: Methuen), p. 103.
2 Interview with John Elsom in a BBC *Kaleidoscope* special, 'A Night Out in Novosibirsk', 17 December 1984.
3 From 'Broadway Baby' in *Follies*.
4 From 'The Little Things You Do Together' in *Company*.

5 Foster Hirsch (1989) *Harold Prince* (Cambridge: Cambridge University Press), p. 120.
6 ibid., p. 75.
7 From 'Waiting for the Girls Upstairs' in *Follies*.
8 From 'I'm Still Here' in *Follies*.
9 From 'You Could Drive a Person Crazy' in *Company*.
10 Stanley Green (1985) *Broadway Musicals* (London: Faber), p. xviii.
11 From the programme for the West End production of *Into The Woods*.

14 THE UNRAVELLING

1 Mikhail Shvydkoi (1987) *The Mid-Eighties: Drama, Theatre, Life* (Moscow: ITI), p. 76.
2 ibid., p. 77.
3 *Time* Magazine (1988) *Mikhail S. Gorbachev* (New York: Time, Inc.), pp. 115–16.
4 ibid., p. 31.
5 ibid., pp. 45–6. See also Mikhail S. Gorbachev (1987) *Perestroika* (London: Fontana/Collins), p. 41.
6 (1988) *Chronicle of the 20th Century* (London: Longman), p. 1264.
7 *Time* Magazine, op. cit., p. 134.
8 Sir Crispin Tickell, address to the British Association for the Advancement of Science, reported in *The Independent*, 27 August 1991.
9 John Elsom, 'Berlin's Theater Festival' in *The World and I*, December 1990, p. 158.
10 Gorbachev, op. cit., p. 49.
11 ibid., p. 37.

15 THEME AND EXPOSITION

1 Robert R. King, 'Coping with Ceauşescu's legacy' in *The World and I*, March 1990, p. 105.
2 *Collier's International Year Book*, 1990, p. 446.
3 ibid.
4 King, op. cit., p. 108.
5 ibid.
6 ibid., p. 109.

INDEX

Abbott, George 7, 8, 17, 23, 32, 100, 102, 103
Abramov, Fyodr 156, 157, 165
Abstract art 8
Abstract Expressionism 51
The Absurd 49–53, 61, 103, 173
ACGB (see Arts Council of Great Britain)
Acheson, Dean 2
An Actor Prepares 19
The Actors' Studio (New York) 18, 20, 51, 164
Adam, Kenneth 111
Adamov, Arthur 53
Adelaide Festival 126
Adenauer, Dr Konrad 91
Adrian, Max 113
Adventure Story 33
Aeschylus 64, 79, 127, 170, 172, 173
Afore Night Come 117
African National Congress (ANC) 166
After the Fall 17
Ain't Misbehavin' 148, 154
Akhmatova, Anna 9
Albee, Edward 100, 103, 108, 117
Aldwych Theatre (London) 65, 109, 123
Alexander, Sir George 31, 32, 34
Ali, Tariq 46, 92, 93, 109, 110
All My Sons 14, 15, 17
Amadeus 138, 142, 143
Amédée 54
America Hurrah 100, 101, 106
The American Clock 21
The American Dream 100, 103
ANC (see African National Congress)
Andropov, Yuri 146, 158–60

Angry Brigade 95
Anikst, Aleksander 73, 76, 78–80, 131
Annie Get Your Gun 1
Anouilh, Jean 30, 53, 121
The Anti-Theatrical Prejudice 176
Anything Goes 148
Archer, William 64, 69, 131
Aristotle 14, 24, 25, 45, 112, 168, 173
Arnold, Matthew 64, 65
Aron, Raymond 51
Artaud, Antonin 53, 68, 86, 90, 97, 109
The Arthur Haynes Show 61
Arts Council of Great Britain (ACGB) 30, 66, 67, 95, 119, 136, 137, 141–3, 154
Arts Theatre Club 34, 66
As You Like It 127
Ashcroft, Dame Peggy 136, 137
Auden, W.H. 60
Avignon Festival 129, 131
Ayckbourn, Alan 135, 136, 138, 139

Baader-Meinhof gang 95
Baal 40
Babbit, Milton 149
The Bacchae 18
Bad Behaviour 154, 155
Badderley, Hermione 113
Bagnold, Enid 33
Bair, Deirdre 50
Baker, Norma Jean (see Marilyn Monroe)
The Balcony 55, 163
The Bald Prima-Donna 54
The Ballad of Clement the Mason 148
Balustrade Theatre (Prague) 82, 139

Bancroft, Ann 19
Banfield, Stephen 154
Bankhead, Tallulah 29
Barba, Eugenio 85, 94
Barefoot in the Park 101
Barish, Joas 176
Barker, Felix 73
Barker, Harley Granville 64, 69, 131
Barker, Howard 95
Barnes, Peter 118
Barrault, Jean-Louis 54, 62, 90, 93, 94, 123
Barthes, Roland 60, 125
Barton, John 139
BBC (British Broadcasting Corporation) 25, 27, 111–13, 140
The Beatles 147
Beaton, Cecil 30
Beaumont, H.B. (Binkie) 25, 28–33, 35, 38, 39, 66, 67, 123, 136, 137
The Beggars' Opera 63
Being and Nothingness 55
Belyakovic 162
Ben-Gurion 93
Benichou, Maurice 129
Benjamin, Walter 42
Bennett, Alan 138
Benning, Achim 130
Bentley, Eric 15, 105, 106
Berlin, Irving 7, 150
Berliner Ensemble 37, 38, 46–8
Bernhard, Thomas 130
Bernstein, Leonard 7, 150
Betrayal 117
Bevan, Aneurin 66
Beyond the Fringe 113
Billington, Michael 109
Biltmore Theater (New York) 107
Birmingham Repertory Theatre 123, 134
The Birthday Party 116
The Blacks 61
Blakeley, Colin 69
Blakemore, Michael 71, 137
Blin, Roger 50
Bochum Schauspielhaus 126, 130
Bogdanov, Michael 139
Bolshoi Opera and Ballet Theatre 162
Bond, Christopher 149
Bond, Edward 95, 117, 118, 120, 122
Born Yesterday 21, 101

Bouffes du Nord Théâtre (Paris) 126, 129, 170
Bradley, A.C. 14, 15
Brandauer, Klaus-Maria 130
Brando, Marlon 19, 20
Brassneck 133
Braun, Volker 47
Breath 59
Brecht, Bertolt 24, 26, 32, 34, 37–49, 56, 65, 71, 76, 79, 80, 97, 105, 109, 110, 120, 121, 150, 161, 172
Brenton, Howard 95, 133, 136, 139, 143
Brezhnev, Leonid 74, 80, 82, 93, 133, 146, 158, 159
Brien, Alan 70
The Brig 97
Brighouse, Harold 75
British Association for the Advancement of Science 178
Brook, Peter 25, 35, 47, 48, 65, 68, 71, 85, 94, 109, 110, 119, 121–30, 144, 163, 170, 173
Brooks, Mel 103
Brothers and Sisters 156–61
Brown, Kenneth 97
Bruce, Lennie 104
Brustein, Robert 101, 104
Bryden, Bill 136
'Bucharest '90' Festival 170
Büchner, Georg 167
Buckwitz, Harry 47
Bukowski, Charles 22
Bulandra Theatre (Bucharest) 170
Bulgakov, Mikhail 9, 162
Burgtheater (Vienna) 130, 131, 167
Buried Child 108
Burrell, John 36
Burton, Richard 30
Butler, Michael 107
Butler, R.A. 67

Cabaret 97, 102, 103
Café La Mama (*see* La Mama)
Cain, Henry 14
Calderón de la Barca 85
Caligula 53
Call Me Madam 7, 150
Callaghan, James 134
Calley, William 104, 105
Camelot 102
Camus, Albert 52, 56

Can Can 147
Capital 43
Caramitru, Ion 168–70
The Caretaker 116
Cariou, Len 151
Carleton-Green, Hugh 112
Carmichael, Ian 26
Carmichael, Stokeley 106
Carrie 154
Carrière, Jean Luc 129
The Carrière Callet 129, 131
Carter, James 152
Carry On (Films) 114
Cartoucherie (*see* Théâtre du Soleil)
Cats 154
The Caucasian Chalk Circle 38, 39, 45
Ceauşescu, Elena 169, 171
Ceauşescu, Nicolae 168–71
Ceauşescu, Nicu 169, 171
CEMA (*see* Council for the
  Encouragement of Music and
  the Arts)
Central Intelligence Agency (CIA) 3,
  4, 23, 99
Chaikin, Joseph 98, 101, 104
The Chalk Garden 33
Chandos, Lord (*see* Lyttelton, Oliver)
Chekhov, Anton 19, 80, 154, 155, 163
Chekhov, Michael 19, 164
Chernenko, Konstantin 75, 131, 146,
  156, 158, 159
Cherry Lane Theater (New York) 97
The Cherry Orchard 163, 164
Chess 154
Chiang Kai-Shek 4
Chicago 154
Chichester Festival Theatre 63
Chomsky, Noam 87, 88
Churchill, Winston 26, 36
CIA (*see* Central Intelligence Agency)
Cieslak, Ryscard 86, 129
CIRT (*see* International Centre for
  Theatre Research)
Citizen Kane 62
Civil Rights Act (US) 100, 105
The Classical Trilogy (Andrei
  Serban) 170–3
The Clockwork Orange 154
Clunes, Alec 34
Clurman, Harold 102–4, 106
Cocteau, Jean 97
Codron, Michael 35

Cohn-Bendit, Daniel 92
Cole, George 25
Colman, Ronald 7
The Comédie Française 64
The Comedy of Errors 136
Comedy Theatre (London) 28
Company 150, 151
The Condemned of Altona 55
The Conference of Birds 120, 126
Congreve, William 75
The Connection 23, 97
The Constant Prince 85, 86, 88, 90
Cook, Peter 113
Cooper, Giles 113
Coriolanus 47, 62, 63
Cottesloe Theatre (London) 132, 136
Council for the Encouragement of
  Music and the Arts (CEMA) 31
A Course in General Linguistics 10
Coward, Noel 26, 30, 33, 35, 119
Craig, Edward Gordon 65, 82
Craiova Theatre (Romania) 171
Crosby, Bing 8
The Crucible 9, 14, 18, 58
Crucible Theatre (Sheffield, UK) 136
Curse of the Starving Class 108

Dadaism 40, 68
Dairy Farm 120
Daley, Richard 107
Dames at Sea 148
Damn Yankees 7, 13
Dangerous Liaisons 53
Daniel, Yuli 77
Darwin, Charles 41
Daubeny, Peter 65
Daumal, René 120
Davis, Ronnie 104
Day, Doris 8
A Day by the Sea 31, 33
de Beauvoir, Simone 51, 57
de Bono, Edward 128
de Gaulle, Charles 58, 91, 92, 96, 111
The Dead Class 82
Dean, James 147
The Death of Bessie Smith 100,
  103
Death of a Salesman 14, 15
Decroux, Etienne 62
The Deep Blue Sea 31, 32
Department of Economic Affairs
  (UK) 66, 111

Department of Education and Science (UK) 66
Department of Trade and Industry (UK) 68
Deutsches Theater 46
Devine, George 34, 37–9, 48, 61
Dexter, John 69, 71
Dibrova, Major-General 46
Dierov, Anatol 144
DiMaggio, Joe 22, 23
The Dirtiest Show in Town 107
Ditch the Bitch 142
Do I Hear a Waltz? 149
Dodin, Lev 156–8
Douglas-Home, Sir Alec (Earl of Home) 66, 74
Douglas-Home, William 137
Dr Strangelove 100
Dr Taranne 53
Dr Zhivago 75
The Dragon 80
Drake University (US) 98
Dreamgirls 153
Dubček, Aleksander 83, 160
Duchamp, Marcel 40
Dulles, Allen 99
Dulles, John Foster 11, 33
Duncan, Ronald 34
Dunlop, Frank 71
Duras, Marguerite 53
Dürrenmatt, Friedrich 67, 121
Dutschke, Rudi 92, 107
Dylan, Bob 104, 147

Early Morning 118
Ecole Normale Supérieure 51–3
Eden, Sir Anthony 32, 33, 112
Edinburgh Festival (UK) 85
Efremov, Oleg 162, 164
Efros, Anatol 158
Einstein, Albert 41
Einstein on the Beach 174
Eisenhower, Dwight D. 5, 11, 18, 21, 23, 150
The Elder Statesman 33
Electra 170, 171
Eliot, T.S. 14, 33, 34, 114
Empress of Persia (see Persia)
Empson, William 81
The Empty Space 47, 125
End Game 58, 61
An Enemy of the People 14

English Stage Company (ESC) 33, 34, 37, 61, 69
The Entertainer 34, 35
Entertainment Tax 29, 67
Epic Theatre 42
Equity (the actors' trade union, UK) 30
Equus 138
Erhardt, Ludwig 92
ESC (see English Stage Company)
Essex, David 148
Esslin, Martin 53
Establishment Club 113
Euripides 79, 170, 172
Evans, Edith 26, 30
Evening Standard 143
Evita 153, 154
Existentialism 52–60
Expressionism 8, 76, 81, 162, 163
Eyen, Tom 107, 153
Eyre, Richard 136, 140

Fabre, Jan 175
Fanshen 133
FBI (see Federal Bureau of Investigation)
Federal Bureau of Investigation (FBI) 9, 23
Fenton, James 138
Fiddler on the Roof 102
Field, Anthony 28
Fields, Gracie 25
Figaro Littéraire 54
Finlay, Frank 69–71
Finney, Albert 136
Flaubert, Gustave 58, 59
The Flies 55
Flint 116
FLN (see Front de Libération Nationale)
Flynn, Errol 8
Fo, Dario 95
Földes, Anna 78
Follies 144, 148, 151–3
Fonda, Henry 14
Fontaine, Lynn 67
Fool for Love 108
Ford, Gerald 152
Ford Foundation 124
Forefathers' Eve 80
Foreign Affairs 1, 5
Formalism 44–6

Fortnum & Mason 30
Fosse, Bob 102
Foucault, Michel 60
France–URSS 56
Frankie Goes to Hollywood 147
Frayn, Michael 138
Freie Volksbühne 47
The French Theatre 64
Freud, Sigmund 18, 19, 51, 58,
    164, 177
Freyer, Achim 167
Friedman, Milton 141, 162
From Protest to Resistance 105
Front de Libération Nationale
    (FLN) 58
Fry, Christopher 34
*A Funny Thing Happened on the Way
    to the Forum* 102, 149
Furth, George 151
Furtseva, Mme 75, 83, 84
Futurism 41, 164

Gaitskell, Hugh 67
Galileo 45, 46, 49
Galin, Aleksander 156
Gallacher, Willie 26
Gamesmanship 26
Gandhi, Mahatma 93
Garson, Barbara 104
Gascoigne, Bamber 116
Gaskill, William 69–71
Gate Theatre (Prague) 82
Gay, John 63
Gelber, Jack 23, 97
Genet, Jean 54, 55, 61, 68, 163
Gershwin, George 150
Gielgud, Sir John 30, 35, 37, 62, 69,
    136, 137
Gilbert and George 174
Gill, Peter 136
Gingold, Hermione 113
Ginsberg, Alan 22
Gladstone, William Ewart 143
Godspell 148
Goethe, Johann Wolfgang 39, 121, 122
Gogol, Nicolai 80
Golden City 115
Golders Green Hippodrome (UK) 30
Gombrowicz, Witold 81, 145
Gomulka, Władyslaw 81
The Good Person of Setzuan 38,
    45, 48, 76

Goodbody, Buzz 136
Goodbye to Berlin 102
Gorbachev, Mikhail 8, 131, 146,
    157–61, 165, 166, 168, 178
Gorki, Maxim 44, 80, 126
Grable, Betty 8
The Grand Magic Circus 94
Granville Barker, Harley (*see* Barker,
    Harley Granville)
Grass, Günter 47
Gray, Simon 138, 139
Grazzi, Paulo 95
Grease 148
The Greeks 139
Grenfell, Joyce 26
Griffiths, Trevor 94
Grishin, Victor 159
Gromyko, Andrei 160
Grosz, Georg 40
Grotowski, Jerzy 82, 85–90, 97, 106,
    115, 123, 170, 173
The Group 30, 34
Group Theater (US) 19
Gruppa Teatre e Arzione (Italy) 95
Guinness, Sir Alec 30
Gulbenkian Foundation 124
Gurdjieff, George Ivanovich 128
Gypsy 102
Guys and Dolls 148

Hair 106, 148
Hall, Sir Peter 34, 50, 63, 68, 69, 71,
    95, 117, 119, 123, 131, 132, 134–40,
    142, 143
Hamlet 18, 63, 68, 78–80, 107, 114, 136
Hammerstein, Oscar 7, 102, 149
Hammond, Jonathan 125
Handke, Peter 126, 130
Happenings 51, 55
Happy Days 58, 59, 137
Haraszti, Miklosz 9, 77, 81
Hare, David 133, 136, 143
Harrison, Kathleen 25
Harrison, Sir Rex 30
Hauptmann, Gerhart 41
Havel, Václav 49, 82, 106, 114,
    139, 145
Haymarket Theatre (London) 30
Haynes, Jim 98
Heart of a Dog 162
Heath, Edward 132–4, 142
Hebbel, Friedrich 39

Hebbel Theatre (Berlin) 37
Hedda Gabler 31
Heilpern, John 125
Heldenplatz 130, 131
Hill, Charles (Lord Hill) 112
Hills, Mr 13
Hinton, William 133
Hiss, Alger 3
Hitler, Adolf 44
Hobson, Sir Harold 69
Hobson's Choice 75
Hochhuth, Rolf 71
The Home 156
The Homecoming 68, 116, 117, 119
Honecker, Ernst 169
House Committee to Investigate
    Un-American Activities (HUAC) 5,
    6, 8, 9, 13, 15, 25, 44
House of Commons (UK) 31,
    73, 74, 137
House of Lords 137
Howard and Wyndham 29
Howerd, Frankie 113
Huggett, Richard 30
Hughes, Ted 124, 170
Humphrey, Hubert 107
Hunter, N.C. 31, 33, 35
Husak, Gustav 169
Husserl, Edmund 53
Huston, John 58

I Am a Camera 102
I Am Right, You Are Wrong 128
Ibsen, Henryk 14, 44, 147
The Ik 126
The Iliad 128
Iliescu, Ion 169
Ilyichev 76
*Imperialism, the Higher State of
    Capitalism* 43
The Importance of Being Earnest 30,
    32
In the Jungle of the Cities 121
Incident at Vichy 21
Innes, Christopher 86, 94
Institute for the Harmonious
    Development of Mankind 128
International Centre for Theatre
    Research (CIRT) 119, 122–6,
    128, 130
International Theatre Institute (ITI)
    90

Into the Woods 154
Ionesco, Eugène 54, 61
Isherwood, Christopher 102, 103
It's That Cat Again 144, 145, 147

Jackson, Sir Barry 123
Jackson, Glenda 68, 109
Jacques 61
Jagger, Mick 147, 148
Jarry, Alfred 53, 97
Jessner, Leopold 40
Jesus Christ, Superstar 148, 149, 153
Johnson, Lyndon Baines 99, 100,
    104, 105
Joint Stock 133, 136
Joking Apart 139
Jones, D.A.N. 109
Joyce, James 51, 114
Jożewicz, Janusz 154
Jumpers 114
Jung, Carl 86, 164, 173
Juno and Avos 148

Kabuki 124
Kadar, Janos 169
Kafka, Franz 53
Kahout, Pavel 82, 114
Kaiser, Georg 41
Kammerspiele (Munich) 95, 120, 121
Kanin, Garson 21, 101
Kantor, Tadeusz 81, 82, 173, 174
Kennan, George 1–6, 10, 11, 27, 43,
    159, 178
Kennedy, Jacqueline 68, 99
Kennedy, John F. 11, 22, 23, 68,
    98–100, 106, 111, 151
Kennedy, Robert 99, 105
Kerouac, Jack 22
KGB (Soviet Committee for State
    Security) 9, 79, 158
Khomeini, Ayatollah 152
King, Martin Luther 100, 105
King Lear 37
King Ubu 53, 126
The Kingfisher 137
Kipling, Rudyard 43
Kiss Me, Kate 148
Kissinger, Henry 11
Knowles, Christopher 174
Koestler, Arthur 18
Komsomol 146, 159
Kosygin, Aleksei 74

Kott, Jan 35, 78–80, 137
Kouate, Sotigui 129
Kowícki, Tadeusz 81
Krapp's Last Tape 58, 61
Kremlin Theatre (Moscow) 73
Kroetz, Franz Xaver 120, 122, 130
Kruschev, Nikita 57, 73–6, 79, 147, 160, 178
Kubrick, Stanley 100
Kulakov, Fyodr 159
Kundera, Milan 82, 114

Labiche, Eugene 126
Laboratory Theatre (Theatre Laboratory, Poland) 85, 86, 97
Laclos, Pierre 53
Lady Windermere's Fan 30
Lahr, John 113
Laing, R.D. 115
La Mama (Café and Theatre) 104, 108, 170
LAMDA (*see* London Academy for Music and the Dramatic Arts)
Langhoff, Wolfgang 46
Lapine, James 154
Lark Rise 136
Larkin, Philip 115
Laughton, Charles 46
Lear 118
Lee, Jennie 66–8, 71, 73, 75
Lehrer, Tom 104
Lehrstücke 44
Leigh, Vivien 35
Lenin, V.I. 43, 79, 114, 164, 166
Leningrad Institute of Theatre 157
Lenkom (Lenin Komsomol) 148, 155, 162
A Letter to Queen Victoria 174
Lévi-Strauss, Claude 60, 87, 88
Libération 56
Lichtenstein, Roy 100
A Lie of the Mind 108
Lifemanship 26
Lincoln, Abraham 98
The Little Hut 123
Little Me 101
A Little Night Music 148, 149
Littler, Emile 68, 117
Littlewood, Joan 34, 115
Living Theater 97, 98, 106, 107, 125
Lloyd-Webber, Andrew 103, 153, 154
Loesser, Frank 7, 150

London Academy for Music and the Dramatic Arts (LAMDA) 68, 123
Long Day's Journey Into Night 70
Lonsdale, Frederick 30, 137
Look Back In Anger 33, 34
Loot 113
Lord Chamberlain's Examiner of Plays 27, 32, 68, 117
Love For Love 75
Love's Labours Lost 123, 147
Lukes, Milan 146
Lulu 40
Lunt, Alfred 30, 67
Lysenko, Trofim 9
Lyttelton, Oliver (Lord Chandos) 35, 36, 63, 71
Lyttelton Theatre (London) 132
Lyubimov, Yuri 65, 76–8, 81, 83, 131, 148, 158, 160, 164

MacArthur, George 4
Macbeth 136
MacBird 104
McCarthy, Eugene 107
McCarthy, Joseph 3–7, 27, 105
MacDermot, Galt 106, 107, 148
McGovern, George 107
Mackenzie, Julia 151
Mackintosh, Cameron 154
Macmillan, Sir Harold 33, 66, 111, 113
The Mahabharata 128–31
The Maids 163
Major, John 143
Malina, Judith 97, 98
Malleson, Miles 62
Malone Dies 51
Malraux, André 91, 93
Maly Theatre (Leningrad) 156, 162
The Man Alive 83, 157
Man Equals Man 43
Man of La Mancha 102
Mao Tse Tung 4, 10, 74, 92, 93, 146
The Marat/Sade (Full title: *The Persecution and Assassination of Marat as Performed by the Inmates of the Charenton Asylum under the direction of the Marquis de Sade*) 68, 110, 111, 117
Marcus, Frank 113
Marowitz, Charles 61, 68, 98
Marshall, George 2
Marx, Karl 18

Marxist-Leninism 2, 9, 28, 42, 56, 146, 157, 162, 166, 175
MAT (see Moscow Art Theatre)
Matthews, A.E. 26
Mayakowsky, Vladimir 75
Me and My Gal 154
Measure for Measure 123
Medea 170, 171
Meetings with Remarkable Men 128
Memoirs (of Peter Hall) 135
The Memorandum 82
Mercer, David 115, 116
The Merchant of Venice 70
Merman, Ethel 6
Merrily We Roll Along 151, 153
Messel, Oliver 30
Der Messingkauf 45
Method acting 19
Meyerhold, V.E. 9, 76
Michigan, University of 9
Mickery (Amsterdam) 122
Mickiewicz, Adam 80
A Midsummer Night's Dream 122, 127
Millar, Ronald 140
Miller, Arthur 9, 13–23, 25–7, 32, 34, 35, 154
Miller, Jonathan 70, 71, 137
Milne, Alastair 140
Ministry of Culture (Moscow) 9, 49, 68, 77, 81, 83, 158
Les Misérables 154
The Misfits 17, 21
Mitterrand, François 92
Mnouchkine, Ariane 94, 122
Modern Times 52, 56
Modernism 40–2, 59, 65, 69, 164, 175
Molière (Jean-Baptiste Poquelin) 80
Molloy 116
Monroe, Marilyn 8, 13, 15, 16, 18–22, 25, 58
Morgan, Hughes Griffiths (see Beaumont, H.B.)
Morgan, Kenneth 32
Morgan – A Suitable Case For Treatment 116
Morrison, Norman 109
Moscow Art Theatre (MAT) 19, 76, 162–4
Moscow State Circus 162
Moscow State University 8, 159
Moss Empires 29
The Most Happy Fella 150

Mother Courage 37, 45
Mozhayev, Boris 83, 84, 157
Mrożek, Slavomir 81, 145
Mulier, Fritz 130
Müller, Heine 47
Murdoch, Rupert 143
Murphy 52
Mutiny 148
My Fair Lady 30
My Life in Art 19
Myers, Bruce 129
The Mysteries 136

National Film Theatre 136
National Salvation Front (NSF) 169
National Theatre (Bucharest) 170
National Theatre (NT) (London, now named the Royal National Theatre) 35, 36, 63–75, 77, 94, 95, 114, 121, 134–40, 142, 143, 154
National Theatre (Prague) 82, 146
National Theatre (Warsaw) 80
National Union of Miners (NUM) 134, 142
NATO (see North Atlantic Treaty Organisation)
Nausea 52
Nekrassov 56
Neuss, Wolfgang 121
The New Objectivity (die neue Sachlichkeit) 41, 164
The New Republic 14
New Statesman 26, 109
New Watergate Theatre Club 25
New York Free Press 105
New York Magazine 151
New York, University of, School for Arts 106
Newman, Paul 19
Nineteen Eighty Four 9
Nixon, Richard M. 107, 150, 152, 161
Nizan, Paul 51
No Exit 55
No Man's Land 117, 137
No, No, Nanette 148
No Time For Sergeants 98
Noguchi, Isamu 37
Noises Off 138
The Norman Conquests 138
Normanbrook, Lord 112

North Atlantic Treaty Organisation
(NATO) 3, 74, 91
Not I 59
Notre Dame (University of Notre
Dame) 6, 11, 178
Nottingham Playhouse (UK) 135, 136
Novello, Ivor 26, 30
Novotny, Antonin 82
Novyi Mir 76, 84
NSF (*see* National Salvation Front)
NT (*see* National Theatre, London)
Nuclear Arms and Foreign Policy 11
NUM (*see* National Union of Miners)
Nunn, Trevor 136, 142
Nuova Scena 96

The Odd Couple 101
Odéon (*see* Théâtre de France)
Odets, Clifford 34
Oedipus 71, 177
Offenbach, Jacques 144
O'Horgan, Tom 107
Oh! Calcutta! 59, 107
Oh, What a Lovely War! 115
Oklahoma! 148, 149
Old Vic Theatre (London) 36, 64,
114, 132
Oliver 102
Olivier, Sir Laurence (Lord Olivier)
20, 34–6, 61–5, 69–73, 78, 90, 94,
114, 117, 118, 137
Olivier Theatre (London) 132
O'Neill, Eugene 14, 23, 70
On The Road 22
On The Twentieth Century 148
*One Day in the Life of Ivan
Denisovich* 76, 84
One Mo' Time 148
One of Us 140
One-Upmanship 26, 114
Open Theater (US) 98, 100
Operetta 145
Oppenheimer, J. Robert 3
The Oresteia 18, 127, 128, 131, 136,
139, 173, 175
Orghast 124, 129, 170
Orpheus in the Underworld 144
Orton, Joe 113
Orwell, George 9
Osborne, John 33, 34
Oswald, Lee Harvey 98, 99
Othello 69, 70, 73, 75

Our Town 16
Over the Bridge 63
Oxford, University of 11

Pacific Overtures 151, 152
Pal Joey 148
Palach, Jan 83
Papp, Joseph 107
The Park 127
Parry, Natasha 122
The Party 94
Pasternak, Boris 75, 78
Peer Gynt 126
Performing Garage (Performance
Group) (US) 85, 104
Persia, Empress of 124
Persia, Shah of 124, 152
Peymann, Klaus 121, 126, 130
The Phantom of the Opera 154
Piccolo Teatro (Milan) 95
The Piggy-Bank 126
Pinero, Arthur Wing 31
Pinter, Harold 68, 114, 116, 117, 136,
137
Piper, John 30
Pirandello, Luigi 53, 55, 97
The Pirates of Penzance 148
Piscator, Erwin 40, 47
Plato 52, 93, 128, 176
Play 58
Plays and Players 117
The Plebeians Rehearse the Uprising 47
Plenty 133, 134
Plowright, Joan 35, 69
Pocket Oxford Dictionary 176
Podgorny, N.V. 74
The Poetics 14, 45
A Policy for the Arts 66
Pollock, Jackson 51
Portable Theatre 136
Porter, Cole 7, 150
Portman, Eric 26
The Postmaster-General 68
Post-Modernism 130, 175
Potter, Stephen 26, 27, 114, 119
The Power of Theatrical Magic
175
Pravda (Soviet Communist Party
newspaper) 76, 84
Pravda 143
Presley, Elvis 8
The Price 21

Prince, Harold 7, 102, 103, 148–51, 153, 154
Prince Littler Consolidate Trust 135
Princess Ivona 145
Princeton, University of and Institute for Advanced Studies 5, 12
Private Eye 113
The Producers 103
Prokofiev, Serge 9
Public Theatre 107
Pure Form in Theatre 81

Quartermain's Terms 139

Rabelais 85, 93, 94
Raceanu, Mircea 169
Rado, James 107
Ragni, Gerome 107
Rame, Franco 96
Rassemblement Démocratique Revolutionnaire (RDR) 56
Rattigan, Terence 30, 31, 33, 35, 139
Raymond, Paul 115
RDR (*see* Rassemblement Démocratique Revolutionnaire)
Reagan, Ronald 6, 22, 153, 161
The Recruiting Officer 71
Red Brigade 95
Red Torch Theatre (Novosibirsk) 145
Redgrave, Michael 69
Reich, Wilhelm 88
Reinhardt, Max 40, 65
Reith Lectures 11
Replica 82
A Resounding Tinkle 61
Restoration 145
The Restoration of Arnold Middleton 116
Revenge 95
Rhinoceros 54, 61
Rice, Tim 153
Richard III 78, 80
Richardson, Sir Ralph 36, 69, 70, 136, 137
Ride-a-Cock-Horse 116
The Rise and Fall of the City of Mahagonny 40
Riverside Studios (London) 136
Robbe-Grillet, Alain 53
Robbins, Jerome 7, 102
Rodgers, Richard 7, 149
Rolling Stones 147

Romanov, Grigory 159
The Romans in Britain 132, 139
Romberg, Sigmund 144, 150
Roosevelt, Franklin D. 2, 3
Rosencrantz and Guildenstern are Dead 114
Rossiter, Leonard 61
Roussin, André 123
Royal Court Theatre (London) 33, 38, 59, 69, 117, 119, 136
Royal Hunt of the Sun 69, 138
Royal Shakespeare Company (RSC) 63, 66, 68, 95, 109, 110, 119, 121, 122, 130, 136, 137, 139
Royce, Carl 13
Rozan, Micheline 123, 126
Rożewicz, Tadeusz 49, 81
RSC (*see* Royal Shakespeare Company)
Ruby, Jack 99
Rudkin, David 117
Rudman, Michael 136
The Ruling Class 118
Rusk, Dean 111
Russell, Bertrand 74
Rutherford, Margaret 30

Saint Genet 54
St James's Theatre (London) 31, 32, 34
St Joan of the Stockyards 43, 44
Sakharov, Andrei 78, 158, 160
Salad Days 25
San Francisco Mime Troupe 104
Sanity, Madness and the Family 115
Sarraute, Nathalie 53
Sartre, Jean-Paul 51, 52–60, 92
Satiricon Theatre (Moscow) 163
Saussure, Ferdinand de 10, 87
The Savage Mind 87
Savary, Jerome 94
Saved 117, 119, 120
Schaubühne am Halleschen Ufer 122, 126, 127, 130, 131, 139
Schauspielhaus (Zurich) 46
Schechner, Richard 85, 104, 105
Schiller, Friedrich 39, 121
Schlegel-Tieck (translations of Shakespeare) 39, 130
Schubert, Franz 40
Schwab, Martin 167
Schwarz, Yevgeny 80

Schwerin State Theatre 167
Schwiedrzik, Wolfgang 121
Schwitkoi, Mikhail 157, 163
Scofield, Paul 136
The Seagull 155
Seberg 154
The Second Mrs Tanqueray 31
The Second Sex 57
Securitate (Romanian Secret Police)
    169
Semaphor Theatre 61, 82
Semi-Detached 61
Seneca 71, 170
Serban, Andrei 94, 170, 172–4
*Sergeant Pepper's Lonely Heart's Club
    Band* 109
The Serpent 106
Seurat, Georges 154
Seven Types of Ambiguity 81
The Seven Year Itch 20
Seventeen Eighty Nine 94
Shaffer, Peter 69, 138, 142
Shah of Persia (*see* Persia, Shah of)
Shakespeare, William 14, 15, 39, 65,
    78–80, 114, 121, 123, 132, 137
Shakespeare Memorial Theatre (UK)
    37, 63, 65, 66, 119, 123, 132
Shakespeare, Our Contemporary 35, 78
Shakespeare's Memory 127
Shakespearian Tragedy 14
Shaw, Bernard 64, 121
Shepard, Sam 108
Shestakova, Eleanor 157
Shiraz Festival 124, 125
A Short Organum for the Theatre 45
Shostakovich, Dimitri 9
Shubert Organisation 142
Side by Side by Sondheim 148
Simon, John 138
Simon, Neil 101, 151
Simonov, Konstantin 76
Simpson, N.F. 61
Sinyavsky, Andrei 77
Situationists 95
A Slight Ache 116
Słowacki, Juliusz 85
A Small Apocalypse 81
Smith, Adam 143
Smith, Maggie 69
So Haltet die Freude recht fest 167
Socialist Realism 8, 9, 42, 44, 49,
    76, 77, 81

Soldiers 71
Solidarity 155, 168
Solzhenitsin, Alexander 76
Sophocles 79, 170, 172
Some Like It Hot 20
Sondheim, Stephen 102, 103, 148–54
Sondheim and Co. 154
Sorbonne, University of 92
The Sound of Music 102
South Bank Board 132
South Sea Bubble 35
Soviet Shakespeare Commission 78
Soviet Writers' Union 76
Sperr, Martin 120
A Spurt of Blood 68
The Stage 34
Stalin, Josef 1, 3, 4, 8, 11, 44, 46, 49,
    73–7, 79, 114, 159, 167
Stanislavski, Konstantin 19, 20,
    76, 163–5
Starlight Express 149, 154
Stars in the Morning Sky 156, 162
Stary Theatre (Cracow) 81, 82
Stein, Gertrude 97
Stein, Peter 95, 120–2, 124, 126–8, 130,
    131, 139, 166, 172
Steinbeck, John 26
Stephen Joseph Theatre
    (Scarborough, UK) 135, 138, 139
Stephens, Robert 69
Stewart, Ellen 104, 170
Stewart, James 8
Stewart, Michael 110
Stockhausen, Karl-Heinz 125
Stop the World – I Want to Get Off 102
Stoppard, Tom 114
Storey, David 115
Stossel, Marleen 127
Strasberg, Lee 18–22, 51, 164
Strasberg, Paula 20
Strauss, Botho 127, 130
Strauss, Johann 145
Street Fightin' Man 147
A Street Scene 45
A Streetcar Named Desire 19
Strehler, Giorgio 95
Stritch, Elaine 151
Structural Anthropology 87
Structuralism 10
Strzełecki, Andrzej 154
The Student Prince 144
Sugar Babies 148

A Suite in Three Keys 33, 119
Summer Folk 126, 130
Sunday in the Park with George 154
Sunday Times 138, 142, 143
Supermanship 26
Suslov, Mikhail 74
Svoboda, Josef 82
Sweeney Todd 149, 151
Sweet Charity 101
Swinarski, Konrad 65
Sylvaine, Vernon 113
Syntactical Structures 87
Szajna, Josef 81, 82

Taganka Theatre (Moscow) 76, 77, 81, 83, 84, 147, 148, 158, 160, 162–4
Tairov, Aleksander 76
Takova, Eleonor 144
Tango 145
Tartuffe 80
Taubert, Richard 40
Teatr Ateneum (Warsaw) 154
The Tempest 156
Tennent, H.M. 29, 30
Tennent, H.M., Ltd 28–30, 35
Tennent Productions Ltd 31
Terry, Megan 100
That Was The Week That Was (BBC programme) 112
Thatcher, Margaret 134, 140–3, 153, 161, 163, 178
Theater Heute 120, 122
Theater am Schiffbauerdamm 38, 46, 47
Theatre of Cruelty (RSC season) 68, 110
Theatre of Death 82, 173
The Theatre and its Double 53, 86
Théâtre de France 54, 90, 93
Theatre Laboratory (*see* Laboratory Theatre)
Théâtre National Populaire (TNP) 48
Théâtre des Nations 85, 90, 91, 98, 123
Theatre Royal (Stratford-atte-Bowe) 34, 142
Theatre School (Warsaw) 154
Théâtre du Soleil 122
Theatre South-West 162
Theatre Studio 164

Theatre Workshop (*see* Theatre Royal, Stratford)
Their Very Own 115
They Are Dying Out 126
The Thief's Journal 54
Thompson, Sam 63
The Three Sisters 73, 164
The Threepenny Opera 43, 44
Tickell, Sir Crispin 178
Time (magazine) 114
Time (musical) 149
Time Out 88
Timebends 14, 15
Tiny Alice 103
Titus Andronicus 35, 118, 123
TNP (*see* Théâtre National Populaire)
Today Is My Birthday 173
Toller, Ernst 41
The Tooth of Crime 108
Topolski, Feliks 26
Torquato Tasso 122
Towards a Poor Theatre 88
Town 104
Traverse Theatre (Edinburgh) 85, 98, 136
Travesties 114
Trinity College, Dublin 51
The Trojan Women 170, 171
Trotsky, Leon 79
True West 108
Truman, Harry S. 1–3
Turnbull, Colin 126
Turner, David 61
Twelfth Night 63
Two-Way Mirror 21
Tynan, Kenneth 35, 59, 63, 69–71, 131, 135, 137
Tzara, Tristan 40, 114

Ubu roi (*see King Ubu*)
Ubu Roi and Scenes from Macbeth 171
Ulbricht, Walter 47, 49
Ulysses 114
Uncle Vanya 164
UNESCO 90, 91
US 68, 109–11, 119, 121

Vakhtangov Institute 76, 77
Vakhtangov Theatre 77
van Druten, John 102
van Itallie, Jean-Claude 100, 101, 106
The Velvet Prison 77

Victor 68
Vietnam Discourse 121
Viet-Rock 100
A View from the Bridge 14, 17, 25, 26, 28
Vilar, Jean 48
The Village Voice 108
The Visit 67
Vitrac, Roger 68
Vladekin 83
Voss, Gert 130
Voznesenski, Andrei 83
Vysotsky, Vladimir 147, 148

Waiting for Godot 34, 49–51, 59, 61, 114
Wajda, Andrzej 65, 81
Waldheim, Kurt 131
Wall Street Crash 42
Wallace, George 100, 107
The War of the Worlds 62
Wardle, Irving 37
Warren, Earl 98, 99
Warren Commission 98
The Water Hen 82
Watkins, Peter 111
Way Upstream 139
Wayne, John 13
The Weavers 41
Wedekind, Frank 39, 40
Weigel, Helene 161
Weill, Kurt 44
Weimar Republic 42, 44
Weiss, Peter 47, 110, 121
Weissmuller, Johnny 8

Welles, Orson 62, 69
Wesker, Arnold 115, 120
West Side Story 7, 102
What the Butler Saw 113
Who's Afraid of Virginia Woolf 103
Wigg, George 112
Wilde, Oscar 30–2, 113
Wilder, Billy 20
Wilder, Thornton 16, 30
Wilkinson, Tom 163
Williams, Nigel 95, 122
Williams, Tennessee 19, 20, 30
Wilson, Sir Harold 66, 67, 73, 74, 91, 110, 111, 118, 132, 133, 134
Wilson, Robert 101, 125, 174
The Witches of Salem 58
Witkacy (*see* Witkiewicz, Stanisław)
Witkiewicz, Stanisław ('Witkacy') 53, 81, 82
Woodrow, Wyatt 31
Workers' Revolutionary Party (WRP) 94
Worth, Irene 124
Woyzeck 84, 167
Writing Degree Zero 125
Wuppertal Dance Theatre 174

Yeltsin, Boris 165, 178
Young, Hugo 140, 142

Zadan, Craig 154
Zadek, Peter 65
Zhdanov 8–10, 42, 44, 68
Zhdanovshchina 8–10
Zolotuchin, Valeri 83